THE TECHNIQUE OF JEWELLERY

Etruscan gold diadem,
4th–3rd century BC

To Virginia for all her selfless dedication and encouragement, and to
Lionel 'Nugget' Paton, the finest craftsman I have ever known.

Bodice ornament with emeralds and enamel flowers. Spanish mid 17th century.

This book is concerned with the craftsmanship of making jewellery, in precious metals. There is no mystique in craftsmanship, only practice, patience and integrity.

Jewellery is an ancient craft, and the techniques described are essentially the same as those used from the earliest civilizations, in which the workmanship and knowledge of the ancient gold and silver-smiths often exceeded ours.

I have not chosen to write about how to design. Art and aesthetics are not easily communicated. Each individual must come to design by himself. The examples illustrated of some of the most magnificent work in precious metals, dating from antiquity to the present day, may help to develop a feeling for creativity.

R.L.E. 1976

'This book is an attempt to communicate the dependable knowledge in the field of technique to the practising artist. It is not intended as a course of instruction in painting, because it is no more possible to learn to paint from books than to learn to swim on a sofa.'

Max Doerner
THE MATERIALS OF THE ARTIST
1935

'There is a human need for the satisfaction of craft. As technocracy widens the distance between our artifacts and the least trace of their makers, the dislocation of man from his nature worsens. . . .'

Hugh Atkinson

THE TECHNIQUE OF JEWELRY

ROD EDWARDS

Charles Scribner's Sons · New York

Acknowledgment

Illustrated by Virginia Smith
Photography by Adrian Flowers

My thanks to the following people for various reasons:
Atkinson, Hugh   *Author*
Collinson, Anthony   *Bank Manager, Barclays, Camden Town N.W.1.*
  'But For Whom'
Coote, Francis   *Design and Research Centre*
Cox, Phil   *Engineer and Craftsman*
Mackay-Edwards, Duncan   *Craftsman*
Gardiner, Marie   *Artist*
Hooton, Harry   *Philosopher*
Hare, Susan   *Librarian, Goldsmiths Hall*
Hughes, Graham   *Art Director, Goldsmiths Hall*
Lewis, Leslie   *Electroformer*
Maryon, John   *Son of the late Herbert Maryon*
Swift, Fred   *Engineer and Craftsman*
Gainsbury, Peter, F.I.M.
Benaim, Silvio Dr.
Grant, Kathleen   *Jeweller*
Thomas, David   *Jeweller*
Donald, John   *Jeweller*
Turk, Geoffrey   *Jeweller*
Grima, Andrew   *Jeweller*

The tables at the end of the book are reproduced by kind permission of
the author, Mr H.R. Neville, and of the publishers, Spink & Son Ltd.

Thanks are due also to the craftsmen who loaned their work to be
photographed, the many manufacturers of tools, equipment and
materials; the Craft Centres and Museums and last but not least to my
students who taught me so much.

1 3 5 7 9 11 13 15 17 19 I/C 20 18 16 14 12 10 8 6 4 2

Printed in Great Britain
Library of Congress Catalog Card Number 77-77547
ISBN 0-684-15309-2

Contents

Gold daisy hairpin, Early Minoan, 2300–2000 BC

I THE WORKROOM, TOOLS AND WORKROOM PRACTICE

The Workroom

A craftsman working alone can make jewellery in a relatively small area with a minimum of equipment. This need only be a strong bench or table, and a dozen basic tools. The quality of handmade jewellery need not be impaired in any way by the fact that it is being done with a minimum of equipment. One has only to look at the work of ancient goldsmiths for this to be apparent.

The chief benefit resulting from extensive equipment is time, it is quicker to polish by machine than by hand. It also offers the opportunity of using methods resulting from modern technology.

If you think that you would like to make jewellery, the initial investment in the necessary tools could be kept to a minimum until you have worked and begun to understand a little of the 'feel' of hand-making jewellery, and decided whether doing it satisfies you. The minimum requirements in tools would be:

1 mouth blow torch that is used with the household gas supply, or a blow torch that is used with bottled gas

1 wooden filing and sawing peg	1 pair AA tweezers
1 saw frame and saw blades	1 pair 'Gilbow' shears
1 pair half round pliers	Borax cone and tray
1 pair flat pliers	1 fine watercolour brush
1 three-cornered file	Alum for pickling
1 half round file	Emery paper

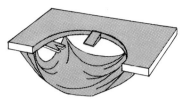

Basle slung below workbench

A work bench with two cut-outs

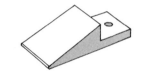

Filing peg

Sawing peg

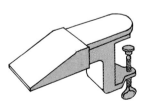

Combination file/saw peg with metal top surface

However, a small space in which to work can have its disadvantages should one want to experiment in a variety of media, such as enamelling, casting etc. This book will therefore deal with the technique of making jewellery on the assumption that the craftsman is genuinely involved, has adequate space and an extensive range of tools. The workroom layout suggested allows for the use of the greater majority of jewellery techniques, but can be adapted or reduced to suit the needs of each individual craftsman.

Workbench

Firstly, one needs a work bench of solid timber, with a semi-circular shape cut out of it. The bench should be of 5·05 cm (2″) thick timber, seasoned and strong enough to withstand fairly solid hammering. A cheaper alternative would be plywood. The dimensions are fairly arbitrary, but the size of the cut-out area and the placement of the bench peg in the centre of it are important, having evolved over a period of years to provide the most comfortable working arrangement.

When working within this area, the hand tools can all be within easy reach, and the sides of the cut-out provide support for your shoulder or elbow. For example, when setting stones or engraving, the cut-out allows maximum freedom of movement and at the same time provides support for one's elbow to rest upon the bench while working at the bench peg. The bench peg itself juts out from the bench, and provides a solid surface on which the filing, sawing and setting are done.

If space permits, it is an advantage to have two cut-outs, one of which would be used only when working with precious metals, and the other for general purpose work which needs to be kept separated from the precious metal area.

The height of the bench is arbitrary, the governing factors being your seated height and the ease with which you can work at chest level. This usually means that the bench is about 90 cm (3′) high. An adjustable chair, preferably straight-backed to prevent a stooping posture, makes it easier to alter position to get the correct focussing distance from the work and the bench peg. (A three-legged stool was the traditional seating for jewellers, but is bad for posture, as well as being reminiscent of Dickensian working conditions.)

Bench pegs

There are two pegs, one for filing, usually made from hardwood as it is longer wearing, and one for sawing, which may be of a softer wood. Both are interchangeable to some degree. If the saw peg is bolted on, under the bench but with the nut not fully tightened, the peg can be swivelled away beneath the bench when not in use.

An alternative type is held on the bench by a G-clamp. When saw piercing, the metal is placed across the V shape, supported on either side by the wood, and the saw cuts through the metal into the space. The saw peg is usually placed slightly to the left of centre, while the filing peg is in the middle in the cut-out.

The filing peg is also screwed onto the bench from underneath, and filing is done on the slanting surface. There is, in addition, a very useful piece of equipment (available in America only at present, from William Dixon Company, New Jersey) that is a combination bench peg and flat iron. The metal surface is useful for hammering, centre punching, etc, and the bench peg is reversible, one side being designed for filing and the other for saw piercing.

Slung beneath each cut-out is a basle (or sheepskin), which collects the lemel (filings) and metal cuttings. Leather made from sheepskin is used as its texture is dense and not even the finest filings will penetrate it, which is an important feature when working with precious metals. Less expensive substitutes for the basle could be made from plastics. If the soldering equipment is close at hand on the bench, care must be taken not to drop any hot metal in the basle when soldering, as this could burn its way through the skin.

Light

It is preferable to have natural rather than artificial light, but if no natural light is present there are a number of counterbalanced bench lights available. A particularly good one is the 'Simplus', which has the added feature of an inbuilt magnifier. For very delicate work, a pair of twin-lensed head binoculars is useful, as well as the traditional jeweller's loupe.

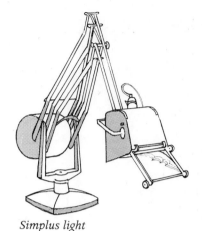
Simplus light

Soldering area

The soldering area can be arranged to one side of the bench. This would consist of a soldering torch fed by a gas supply. Gas alone will not generate sufficient heat for soldering, so it is mixed with air to increase its heat. The soldering torch uses this combination of gas and air, either in the form of a mouth blown torch, or a torch that uses compressed air or oxygen. If compressed air is to be used with coal gas or natural gas, a safety measure in the form of a blow-back cock must be fitted to the gas supply. If there is no access to coal or natural gas, then bottled gas could be used with its appropriate torch.

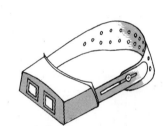
Head binoculars

It is essential to be able to subdue light in the area in which one is soldering or annealing, so that the colour change that takes place when metal is heated becomes more apparent. This can be arranged by making a shield, to subdue the light source, from almost any light gauge metal. Overheating can burn the alloy in the solder, leaving 'pit' marks and/or weakening the solder joins. Asbestos can be used as a base for the soldering area to protect the bench from heat, but it must be industrial asbestos. Never use builders' asbestos, as under heat it may shatter.

Instead of working on an asbestos base, one can use a metal turntable for soldering on. It is the type of revolving table used by potters, or cake decorators, and is about 15 cm (6″) high and 18 cm (7″) in diameter. On top of this an ordinary household asbestos mat can be placed to prevent the turntable from heating, and the actual soldering done on a pure charcoal block placed on top of the asbestos mat.

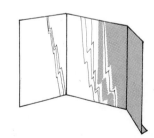
Soldiering shield against light

The Heneage Jewel. Given by Queen Elizabeth to Sir Thomas Heneage, the miniature dated 1580, the jewel 1585 both by Nicholas Hilliard

Pure charcoal is the best material to solder on, although it is expensive. It must always be warmed before use with the soldering torch. This is because it attracts moisture when not in use and if heated too quickly it will crack, either in half or in a number of pieces. One way of keeping the charcoal intact is to coat it with investment plaster on its four sides and base (to about halfway up the sides), and it will then last for a considerable period. After use its roughened top surface can be smoothed down with coarse emery paper or a rough file.

Should lead in any form have been used, always make sure that no trace of it is left behind on the soldering area. If even a particle of lead comes into contact with heated gold it will penetrate deeply into the gold, and will damage the surface.

Soldering and soldering torches will be described later. A soldering flux will be needed and brushes with which to apply it. The flux for precious metals is usually borax, which can be bought in cone, lump or powder form.

Pickle

When annealing or soldering platinum, gold, silver, brass, copper or nickel silver, oxidization takes place, and this must be removed. This is done by submerging the work in a diluted acid, known as pickle. Pickle is made by adding one part of sulphuric acid to eight, ten or twelve parts of cold water.

It is vital that the acid is always gently added to the water, rather than vice versa, otherwise the combining of the two could cause a mild explosion, perhaps resulting in damage to eyes or clothing. For advice on First Aid in such circumstances, see the section on First Aid. As a reminder of the fact that acid must be added to water, think of it alphabetically – as adding A to W.

The pickle should be used in a lead or pyrex bowl. Prior to use the pickle must be warmed. A bunsen burner is used for this, with a tripod placed over it, and an asbestos mat to protect the bowl from the naked flame. When working, keep the pickle at a low even temperature, otherwise the water content will evaporate and the acid become too strong. Should this happen, allow the acid to become cold. Because the water content has evaporated, the acid will have reverted back to its almost undiluted state. It can be restored to the correct proportions by adding it to water (A to W).

Before adding acid to water, let the water stand for four to five minutes, in which time it will begin to de-oxygenize and the acid can be added slowly but with more safety.

After work has been pickled to remove oxidization, wash it thoroughly in clean water and dry it. If it were allowed to remain damp and carried on to the next process, it could rust the machinery or tools involved.

When taking work to the pickle, remember to use only brass, copper or nickel silver tweezers, not iron or steel. Putting iron or steel tweezers or other ferrous metals such as binding wire into the pickle will stain precious metal. This can be difficult to remove from under-cuts or

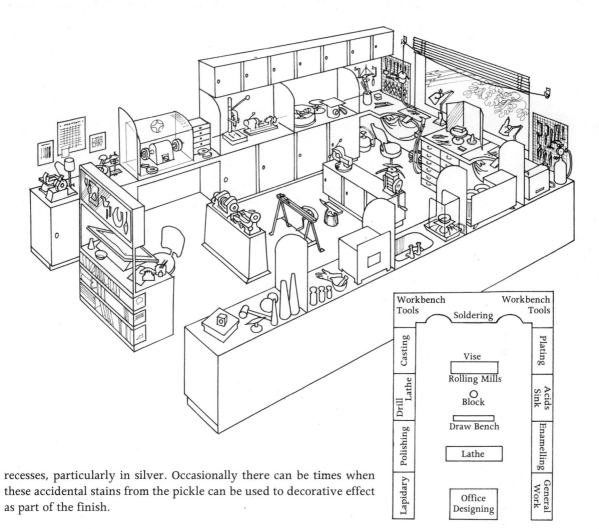

Workbench Tools	Soldering		Workbench Tools
Casting	Vise		Plating
Drill / Lathe	Rolling Mills		Acids / Sink
Polishing	Block		Enamelling
Lapidary	Draw Bench		General Work
	Lathe		
	Office Designing		

The work-room plan

recesses, particularly in silver. Occasionally there can be times when these accidental stains from the pickle can be used to decorative effect as part of the finish.

Acid-free pickle

Alum comes in a powdered or lump form and when dissolved in hot water and kept hot, provides an acid-free pickle that is, of course, safer to handle than the pickle made from acid as it is non-corrosive. Another type of acid-free pickle is made by Hoben Davis, England.

Plan of workroom

The plan of the workroom will be centred around the work bench, for here the basic processes of sawing, filing and soldering are done. The placement of the areas for other work can be arranged to suit the room, provided that the work areas where cleanliness is essential is well separated from the others. (For instance, enamelling must be kept away from polishing.)

The area for pickling needs to be near a water source and securely housed to avoid spilling or splashing. Polishing, of course, must be separated from all other processes because of the fine, pervasive powder

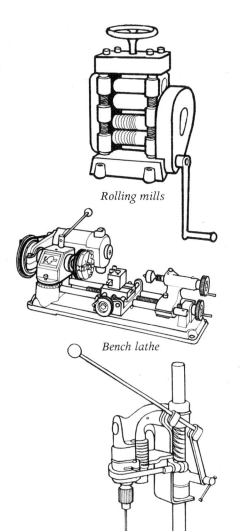

Rolling mills

Bench lathe

The Desoutter drill

thrown off. An extractor fan is invaluable for this and if the polishing motor is housed in a box, it will help to contain the polishing waste.

The rolling mills can be bolted onto a strong table, or may have a stand on steel legs that can be bolted to the floor. Similarly, the draw bench has steel legs for bolting to the floor.

The casting area will include equipment for centrifugal casting, as well as the other casting processes.

The plating and enamelling areas can be side by side, as absolute cleanliness is essential in each process.

The area for lapidary work will include equipment for slabbing, cutting, grinding and polishing gem stones.

The bench lathe and the drill can be used in proximity to each other, as their purposes are not dissimilar, but the larger, more comprehensive lathe will usually be free-standing.

For exceptionally heavy hammering, it is necessary to have a stout table, or a section of a seasoned tree trunk. This will support the use of an anvil, which is very heavy, or of a bick iron or sparrow hawk, which are smaller types of anvil.

Cupboards and shelves can be built in under the main working area to take tools, equipment and chemicals, and a large sheet of pegboard on the wall is useful to hold small tools in constant use, pliers, drill stocks, hammers, etc.

As a number of gas cocks will be needed, the simplest solution is to use a four-way gas unit, such as those available from laboratory equipment suppliers. This will allow for the use of four gas pipes and avoid the confusion of a number of loose pipes tangling in the working area. The same principle can be used to reduce the number of electrical fittings. A box can be made by an electrician, into which the supply comes direct from the power mains and feeds half a dozen other power points.

The equipment that has been itemized here is necessary for a craftsman to be able to utilize all the available techniques and skills involved in making jewellery and metal work. However it is possible to work satisfactorily on a very reduced scale, as I have described. A craftsman working in this simplified way will have to have many processes done for him outside the workroom, by lapidaries, platers, casters, enamellers and other specialists, but it will still be possible to produce the highest quality handmade work, despite limitations of equipment.

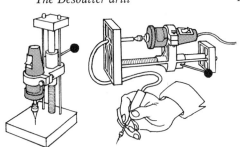

The miniature precision drill can be used vertically or horizontally with a flexible shaft

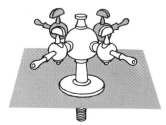

Fourway gas cock

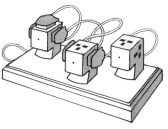

Bank of nine power points

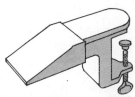
Combination file/saw peg with metal top surface

Tools used in Jewellery making

Sawing peg

PEGS

1 wooden filing peg
1 wooden sawing peg
1 Dixon combination bench peg for filing and sawing

Filing peg

PLIERS

Pliers – Half Round
    – Round Nose
    – Flat
    – Parallel jaws
    – Pointed flat
(All the above are smooth-jawed box jointed pliers
in large, medium and small sizes)
    – 1 pair strong all-purpose pliers

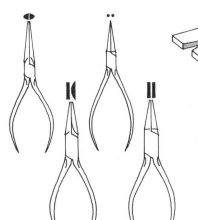

Pliers

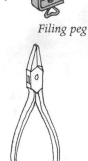

All-purpose pliers

SHEARS

Shears – 1 pair large
    – 1 pair small
    – 1 pair curved
(Trade name 'Gilbow')
All for both left and right hand

Large shears

Small shears

TWEEZERS

2 pairs tweezers (A.A. brand name)
1 pair iron tweezers, approximately 21 cm (8")
1 pair brass or copper tweezers
Several types of adjustable tweezers or locking tweezers

Sliding tweezers

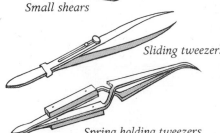
Spring holding tweezers

17

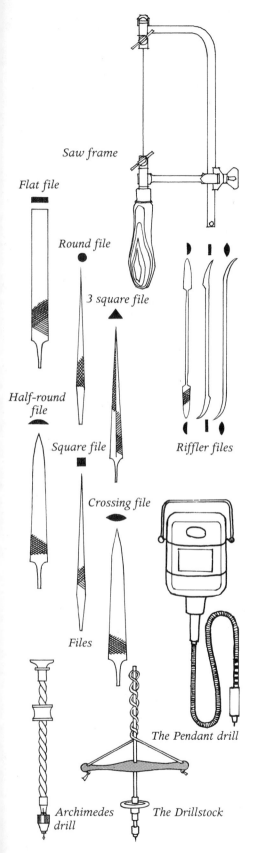

Saw frame

Flat file

Round file

3 square file

Half-round file

Square file

Riffler files

Crossing file

Files

The Pendant drill

Archimedes drill

The Drillstock

SAW FRAMES

1 Saw frame, adjustable, French, 5·05 cm (2")
1   ,,   ,,   ,,   6·3 cm (2$\frac{1}{2}$")
1   ,,   ,,   ,,   10·15 cm (4")
1   ,,   ,,   ,,   15·2 cm (6")
(The above have the trade name 'Bull's Head')
1 Saw frame with adjustable tension screw at top of frame (German)

SAW BLADES

Saw Blades, 1/0, 2/0, 3/0, 4/0, 5/0, 6/0, 7/0, 8/0, 1, 2, 3, 4
(The above blades are Swiss, German, English, French)

SOLDERING TORCHES

1 'Flamemaster' blow pipe for annealing, melting and soldering, with seven extra nozzles
1 Soldering blow pipe, French pattern
1 Large soldering torch for heavy work and melting
1 Swivel soldering burner
1 Mouth blow pipe

FILES

Files in the following shapes, fine, coarse and medium cut, size 21 cm (8")
3 square tapered
Round (or rat tail)
Half-round
Crossing (or double half-round)
Square tapered
Flat

Needle files in the above shapes, in fine, coarse and medium cut, size 15·2 cm (6")
The following in fine cut –
Gapping files
Set of escapement files (Swiss)
Set of watchmaker's files (Swiss)
Set of riffler files ('Stubbs')

DRILLS

Assorted twist drills from 0·4 mm ($\frac{1}{64}$") to 6·4 mm ($\frac{1}{4}$")
1 Pendant drill
1 Desoutter drill
1 Archimedes drill
1 drill stock with three chucks
Assorted watch pivot and clock drills for drill stock

HAMMERS

1 Chasing hammer
1 Ball pein hammer
1 Watchmaker's hammer
1 Warrington hammer No 1
2 Planishing hammers No 130
1 Collet hammer No 131
Set of 'Thor' hammers
1 Creasing hammer
1 Cross pein hammer

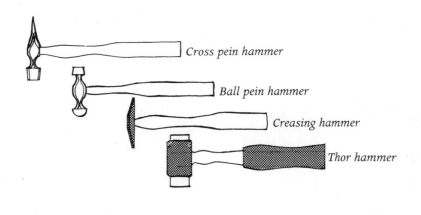

Cross pein hammer

Ball pein hammer

Creasing hammer

Thor hammer

MALLETS

1 Rawhide mallet, 4 cm ($1\frac{1}{2}$") diameter
1 Boxwood mallet, 4 cm ($1\frac{1}{2}$") diameter
1 Boxwood bossing mallet, 6 cm ($2\frac{1}{2}$") diameter
1 Horn mallet

Bossing mallet

Leather mallet

Horn mallet

SAWS

1 Back saw with interchangeable blades
1 Hack saw frame and blades
1 Miniature hack saw frame with blades

1 pair end cutters
1 pair side cutters

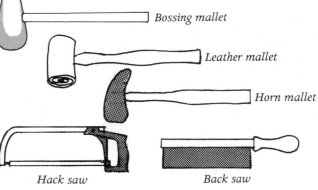

Hack saw

Back saw

SOLDERING

1 Pure charcoal block
1 Borax tray
3 Borax brushes
1 Borax cone
1 Tin Argo-tect
1 Tin Easy Flo
1 Bottle Auflux
1 Wig for soldering

4 Pin tongs, sizes 1 – 2 – 3 – 4
2 Pin vises
1 Hand vise
1 Tripod for bunsen burner
1 Bunsen burner
2 pair toolmakers dividers, 1 × 7·5 cm (3"), 1 × 15 cm (6")
2 pairs sliding tongs
1 Micrometer
1 Automatic centre punch with three spare punches
1 Draw bench
1 pair draw tongs

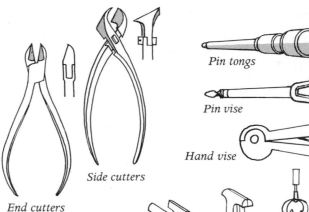

Side cutters

End cutters

Pin tongs

Pin vise

Hand vise

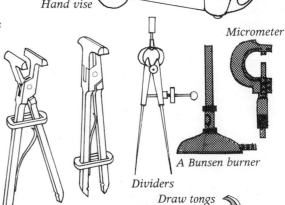

Micrometer

A Bunsen burner

Dividers

Draw tongs

Sliding tongs

Felt cone for polishing inside rings

Solid felt bobs

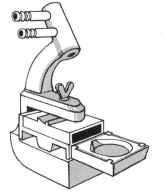

Melting apparatus with crucible

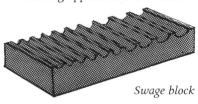

Swage block

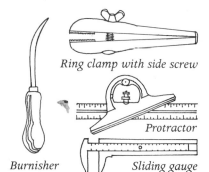

Ring clamp with side screw

Burnisher   *Protractor*

Sliding gauge

Protractor centre finder   *Spring gauge*

POLISHING MATERIALS

2 Black bristle brushes, 7·5 cm (3″) diameter
2 Tripoli brushes, 7·5 cm (3″) diameter
2 Rouge brushes, 7·5 cm (3″) diameter
2 Felt bobs, 5 cm (2″) diameter × 2·5 cm (1″), 2·5 cm (1″) diameter × 1·25 cm ($\frac{1}{2}$″)
2 Inside felt cones, 5 cm (2″) × 2·5 cm (1″)
1 Brass scratch brush, 7·5 cm (3″) diameter
1 Bar Rouge or 1 bar Polierpaste, pink
1 Bar Tripoli or 1 bar Polierpaste, white
1 Bar Carbrax for polishing steel
1 Hank each of polishing threads, fine, medium, coarse
1 Bag boxwood sawdust
1 Double boiler for heating boxwood sawdust
1 Carborundum stone (medium/fine, coarse/medium, coarse/fine)
1 Arkansas Oil stone, 15 × 5 × 2·5 cm (6″ × 2″ × 1″) boxed
Various sizes of Water of Ayr stone
Emery paper in very fine, fine, medium and coarse grades

1 Tip-up melting apparatus and 'Fletcher' crucibles with holders
1 Tap holder, bar type, 1·6 mm ($\frac{1}{16}$″) to 6·4 mm ($\frac{1}{4}$″)
1 Tap holder, chuck type, 1·6 mm ($\frac{1}{16}$″) to 3 mm ($\frac{1}{8}$″) − 3 mm ($\frac{1}{8}$″) to 5·5 mm ($\frac{7}{32}$″)
1 Die holder for Dies 20 mm ($\frac{13}{16}$″) diameter
1 Bick iron with base, 4 lb
1 Anvil, $\frac{1}{4}$ cwt
1 Bench block 7·5 × 5 × 2·5 mm (3″ × 2″ × 1″)
1 Ring clamp with end screw
1 Ring clamp with side screw
1 Ring clamp with wcdgc
1 Scriber
1 Curved polished steel burnisher
1 Large doming block of brass or steel
1 Small doming block of brass or steel
2 Swage blocks
1 Set of steel doming punches
1 Set of steel cutting punches
1 Set of boxwood doming punches
1 Ring triblet, steel 12″/15″
1 Size stick, A to Z+$\frac{1}{2}$ sizes
1 Set ring sizes, A to Z+$\frac{1}{2}$ sizes
1 Set scales and weights with stand and drawer, to weigh up to 20 oz TROY (metric)
1 Spirit lamp
1 Magnifying lens on stand, 4″ diameter (× 10 magnification)
1 Steel rule, metric
1 Brass sliding gauge, metric
1 Spring gauge, in Douzieme/Dixieme (12ths/10ths)

DRAW PLATES

1 Draw plate, with 20 round holes   0·6–0·1 millimetres
1   „   „   20   „   1·0–0·4   „
1   „   „   20   „   2·0–0·7   „
1   „   „   20   „   3·0–1·5   „
1   „   „   20   „   7·0–5·0   „
1   „   „   20   „   9·0–7·0   „
1   „   „   20 square holes   7·0–5·0   „
1   „   „   30   „   3·5–1·0   „
1   „   „   50   „   5·0–1·0   „

There are other shaped holes available in draw plates, e.g., 3 square, knife-edge, $\frac{1}{2}$ round, etc.

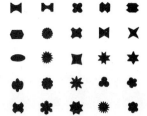

A few of the available drawplate shapes.

Vernier gauge

1 Vernier Gauge
3 Mill grain wheels, No 5 – 7 – 9
1 Wooden handle with chuck, for mill grain wheels and grainers
1 Adjustable steel square, 90° to 45°
1 Headband magnifier
1 Loupe (or eye glass) × 10 magnification
1 Triangular scraper
1 Curved scraper
1 Set of graining tools
1 Fion for graining tools
2 BA screwplates (Swiss) with taps, for holes 1–9 BA and 10–20 BA
      (or the equivalent in metric sizes), or a set of taps and dies in the
      same sizes, with a tap wrench and a die stock
1 Vee block and clamp
1 Drilling machine vise
1 Instrument vise (small bench type)
Assorted steel fraizers or dental burrs, for use in a pendant drill or in a
      flexible shaft fitted to a motor
Assorted rotary files, discs and grinding points
Assorted dental polishing brushes and felt wheels for use in the pendant
      drill or flexible shaft
Set of three pin chucks for use in a drilling machine for holding very
      fine drills (trade name 'Eclipse')

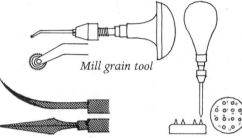

Mill grain tool

Curved and triangular scrapers   *Graining tool and fion*

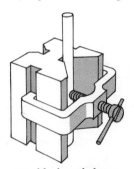

Vee block and clamp

GRAVERS OR SCORPERS

1 Graver (or scorper), square No 6
1   „   „   „   flat edge No 6
1   „   „   „   round edge No 6
1   „   „   „   bull stick No 4
1   „   „   „   spit stick No 6
1   „   „   „   knife edge No 3
6 handles for the gravers or scorpers (There are other shapes and cuts of scorpers available)

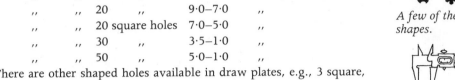

Mole Wrench

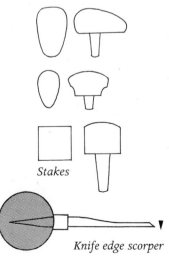

Stakes

Knife edge scorper

21

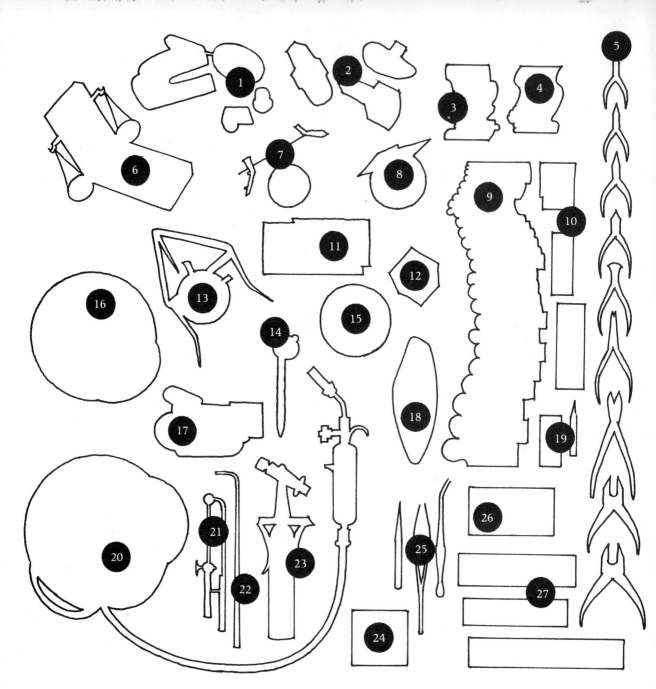

1. Magnifying glasses
2. Stakes
3. Cutting punches
4. Steel doming punches
5. Pliers, cutters and shears
6. Stone scales
7. Adjustable clips
8. Bick iron
9. Boxwood doming punches
10. Swage blocks
11. Asbestos pads
12. Doming block
13. Bunsen burner and tripod
14. Bench swivel burner
15. Borax tray and brush
16. Charcoal, asbestos and turntable
17. Melting apparatus and crucible
18. Cuttlefish
19. Collet plate and punch
20. Butane gas and Sievert torch
21. Mouth blow torch
22. Mouth blow pipe
23. Ronson gas and torch
24. Bench block
25. Tweezers
26. Doming die
27. Draw plates
28. Drill stock and chuck
29. Saw frame and blades
30. Brushes
31. Buff sticks
32. Pendant drill
33. Jointing tool
34. Ring sizes

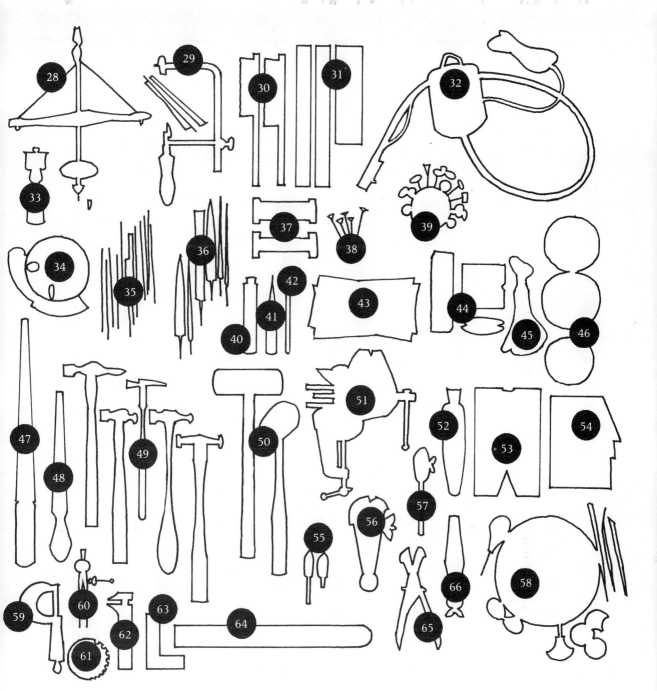

35. *Needle files*
36. *Assorted files*
37. *Binding and copper wire*
38. *Miniature screwdrivers*
39. *Dental polishing brushes*
40. *File handle*
41. *Automatic centre punch*
42. *Scriber*
43. *Modelling wax and knife*
44. *Water of Ayr stone,*
    rouges, felt bobs

45. *Polishing strings*
46. *Polishing mops*
47. *Ring triblet*
48. *Size stick*
49. *Hammers*
50. *Hide and wood mallets*
51. *Swivel bench vise*
52. *Wedge ring clamp*
53. *Saw Peg*
54. *Filing peg*
55. *Pin tongs*

56. *Hand vise*
57. *Pin vise*
58. *Engraving pad, scorpers and*
    burnisher
59. *Micrometer*
60. *Dividers*
61. *Standard wire gauge*
62. *Sliding gauge*
63. *Steel square*
64. *Steel rule*
65. *Sliding tongs*
66. *End screw ring clamp*

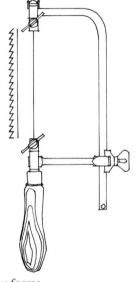

Saw frame

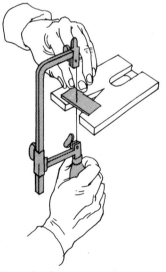

Saw piercing

Workroom Practice

THE SAW FRAME

The jeweller's saw is probably the most important tool used in making jewellery. It is the main cutting tool, either for the outside shape or the detail within the design, and is highly versatile because it can be used on all gauges of metal. It makes a clean precise cut that requires very little subsequent work.

Unlike a woodsaw, which saws horizontally as it is pushed away from you, the jeweller's saw is held vertically and cuts on the downward stroke. (For this reason always make sure the saw blade teeth face down and out of the frame.)

The versatility of the jeweller's saw is clearly shown in instances where it can be used to open a narrow aperture; this would usually be done with a file but if the aperture is too fine for a file, the saw blade can be used instead, by slightly angling the blade so that only one edge of the face of the blade is cutting, and the delicacy of this cut will allow enlargement of even the finest slot.

The most useful saw frame for general jewellery work has a distance of 7·5 cm (3″) from the blade to the spine of the saw frame. For very fine work a 5 cm (2″) width frame will give greater control. A 15 cm (6″) width will encompass work up to 15 cm (6″) square, while accordingly larger frames must be bought for larger work. Choose a saw frame with an adjustable spine to accommodate the varying lengths in which manufacturers make saw blades.

Saw blades are made in at least twelve different cuts. The finer the blade, the more teeth per inch it will have, and the narrower the face of these teeth will be. Conversely, the coarser blades will be thicker, with less teeth to the inch. Fine blades are numbered from 1/0 to 8/0 and the coarser blades are numbered from 1 to 4. The best blades are generally Swiss, German or French.

A good rule to follow is 'the thicker the metal, the coarser the blade'. If it is hard to see the teeth in a fine blade, hold it up to the light or test it with a finger nail to feel if the teeth are facing downwards.

PLIERS

The main purpose of all pliers is to bend, hold or curve metal.
Half-round pliers are for curving metal.
Round nose pliers are for curving wire and curving fine settings.
Flat pliers, parallel-jawed pliers and pointed flat pliers are for bending and holding metal, as are strong all-purpose pliers.
Pliers with serrated inside jaws are unsuitable for jewellery unless the serrations are removed.

SHEARS

There are straight shears and curved shears, and they are used for cutting metal (as it is quicker than sawing) and for cutting solder for paillons.
When shears are used to cut metal the action of the jaws will distort the edges, by compressing them as the cut is made. For this reason it is not advisable to use shears to cut an edge that is to be soldered. By comparison a sawn edge will be a clean undistorted cut and so can be soldered without further work on it, other than removing the slight burrs left by the saw. Both straight and curved shears can be bought for left-hand or right-hand use.

DRILLS

The Drill Stock

One of the most ancient tools used by primitive man was the drill. According to early records the ancient drill resembled in its proportions a bow and arrow, but its principle was the same as the drill stock used today. It is remarkably simple and efficient, and as it is worked by hand is highly manoeuvrable, easy to manage and convenient. Holes can be drilled quickly and accurately at the bench, as the drill stock is as conveniently at hand as the saw frame or the file, ready for immediate use. Given the choice on a particular job, I would prefer to use this simple drill to a power drill.
It is used primarily for drilling small holes quickly. It was used by stone setters for many years to make tapered holes for setting stones, but has been superseded in this case by the flexible shaft drill. (The drill stock was also used by clockmakers and watchmakers to drill holes for the pivots of clocks and watches.) It is still superior to a flexible shaft drill when a straight hole is required because it can be used with greater accuracy.
The drill stock has three interchangeable chucks to hold a range of drills for different purposes.

Using the Drill Stock

The drill stock consists of a steel rod with a wooden cross bar and a fly wheel and a chuck to hold the drill. There is a leather thong

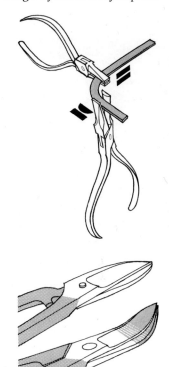

Provided a strip of metal is narrow enough (6 mm/¼ in) it can be curved horizontally using half round and flat pliers

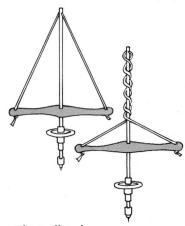

Straight and curved shears

The Drillstock

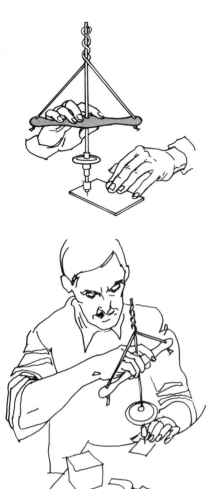

Using the drill stock

attached to each end of the wooden cross bar and it passes through a hole in the top of the steel rod. In use, this thong is twisted up and down the central rod, causing the rod to revolve and in turn this causes the fly wheel to revolve backwards and forwards. This then causes the chuck holding the drill to revolve. The revolution will be of a full circle or more, and then reversing into a full circle back in the opposite direction.

The driving force is the leather thong. In action it is caused to twist up the central rod or shaft to the right. At the peak it is fully twisted and then reverses, coming down the shaft twisting to the left, and this up-and-down, left-right-left-right twisting is the drilling action. The thong is worked by your hand lightly pressing on the wooden cross bar. To acquire the technique let us suppose that you have twisted the thong and the cross bar up the shaft as far as they will go. Now, the lightest pressure of your hand on the cross bar will bring it down, twisting the thong. As it nears the bottom of the shaft, the momentum of the fly wheel will cause it to wind up again, but on the opposite twist. With practice you will now be able to manage a regular movement that keeps the thong winding evenly up and down the shaft, and this causes the drill to cut. It can be difficult to acquire this technique but once you have done so it is surprisingly easy to work. No effort is required as light pressure is essential and it can be manipulated by one hand only. With experience, it can be worked with two fingers only.

Twist the thongs at first in the way you find easiest to handle and you will in time develop your own method of using the drill stock. The diagram shows my method of using it.

There are a few points to remember:

Do not allow the thong to overlap on itself at the top of the shaft. It must be threaded smoothly through the hole or it will tangle and impede the action.

In time the leather thong will stretch, allowing the cross bar to drop and thereby bind on the fly wheel. This will impede the smooth flow of the twisting of the thong and prevent the drill from functioning, so the thong must be shortened. This is easily done as the thong is only knotted below the crossbar. Pull it out a little further and knot it again.

When putting a new drill in the chuck, tighten the chuck with hand pressure only. Using pliers to tighten it would strip the thread on the pin chuck and damage it. Never force a drill into a chuck. If it doesn't fit comfortably, select another size of chuck that will accommodate the drill easily.

Keep the central shaft of the drill stock clean and lubricated with vaseline.

When manipulating the drill stock keep your fingers away from the shaft, as if they are in contact with it they will prevent it from revolving.

Ensure that the drill is relatively short where it projects from the chuck, as too long a drill will be subject to too much torque in movement and may break.

The Archimedes Drill Stock

Archimedes Drill

The Archimedes drill stock functions in the same way as a drill stock, in that it is operated manually, to cause the drill to cut clockwise and then anti-clockwise.

In the drill stock this was caused by the leather thongs twisting up the stem. In the Archimedes drill stock, a collet is made to run up and down the stem. This collet is hand held. The Archimedes drill stock consists of a twisted square rod of metal, with a chuck to hold the drill at one end, and at the other, a loose knob that allows the rod to twist. The collet fits the rod with a matching inside twist, rather like a nut and bolt, and is manually worked up and down the stem, causing the drill to cut. It has three chucks to hold drills of different sizes.

The Pendant Drill

The Pendant drill

The pendant drill has a flexible shaft driven by a small electrical motor. The motor is suspended so that the flexible shaft can fall freely without twisting. This flexibility is a great advantage because of the freedom of movement it allows – in effect the drill can be manipulated as freely as a pen or pencil.

There are interchangeable chucks that hold drills of varying sizes, small grinding points and polishing wheels and fraizers for texturing the metal or tapering holes.

The power for the pendant drill is controlled either at the end of the flexible shaft, or by a foot control, and some types of pendant drill have variable speeds.

As this is a piece of equipment that is being developed and improved all the time, it is worthwhile buying the newest model and, as with all tools, if possible, always buy the best.

Desoutter Drill

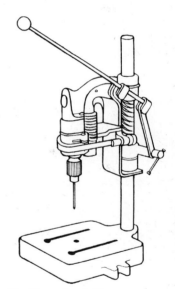
The Desoutter drill

There is another type of drill which is an electrically powered drill gun. It can be hand-held or clamped onto a drill stand, and used vertically as a drill, or can serve a dual purpose as a polisher if clamped horizontally. For fine work Desoutter drills are extremely accurate.

Twist Drills

Twist drill

Twist drills are that part of a drill that does the actual cutting. They are fitted into the chuck of the drill stock, the pendant drill or the drilling machine and are available in many different sizes.

For perfect drilling the cutting edges should be at an angle of 59° to the shaft. In jewellery making this angle is not critical and could range to 45°.

Scorpers or Gravers

Angle of 59° at apex of twist drill

Small cutting tools covering an extremely wide range of uses and available in about 12 different shapes.

Flat file

Round file

3 square file

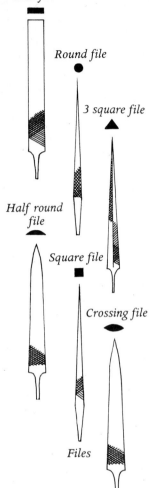

Half round
file

Square file

Crossing file

Files

File in a sweeping movement
rather than a series of straight
strokes

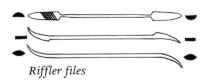

Riffler files

Files are used basically for smoothing or trimming off rough edges. The six main types of file are:

1. The flat file. Because of its broader surface, this is ideal for smoothing large flat areas, as when removing surface marks caused by hammering, etc or for trimming up the edges of a piece of metal.
2. The 3-square file is triangular in shape with a filing surface on each side. It is mainly used for filing flat surfaces or inside angled corners.
3. The round or rat tail file is for trimming up round holes.
4. The half round file is used for filing out a curved shape, as in the shank of a ring. Its flat side can be used for ordinary flat filing.
5. The crossing file (or double half round) is used for curving shallower shapes, and both sides of it are shaped to slightly differing curves.
6. The square file is used for trimming up square holes and inside right angles.

All the foregoing files are approximately 20 cm (8″) and tapered, except for the flat file which has parallel sides. Needle files are a replica of those shapes and cuts but are usually about 15 cm (6″) long and are used for finer work. There are files even smaller than needle files, such as escapement files and watchmaker's files for extremely fine work, and other specialist files for particular techniques – they are not essential for average jewellery work but will be mentioned in the section on the relevant technique.

The particular advantage of using files is that after using a coarse file, the work can be gone over again with the same shaped file but finer, which allows for easier finishing with emery paper. The fewer marks left by a file, or saw, the better and the less work involved in the finishing processes. It takes a lot of hard work and emery paper to remove the effects of coarse files or saws, so use the finer files when possible.

As an example of the correct use of files, if a plain strip of metal were turned up into a wedding band, the half round files would be used to smooth the inside of the ring, starting with a medium cut file and progressing to a fine cut. To avoid scoring the surface with the files, use the half round files in a diagonal motion that sweeps across the inside curve of the ring. As there is no file that can follow the outside contour of the ring, use a flat file, again progressively reducing the coarseness, but run the file along the curve of the ring following the contour in a series of sweeping movements rather than straight strokes that would give a series of flats or facets.

Files should always be put into a handle to protect the palm of the hand in case the file catches in the metal. This is the safest way to use a file. However, I prefer to work without a handle, because it means that I can hold the file closer to its tip and consequently feel it more as an extension of my fingers, giving greater sensitivity. If you choose to work in this way, always make sure that you hold the file more or less in the middle, so that its sharp handle or tang protrudes well beyond your palm.

Another set of small files (12·7 cm (5″) to 15 cm (6″) long) are riffler files, which come in 18 or more different shapes, all with curving ends designed for filing into the cavities of bowls, domes, or awkward shapes.

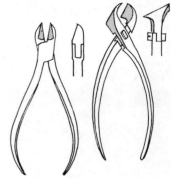

END CUTTERS

These and side cutters are for cutting wire. Their design allows you to get closer in to the work than shears would, and as an example, are particularly useful in shortening a rivet. Their differing design allows you to use them in places that would be inaccessible to shears.

End cutter and side cutters

PIN TONGS

Pin tongs come in four or more different sizes, and are used primarily for holding wire while it is being worked on.

Pin tongs

PIN VISE

This is for holding small pieces of metal for filing or sawing, and is an excellent clamp when several sheets of metal must be held together – for example, in duplicating a shape by both sawing and filing it out. Some pin vises are also designed to hold wire.

There are two other types of small vise, one is a hand vise, which serves the same purpose as a pin vise, but for larger pieces of metal. The other type are sliding tongs, in which the grip is effected by a sliding rectangular washer, whereas the hand vise is simply screwed up to grip.

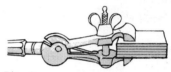

Pin vise

A MICROMETER

Used for measuring the thickness of metals, it is a delicate instrument and should be carefully handled, as dropping it could upset the gauging mechanism. When not in use, keep it boxed.

Micrometer

BACK SAW

This is not dissimilar to the ordinary Tenon wood saw in shape, but smaller. In complete contrast to the flexibility of the jeweller's saw frame, the back saw is a rigid blade, designed simply to cut an unvarying straight line of even depth. For example, if one wants to groove metal along a straight line preparatory to bending it at right angles, as in making the side of a box, the back saw will give a straight even cut, whereas a jeweller's saw will cut onto both edges but bow over the middle.

The back saw is equally useful in cutting along the join of a chenier as the cut does not waver. It is invaluable when slotting or making hinges, and its use is described in the section on box-making.

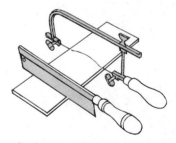

A back saw will make a straight cut, but a jeweller's saw will bow over the middle

Binding Wire

Iron binding wire is used to hold work together while soldering.

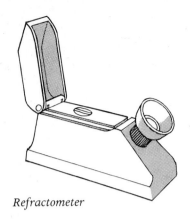

Refractometer

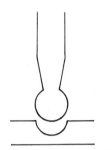

Doming punch and doming die

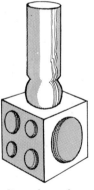

Doming die and wooden punch

Fraizers

Refractometer

Used to identify gem stones. It has a scale which shows the refractive index of the stone being tested. This is then checked with a table of the refractive indices of stones. This may not provide totally conclusive proof of the identity of the stone, without cross-checking, but will establish the type of stone.

Copper Wire

Copper wire is used to suspend work in pickle.

Stone Scales

A set of stone scales are for accurate weighing of stones.

Miniature Screwdrivers

May be necessary if very fine work has to be screwed together instead of being soldered or rivetted.

DOMING PUNCHES

These match the sizes of the depressions in the doming block, and are made of steel or boxwood. The steel punches are bought as a set graduated in size from 16 mm ($\frac{1}{16}$″) to approximately 18 mm ($\frac{3}{4}$″), whereas the wooden punches range from a relatively small size up to $1\frac{1}{2}$″ diameter. If you need to dome up a shape larger than this diameter, it may be necessary to improvise your own doming die and punch.

DOMING BLOCKS

Used for doming up flat metal, using the corresponding doming punch of wood or metal. The doming block itself is of brass or steel, and has a series of graduated depressions that will produce a domed or a hemispherical shape.

In doming, a flat metal disc is placed just inside the bowl and the matching punch positioned on it and struck with a hammer. This will force the disc to take the shape of the dome. Proceeding through the graduated diminishing depressions using the appropriate punches will finally round the dome into a hemisphere. Soldering two of these together will, of course, produce a sphere. It is essential to use the matching punch for each bowl (ie, the same diameter) if you are using a metal punch, otherwise both punch and bowl will be damaged. Using a wooden punch of the wrong size will undoubtedly damage it. The larger punches are usually wooden and the smaller ones are metal.

FRAIZERS OR BURRS

These can be of steel or carborundum, and are used in the flexible shaft or the lathe to enlarge or taper holes, and can also be used to texture the surface of metals. Rotary files, emery discs, grinding points and rubber wheels impregnated with fine emery powder are for the same purposes, and are obtainable from dental and jewellery suppliers.

V-BLOCK AND CLAMP

A V-block and clamp are used to hold a small piece of metal firmly when drilling, eg when drilling a hole through the length of a piece of wire, it would be too difficult to hold the wire by hand and drill it at the same time. To hold larger work steady when drilling, a machine vise can be used.

V-block and clamp

AN ANVIL

Provides the base on which heavy hammering, shaping or stretching of metal is done. It is usually of iron and a suitable weight for a jeweller's anvil is 60 kg ($\frac{1}{4}$ cwt). It is generally placed on a wooden block (or section of tree trunk) on the floor.

A smaller type of anvil which is used on the workbench may only weigh 4·5 or 6·5 kg (2 or 3 lb), and is called a Bick Iron. This is used for similar but finer work, and the more expensive ones are of hardened, tempered, polished steel.

A BENCH BLOCK

Is also of hardened, tempered steel, perhaps 7·5 cm (3″) square by 2·5 cm (1″) deep, with at least one surface polished, and is used when work needs to be hammered flat. The edges can be used when hammering metal to a rightangular shape.

EMERY PAPER

Emery paper is similar to sandpaper but of a better and more enduring quality, and comes in a number of grades from coarse to very very fine (this latter is known as flour emery). The paper backed type is most suitable for jewellery. Its main purpose is the removal of file marks prior to polishing.

EMERY PAPER STICKS

Emery papering difficult corners is easier with an emery paper stick. I make these by folding emery paper tightly around a three-sided wooden stick. Lay the stick along one end of the back of the paper and score along one side with a sharp point. Score lightly so that the surface of the paper is not broken, and then turn the stick over onto its next face, creasing the paper on its score line. Continue to score and wind the paper onto the stick in this way, and when complete, secure it at its centre with binding wire. One then has a three-faced emery stick, similar in principle to a three-cornered file. (The file, however, is tapered.) After the first layer has been fully used, it can be torn off,

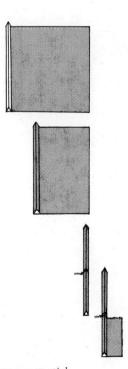

Emery paper stick

Ring clamp with side screw

Curved and triangular scrapers

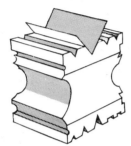

Right-angled shape formed in swage block

Swage block

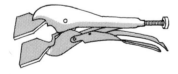

Mole Wrench

Flux

down to the binding wire, exposing a fresh surface. Although it may seem tedious, this simple process will give you approximately forty emery paper surfaces. Emery sticks could be made in the same way from round, half round or square dowel sticks.

RING CLAMPS

Ring clamps are for holding rings when setting stones. There are three types, one with a side screw, one with an end screw and one with a wedge. They can also be used as a clamp to hold two or more pieces of metal together while sawing or filing duplicates. They are designed to hold a narrow shank but can be adapted to hold a wider one.

SCRAPERS

A triangular scraper or a curved scraper is used to remove burrs from the inside of holes or inaccessible places or from the edges of metal, and have highly sharpened cutting edges.

SWAGE BLOCKS

The swage block is for shaping strips of metal into curved or angular shapes with the corresponding former. As opposed to the doming die with bowls for shaping, the swage block has channels for shaping, and these are used for trueing up the shape of settings, cheniers, angles etc.

If the backsaw had been used to make a groove for a right-angled strip, the shape could then be formed in the swage block with the appropriate former. While all swage blocks are not available in hardened or tempered steel, if there is a choice, buy those that are, as it is almost impossible to damage them.

MOLE WRENCH

A mole wrench can be used for the same purposes as a pin vise or hand vise, but for larger scale work. For instance, if cutting or filing duplicate shapes, the mole wrench can be locked on to the stacked metal sheets to grip them firmly throughout the operation. Mole wrenches are available in different shapes and sizes.

CUTTING PUNCHES

These are hardened, tempered steel rods with a hollow in one end shaped as part of a hemisphere. The edge of this is sharpened and the tool is used hammered to cut discs from metal of a limited thickness, (ie ·025 gauge). They are generally bought as a set, in graduated sizes, as are doming punches. They can be used as a chasing or texturing tool, and in making round links for a chain.

FLUX

Flux is used in soldering with a borax tray and brush.

A RING TRIBLET OR MANDREL

This is a long tapered steel rod. It is used for rounding up the shank of a ring, or for rounding a bezel for a setting. Apart from this round triblet, there are oval and square shaped triblets, and larger sizes are available for forming these shapes, as in bracelets, lockets or boxes.

A set of ring sizes are used when measuring the finger size for a ring. They are a graduated set of rings that range through 26 sizes. In Britain they are arranged alphabetically from A to Z, but in Europe they are numbered. An alternative set will have the half sizes between, ie A, $A\frac{1}{2}$, B, $B\frac{1}{2}$, etc, or 1, $1\frac{1}{2}$, etc.

Ring sizes

A RING STICK

Is a tapered steel tube used to measure the size of a ring. It has a graduated scale from A to Z, and half sizes between, incised along it, and these correspond to their equivalent in the ring sizes. Ring sticks may be either hollow or solid. Never hammer a ring on a hollow one, although the solid type may be used in place of a ring triblet or mandrel, provided it is hardened and tempered.

A ring stick

DRAW PLATES

A craftsman may find it necessary to reduce or reshape wire and this is done by pulling it through a draw plate. This is a steel plate with a range of diminishing holes (circles, squares, triangles, double half rounds, diamond, and various other shapes).

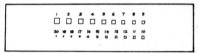

Square drawplate

A PAIR OF DRAW TONGS

These are necessary to grip the point of a wire as it is pulled through a draw plate, and they resemble a large pair of pliers. Alternatively, if you have a draw bench for drawing wire, the tongs will be supplied with it.

Basic drawplate shapes

A DRAW BENCH

This is essential if you wish to draw wire that is over 3 mm ($\frac{1}{8}''$) thick. It is also impossible to pull this gauge of wire through a drawplate by hand, even if the draw plate were to be held in a bench vise and draw tongs were used.

Draw tongs

Polishing Materials

The brushes and mops used on the polishing machine range from a black bristle brush, which is coarse textured, to a tripoli mop and finally to a soft rouge mop. Inside felt cones are used when polishing the inside of a ring. Replicas of the standard bobs, mops and felts can be obtained in miniature to use with a flexible shaft.

Other types of bobs or mops can be made of felt or chamois leather,

Polishing mops

A Bench Vise

and they are all used in conjunction with the appropriate polishing compound (tripoli in the early stages, and finally rouge). There are other polishing compounds, such as *Polierpaste* (white is the equivalent of tripoli, and pink the equivalent of rouge). For a satin finish (a sheen finish rather than a brilliant finish) use a brass bristle mop or a steel mop with water, softened with a detergent.

Polishing threads are used for apertures that are too fine for a mop to penetrate. The threads, which come in three grades, are charged with the appropriate compound, threaded through the aperture, and the work is then shuttled backwards and forwards on the taut string to polish the recess.

Carborundum Stone

Because of its hardness this is used for sharpening tools, and can be bought either as a block with one grade of abrasive surface, or in combinations of fine and coarse surface. This can also be used in place of a file for levelling off a collett or setting.

Arkansas Oil Stone

This is an even harder stone than carborundum and is used for the final sharpening of cutting tools such as scorpers or chisels.

Water of Ayr Stone

This is of a softer nature and a finer texture than the preceding stones, and where a particularly fine finish is required, rubbing with this stone and water will remove even the finest emery paper marks, and it is the most effective way of removing fire-stain.

The die will cut a thread on wire

CHARCOAL BLOCKS

These are the best material for soldering on, but they must be pure charcoal blocks, not compressed charcoal.

Tap and tap holder

Die and die holder

THE HACK SAW FRAME

The hack saw frame and the miniature hack saw frame, both with the appropriate blades, are used for heavier or coarser work than the jeweller's saw could comfortably cope with.

Taps and Dies

These are used for making the equivalent of fine nuts and bolts in precious metal, as for instance in making a pair of screws for earrings.

The tap makes the inner thread as in a nut, and the die makes the outer thread as on a bolt. Taps and dies are held in tap and die holders. They are available in a large range of sizes, and in a range of threads to the inch in each size.

Tap and tap holder

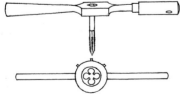

Die and die holder

Measuring Devices

These include a steel rule, a pair of dividers (toolmaker's type), a sliding gauge, a spring gauge, a Vernier caliper gauge, an adjustable steel protractor (from 0° to 180°) a set square, dividers and a compass.

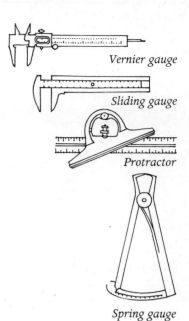

Vernier gauge

Sliding gauge

Protractor

Spring gauge

A Scriber

This is, in effect, a steel pencil and is used for inscribing on metal.

A Straight and a Curved Steel Burnisher

These are used in finishing and polishing fine work, such as the edge of a setting, or to polish otherwise inaccessible places. Burnishers are also made of hard stone, such as hematite and agate.

Boxwood Sawdust

This is the purest sawdust available, and is invaluable when drying out work after the final washing. The sawdust is put in the top half of a double boiler and the water in the bottom half is heated. When the sawdust is moderately hot, it will absorb any remaining moisture in the work put into it.

Melting Apparatus

For melting small amounts of metal a 'Fletcher' tip-up ingot mould is used, with its own crucible.

It has gas and air inlets to produce a flame for melting, and this flame is directed down in the crucible. When the metal is molten, the stand is tipped backwards on its hinged base and the metal flows out of the crucible into the ingot mould. The width of this mould is adjustable, but not its length.

The principle of melting is to try and fill the ingot mould completely with molten metal. With experience one will learn how much metal will fill a given size. Initially one will have to estimate. With a small amount of metal the width of the ingot must be narrowed, as it is preferable to have a long narrow mould filled to the brim rather than a half-filled mould. If the gold fills the ingot its molecular structure will remain intact in rolling, and it is less liable to crack. It should be rolled in the same direction as it was poured into the mould, ie along its length.

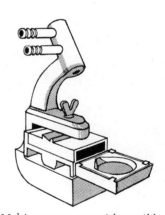

Melting apparatus with crucible

There is another ingot mould, used when making wire. In this the molten metal is poured into small troughs. This rod of metal is subsequently rolled in the square rolling mills to the required diameter and then pulled into wire of the desired shape through the draw plates.

Scorpers or Gravers

Small cutting tools covering an extremely wide range of uses – carving, engraving, texturing and setting. The cutting edges are available

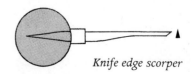

Knife edge scorper

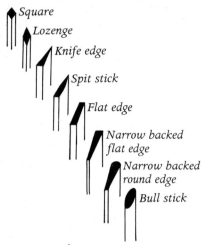

Square
Lozenge
Knife edge
Spit stick
Flat edge
Narrow backed
flat edge
Narrow backed
round edge
Bull stick

Gravers and scorpers

Graver or scorper handle

*Graver handle with
interchangeable chucks to hold
small tools, such as beading
tools and mill grain tools*

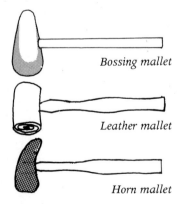

Bossing mallet

Leather mallet

Horn mallet

in about a dozen different shapes with five or six sizes in each shape, eg flat scorper, half round scorper, knife-edge scorper and a lining scorper. The cutting face of the lining scorper has parallel grooves for texturing.

Gravers serve the same purposes as scorpers but the cutting edge is differently angled for engraving.

A Grain Tool

Used in stone setting. The small hollow in its end is used to make the grain in a thread and grain setting, as will be described in the appropriate section. A fion is a matched tool for polishing the inside of the grainer.

A Mill Grain Tool

Used to obtain a beaded edge on a setting. It resembles a graining tool, but a miniature wheel is slotted into its end, and the face of this has indentations around it (like the indentation in a graining tool) and when the wheel is run around the edge of a setting, it leaves a beaded edge. However, unlike the graining tool, the purpose of this is purely decorative.

Scorpers, gravers, grain and mill grain tools are not supplied with a handle, but must always be used in a handle. They should not protrude more than 7·5 cm (3″) beyond the ferrule of the handle, and with very fine scorpers no more than 5 cm (2″).

Hammers

Hammers are extensive in design and function. A planishing hammer is the one most frequently used in jewellery – predominantly for stretching, flattening and doming. A repoussé hammer is used in conjunction with punches for repoussé work.

Ball Pein hammers and Warrington Cross Pein hammers are for general work where it is not essential to leave the surface of the work unmarked. Planishing hammers, because of their slightly curved and highly polished heads are less likely to mark work.

A creasing hammer can be used for making channels in metal or adapted as a texturing hammer. A watchmaker's or riveting hammer is used for very delicate work.

'Thor' hammers are particularly well designed. There are a number of hammers in this range and one of the most useful has a leadshot-filled head. This design prevents the hammer from bouncing, which is most important when stamping metal, either for hallmarking or texturing.

Mallets

Are of softer materials than hammers to prevent bruising of metals. They are made of boxwood, hide, rubber, horn, plastic, ebony, nylon and copper. 'Thor' mallets are available with interchangeable heads of aluminium, rubber, wood and plastics.

Stakes

These serve a similar purpose to doming punches, but their heads are of varying curved shapes, unlike the spherical head of the doming punch. They are considerably larger than punches and do not generally have a matching die.

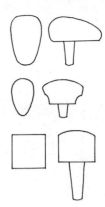

Stakes

Rolling Mills

Used for rolling sheet metal or wire thinner. The mills can be used manually or power driven. There are two steel cylinders through which the metal is rolled to make it thinner, or other cylinders with graduated grooves for reducing square, round or half round wire. There are also engraved cylinders for patterning wire (eg wedding rings).

In rolling metal, the thinning process must be accomplished gradually, by passing the metal through the mills a number of times, adjusting and diminishing the space slightly each time. The top centre gear controls the aperture, and if this were to be turned to leave an aperture considerably smaller than the thickness of the metal, while it may be possible to insert the metal, it will either jam or may be rolled thinner than intended.

In thinning the metal it will lengthen but not widen, ie it will extend in the direction you are rolling it. If you wish to increase the width of the metal, it must be inserted sideways. The metal will be hardened by continued rolling, and must therefore be annealled occasionally or it will crack.

Mills are available with combined sheet and wire rollers. If mills are power driven, they must, by law, have a guard for protection. When the mills are not in use keep them slightly greased or oiled.

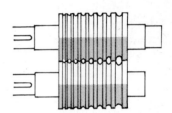

Mills for rolling and reducing wire

Engraved mill rolls for impressing patterns on wire

Sawing and Slabbing Machines

For lapidary work, one needs a sawing or slabbing machine to cut the rough stone. It is subsequently ground with emery wheels and then polished using copper laps and finished with a felt polishing wheel. One can buy this slabbing and polishing machine as one unit, or as two separate units. This type of machine will only cut and polish cabochon stones (ie with a smooth rounded surface). For faceted stone cutting, a machine with a faceting head is needed.

A Bench Vise

This has a revolving head which allows you to position work held in it, throughout a circle of 360°. An improvement on this is the ball base vise, which will swivel in any direction. As the jaws of a vise consist of hardened and tempered steel (and may be serrated) it is advisable to cover them with detachable fibre grips, which will protect the metal from bruising while it is held in the vise.

A Hand Vise

Usually of intermediate size, between a pin vise and a bench vise.

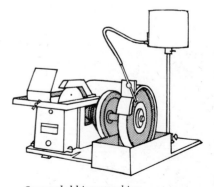

Stone slabbing machine

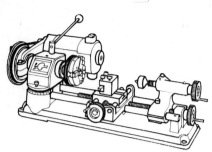

The Emco Unimat small bench lathe (approx. 45 cm long) converts to drilling machine, thread cutting, grinding and polishing machine, and works metal, wood and plastic

The Lathe

A lathe is a very useful adjunct to the jeweller's range of equipment, primarily because it can be used to make tools for specific purposes. The large lathe shown in the drawing of tools (page 45) is a major piece of equipment but the cost of it would be warranted in a workshop with sufficient turnover, or for a manufacturing jeweller and silversmith. The small lathe shown here is ideally suited to the smaller workshop of a craftsman jeweller and is reasonably priced.

The basic purpose of the lathe is for making and repairing tools. Its cost will be covered in time, as you will not need to buy expensive specialist tools, but can make them yourself. It will be particularly useful for larger work – necklets, bracelets, bowls, ceremonial cups, rods or maces, and trophies where the work is bordering more on gold or silver smithing than jewellery. When you are designing a work piece, it may become apparent that the whole process could be facilitated by a tool specially shaped for that particular piece, and this could be made on the lathe.

Standard jeweller's tools such as doming blocks, doming punches, tapered punches, ring mandrels and square, hexagonal, octagonal mandrels are available in a limited number of sizes only, and if the maximum size were not big enough a larger version could be turned up on the lathe. Equally, there are standard tools that may not be small enough for your requirements and these can be reduced to the required size on the lathe. For example, tapered punches (used in making a tapered setting) are only available in two degrees of taper – one is 45° and one is 30°. You may need a taper of a different degree, say 60°, or a smaller taper, say 20°, and this can be made up on the lathe.

There are a considerable number of attachments that can be used with the lathe that greatly extend its range of operation. The most useful attachments may be those for drilling, grinding and shaping, particularly in tool making where the precision of the machine is a great asset. It can be used for these same purposes in jewellery making but it is more convenient to use the traditional methods when making a single piece, although the lathe would be much faster if one were making multiples. The attachments allow the lathe to be used in all the following ways: as a circular saw for wood and metal, as a jigsaw, as a drive for the flexible shaft, as a screw-cutting machine, a drilling and milling machine, a grinding machine, a wood-working lathe, a routing and planing machine. One of the attachments is a dividing head which is calibrated to mark absolutely precise divisions. The dividing head can be used equally well for steel, wood or plastics.

The method of using a lathe is too complicated to describe here, but I recommend an excellent book on the subject: *The Amateur's Lathe* by Lawrence H. Sparey. There are courses of instruction in the use of the lathe, and you would be wise to attend one of these to learn how to make the best use of the machines' potential. Whilst lathes are a most useful adjunct in a workshop, they are expensive, take time to set up, and unless you intend to make a lot of jewellery using the lathe, think twice before investing in one.

SCALES AND WEIGHTS

A set of scales and weights are needed if you intend to alloy your own metal, or to use the lost wax method for casting. It is also an advantage to be able to weigh up small quantities of chemicals for different formulae (as in niello alloys). The scales should be able to weigh up to at least 5 oz Troy or 155·5 grams.

A SPIRIT LAMP

A spirit lamp is used with methylated spirits when heating the knives or other implements used in wax modelling or for melting pearl cement for pearl setting.

A MAGNIFYING LENS

A magnifying lens on a stand can be a great help when doing very fine work where attention to detail is vital, as in setting. Head binoculars serve the same purpose, as do smaller magnifying glasses known as loupes.

A WIG

Is used for soldering on, where it is necessary for the flame to get beneath as well as on top of the work. It is a thick circular mat of loosely woven iron wire, with a handle. It can be hand held or supported on a tripod.

BUNSEN BURNER

This is used predominantly to provide a gentle heat – for example: keeping pickle warm, or keeping the boxwood sawdust warm. The gas of the Bunsen burner alone will only give a diffuse gentle flame but combined with air the flame can be intensified. There is a hole at the base of the Bunsen burner, covered by a regulating sleeve, which can be moved around to cover or expose the hole, and consequently govern the air intake through the hole. A tripod is placed over the burner to hold an asbestos mat and a Pyrex or lead bowl. Should you not have a soldering torch a Bunsen burner could be used instead, within its limitations. To obtain its maximum heat the sleeve must be turned to expose the hole completely.

Oxygen

Oxygen can be combined with gas or hydrogen or acetylene for melting or soldering when an intense or localized heat is required. This is essential when working with platinum and may be necessary for some white golds. The type of torch generally used with gas is unsuitable for use with oxygen, and a specially designed torch must be used with the oxygen cylinder.

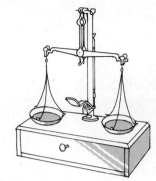

Scales

Spirit lamp

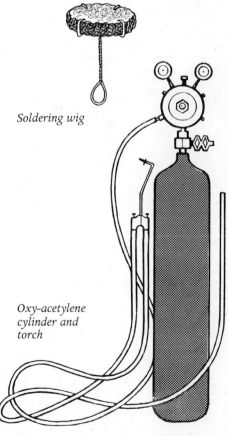

Soldering wig

Oxy-acetylene cylinder and torch

41

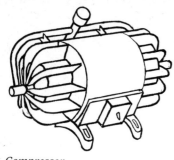

Compressor

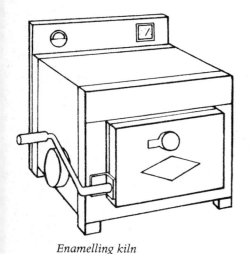

Enamelling kiln

Compressor

A compressor is necessary when soldering or melting requires greater heat than one can obtain by using the mouth blow torch. Compressed air can be mixed with gas to give a high degree of heat, but for work requiring really intense heat, oxygen and gas will need to be used. The compressor can also be used to drive pneumatic grinders and drills, and for sand blasting. The 'Reciprotor' (Model 506R) is a very small but powerful machine that would supply enough air for 4 to 6 hand torches to be used simultaneously.

TWEEZERS

These are made in many shapes, generally pointed, to facilitate the handling of fine pieces of metals and the placing of paillons for soldering. Other types, such as sliding tweezers, spring-holding and adjustable tweezers are designed to grip without being held. There are some tweezers that have a heat-resisting material on the handles; these are particularly useful when a lot of soldering is being done, as tweezers can become too hot to hold. If a fierce flame is being used, the usual short-handled tweezers are not suitable, and there are long tweezers available for this purpose.

Polishing Machine

A polishing machine is necessary for finishing jewellery to a high standard. For preference it should be a double-ended machine, thereby giving two spindles with tapered, threaded ends, onto which the polishing mops are screwed. The virtue of a double-ended machine, as opposed to a machine with only one spindle, is that each end can carry a different type of mop, which will save time and wear on the motor. It should be capable of 2,750/3,000 rev/min.

Enamelling Kiln

For enamelling a kiln is essential. One that is capable of controlled temperatures up to 1030°C can also be used for burning out wax in the lost wax casting process and for niello work. Choose a kiln that is fitted with a temperature control and cut-out gauge.

Plating

The plating process is used to deposit a film of one metal upon another metal. It usually follows that the lesser alloy is coated with the higher quality alloy; for example, silver can be plated with gold, or 9 carat gold plated with 18 carat gold, etc.

Cuttlefish

This is used for simple casting in gold or silver.

A Collet Punch and Plate

These are used to taper collets or settings. The plate has a range of tapered holes of 30° or 45° angles, and there is a corresponding punch. It is quicker, and wastes less metal, to make a cylindrical setting and taper it with the collet punch in the plate to the required shape, than to cut out the curved pattern necessary for a tapered setting.

Horizontal centrifugal casting machine

An Automatic Centre Punch

This can be used to accurately position a dimple in metal for subsequent drilling. Because of its spring-loaded action it will make a dimple of varying depths (regulated by an adjustable head) in which to locate the point of a drill. An alternative type of centre punch, which is not automatic, can be hammered to make a depression.

Centrifugal Casting Equipment

Centrifugal casting equipment allows for the high precision casting of silver, gold, platinum and palladium. If one were specializing in this technique equipment would include a centrifugal casting unit, a vulcanizing press for making rubber moulds, a vibrating table and a vacuum bell, as well as other equipment.

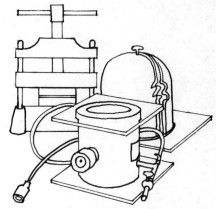

A centrifugal casting unit

Adjustable Clips

Used to hold work steady while soldering.

Felt Sticks

A felt stick, coated with rouge or tripoli powder, is used after emery papering, for polishing.

Buff Sticks

Buff sticks have emery papered surfaces of varying grades for removing file marks.

A typical workbench situation

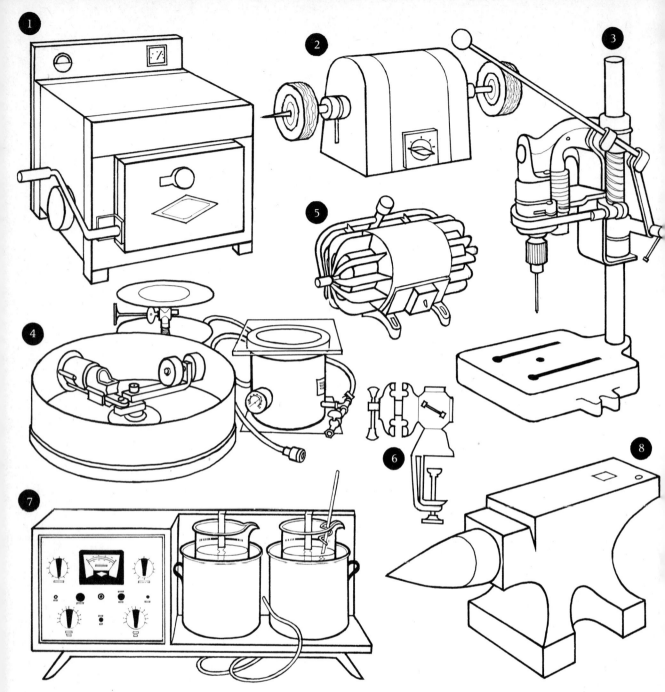

1 Enamelling kiln

An enamelling kiln capable of controlled temperatures up to 1030°C could also be used for niello work or in the lost-wax casting technique

2 Double ended polishing machine

A double-ended polishing machine ('Jugodent') with tapered spindles and capable of 2,750/3,000 rev/min

3 Upright hand operated drill

4 Centrifugal casting machine and vacuum chamber

Casting equipment includes a centrifuge and a vacuum investing and casting unit

5 Compressor

A compressor ('Reciprotor') supplies a powerful stream of air to be mixed with gas for soldering

6 Bench mounted hand vise

A bench vise with an adjustable swivel head and two different sized jaws, one of which is grooved to hold wire

7 Electroplating equipment

A plating bath deposits a film of metal (usually gold, silver or rhodium) on a base

8 Anvil

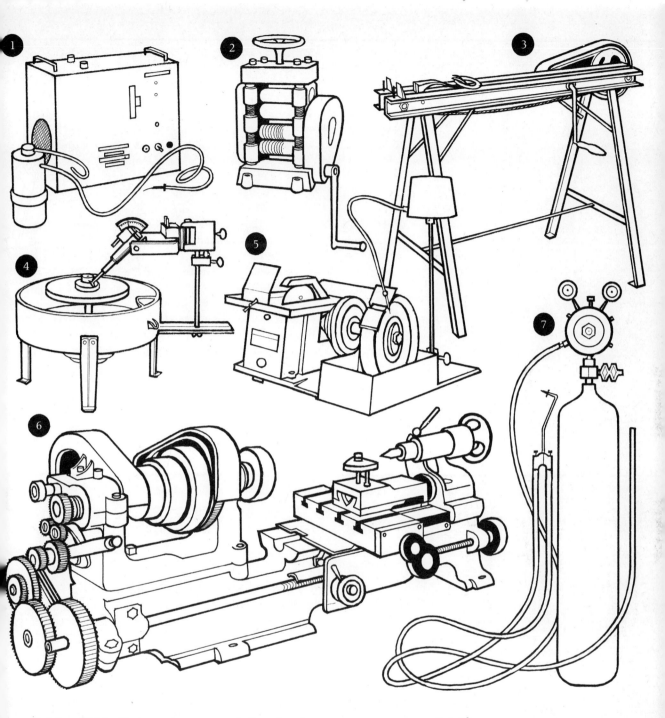

1 Micro Weld soldering equipment

A Micro Weld Micro Flame Gas generator is a sophisticated soldering apparatus for very fine work

2 Rolling mills

Rolling mills. This combined set is used for rolling sheet or square wire

3 Drawbench

4 Stone cutting machine

5 Slabbing and grinding machine

For lapidary work; a Robilt slabbing machine for cutting stones and polishing cabochon stones and a faceting machine

6 Lathe

7 Oxy/Acetylene cylinder and torch

An oxygen cylinder combined with gas and its particular torch is used for soldering or melting when extremely high temperatures are required

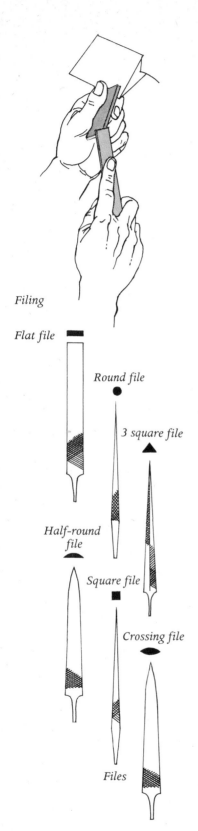

Filing

Flat file

Round file

3 square file

Half-round file

Square file

Crossing file

Files

Filing

The basic ways of shaping metal for jewellery are by sawing and filing. Once the shape has been sawn out, the file is used to smooth off rough edges that may have been left, and to refine the detail of the work. The principle with filing, as with sawing, is to match the grade of file to the gauge of metal, using a heavy file for a thick metal and, if the work requires it, gradually coming down through the range of files, using finer and more specific files as the work is refined and becomes more precise.

There are literally hundreds of different types of file available, each for specific jobs, and within each category there will be a range of coarse, medium and fine files. There is a need for such a very large range, for a basic requirement is that the right file be used for each aspect of the work as it progresses. There will be a shape of file that most adequately cuts the shape that you require, and it wastes time to use a file designed for another purpose. It may also diminish the quality of the finishing.

The file cuts on the forward stroke, and it should be used in a stroke that follows along the contour of the work, not across it, other than minimally. If one were filing a large outward curve, a flat file should be used in long strokes, working evenly forward. For an inner curve a half-round file would be used, with the same smooth even strokes. Erratic filing, or filing diagonally across the edge, could produce a series of flats rather than the required curve.

Should the teeth of the file become clogged with filings, they can be brushed clear with a wire brush.

Sawing

To fit a saw blade, put it into the top jaw of the frame as far as it will go. The teeth must be facing out, away from the frame and slanting downwards, as when sawing the teeth cut on the down stroke. Not all saw blades are the same length, but the saw frame can be adjusted to the required size, using the screw clamp on the spine, through which the spine can slide to lengthen or shorten it.

It is essential to have a taut blade – a flaccid one will not saw accurately and will break. To give this tautness and tension in the blade, the frame has been designed to allow for a certain flexibility, by the introduction of the curve at the top of the spine which gives springiness. The point is to compress the frame while inserting the blade. On release the blade will be taut.

The length of the blade should be 3 mm ($\frac{1}{8}''$) shorter than the length allowed for in the frame, so that when it is tightened into the bottom jaw as far as it will go, the frame is still slightly compressed and the blade taut.

The best way to fit a blade is by placing the handle of the frame against your chest, and holding it horizontally with the top end resting against the bench peg, insert the saw blade into the top jaw. Having tightened the top nut, gently lean on the handle to compress the frame, insert blade into lower jaw and tighten that nut. Release pressure on saw frame slowly as a quick release may break the blade. The blade will now be taut. When flicked with a finger nail, it should give a slight ping. Failure to do this means the saw is not taut and will not cut straight, and will probably break.

Do not tighten any screws on a saw frame with pliers, as this will in time strip the thread from the screw.

When the saw frame is not in use, release the blade from the lower jaw, otherwise a tool accidentally dropped on it will probably break the blade.

The virtue of an adjustable saw frame is that even a short length of broken saw blade can still be used.

When sawing, as far as possible keep the blade perpendicular (ie at right angles to the work), and try to use the full length of the blade. The cutting is always on the downward stroke. There should be no need to force the blade through the work, or to use quick up and down strokes.

To make a right-angled cut in a piece of metal, saw to the corner and then, keeping the saw frame moving up and down but not forward, gently turn the frame to the direction in which you wish to go. This clears the corner of metal to allow the saw blade to negotiate it. With practice one can move the metal rather than the saw frame, or both metal and saw. This is a particularly useful technique when sawing a curve.

When sawing thicker metal, occasionally stroke the saw very lightly on a piece of beeswax to lubricate it. When you became more adept at sawing, there are occasions when the saw can take the place of a file – for instance, in a very fine slot where one could not fit a file, to straighten up the edges.

If the design does not permit sawing from the edge of the metal into the centre a hole must be drilled, and the saw blade inserted through the hole before the blade is tightened in the lower jaw, and then proceed to saw out the design.

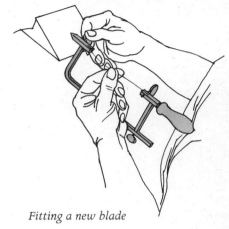

Fitting a new blade

Annealing

Most metal will have been bought in sheet form from a bullion merchant. In its manufacture it will have been rolled flat through rolling mills, which will have altered its molecular structure and thereby been work-hardened. Before it can be worked it must be softened, by annealing, to restore it to its natural state. When buying metal there is a choice between 'hard rolled' or 'soft rolled', ie un-annealled, or annealed. However, despite the state in which metal is bought, I would, as a precaution, recommend annealing it prior to working with it.

Gain experience of saw-piercing using simple designs

47

Metal is annealed by heating to a dull red and then being allowed to cool. It will then be soft enough to work. Over-heating, for instance to white hot, will not make it softer but will damage it. Some alloys may be quenched when hot, but usually the bullion merchants will advise you on this point.

Soldering

Soldering need not be difficult provided a basic set of rules is followed. There are several alternative methods of soldering and each may be successful in the hands of an individual craftsman.

In my teaching I have found that the most common problem students have is to solder correctly. The master craftsman to whom I was apprenticed taught me a method of soldering that I have found faultless, if followed meticulously. If you follow the procedure I describe, your soldering should be totally successful.

Soldering is the technique of joining two pieces of metal together by flowing another molten metal between them which, on cooling, unites them wholly. The metal to be made molten is solder. It will be of the same type of alloy as the work it is being used on (gold on gold, silver on silver) but of a lower quality and having therefore a lower melting point than the work piece. When heat is applied the solder will melt first, before the heat can affect the work piece, and it will flow into the join, penetrating slightly into each face of the join and fusing the faces together.

The strongest join will be one in which the melting point of the solder is only slightly below the melting point of the metal. Solder is composed of the metal to be soldered and a proportion of a baser metal. The addition of the baser metal reduces the quality of the alloy, allowing it to melt more easily than the metal. The less the reduction in quality, the harder the solder will be. The greater the reduction of quality, the lower the melting point and consequently the easier flowing the solder will be. The degree of reduction will therefore produce hard, medium and easy solder. As an example of reduction in quality, 18 carat gold can be used to solder 22 carat. There are specific solders for each metal and detail of their constituents are given in the section on alloys. Solders can be bought ready made, or you can alloy them, ie, make them yourself.

When making a solder it is essential to remember that if the quality of the solder becomes too low the work piece as a whole may not pass the assay test. Too great a proportion of solder on the work may reduce the total precious metal content so much that it will be beneath the assay standard and therefore would not be hallmarked. It is also unnecessary and shows poor craftsmanship to use too much solder.

Soldering is not intended to fill a space – on the contrary, the join to be soldered must be closed as tightly as possible with no visible gap – preferably one should not be able to see light through the join. To endeavour to fill a gap with it would give a weak and unsatisfactory join. A correctly soldered join will be one in which a mere film of solder covers each face and penetrates slightly into the metal when fused, bringing about a homogeneous join.

Having made it clear that solder is not a gap filler, and that any space between the faces to be joined must be minimal, one may wonder whether and why the solder should penetrate this minute area. It does so, firstly by its nature and secondly by capillary attraction.

CAPILLARY ATTRACTION

Capillary attraction is the process whereby a fluid substance will flow into and even up a narrow gap between two solids. As a simple example, if a clean sheet of glass, lying horizontally, had a little pool of water placed on it and another clean piece of glass was laid on top of the first, and moved until its edge touched the water, some of the water would immediately flow into the minute gap between the two sheets of glass. The water is 'pulled' into the gap by capillary attraction. Provided the gap is minute, the effect will be the same even when the glass sheets are held vertically, and the water will remain within the gap.

The same effect occurs when a join or gap is being soldered. The fluid solder is attracted, even against gravity, into the 'capillary' gaps and remains there.

Solders

A clear example of the principle of soldering is as mentioned earlier – the fact that 22 carat gold can be soldered with 18 carat gold – 18 carat gold can be soldered with 14 carat gold. While the principle would still prevail in that 14 carat gold can be soldered with 9 carat gold, I would not recommend this because of the colour difference in the 9 carat, but I would use the specific soldering alloy for 14 carat.

Hard solder for a given metal will most closely resemble the metal in colour, as it contains the highest proportion of this metal. As the easier solders contain less of the metal and more of the other alloying metals, they will be that much further removed in colour.

I strongly recommend that hard solder be used whenever possible because of both its matching colour and its strength. It should be used through as many stages in making a piece of jewellery as is feasible.

However, if many hard solderings are going to be necessary, there will come a point when the repetition of soldering and the intensity of heat required for it will begin to affect the earlier solderings adversely. In effect, the base metals in the alloy, which melt more easily, are being burnt out and this results in pitting and weakening in the soldered area. At this point one would have to begin to use medium solder. It will be difficult for the student to judge when this is necessary but at any sign of the slightest pitting a change to medium solder should be made at once.

Medium solder is then used until it too is likely to be adversely affected by the heat required, and the soldering is then finished with easy solder.

FLUX

Soldering cannot be done without the use of a flux. The function of flux is to keep the cleaned surface free from oxidization (which occurs when heat is applied) and to assist the flow of the solder.

For most gold and silver work, borax mixed with water has proved to be an ideal flux for jewellery working, known over many, many years. It was possibly the first known flux.

Borax can be bought as a powder, in lump form, or in a compressed cone. The cone or lump borax needs to be rubbed on the slightly abrasive surface of a borax tray or a piece of ordinary slate to grind a little of it off, and this is then mixed with distilled water to the consistency of milk. Avoid using tap water as it contains lime. There are proprietary brands of flux available in both powdered and ready-mixed liquid form. *Easy-flo* is a powder flux, and *Auflux* a fluid, and other brands of flux are available.

It is essential in soldering to make absolutely sure that everything is perfectly clean – implements, metals, hands and materials. If a metal surface becomes dirtied in any way, the borax and the solder will not penetrate through the dirt. This is one of the most common causes of unsuccessful soldering. Even the natural oil from one's hands is sufficient to interfere with the flux and the solder.

PAILLONS

Solder generally comes in strip form of varying widths and is fairly thin and therefore suitable for most purposes. However, for very fine work it may need to be rolled thinner.

If the solder has been left in the open (particularly silver solder) for any length of time, it will have become oxidized or dirty, and must be either pickled or lightly emery papered to remove this film before beginning to work with it. Only a very small amount of solder is needed to fuse a join, and the solder strip must therefore be cut into extremely small pieces. These are called paillons.

The most efficient way of cutting them is by using shears and holding the strip of solder between thumb and first finger, steadying the bottom blade of the shears on the second finger, and cutting a series of strips into the length of the solder piece. Then turn the solder so the shears will cut across at right angles, still with the bottom blade on the second finger, and now with the solder pressing against the finger, cut through the solder strips and in doing so, press the cut pieces onto your finger by turning the shears to hold them, and transfer them to the borax tray. This method of cutting and holding solder will prevent the paillons

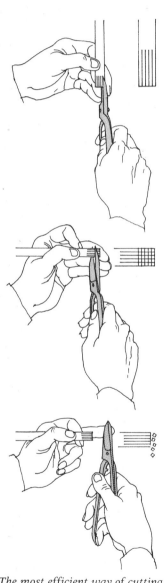

The most efficient way of cutting paillons

50

from flying in all directions.

It is important to be able to cut solder into these equally sized pieces. When cutting the strips into the piece of solder, the right-handed shears in general use allow you to see the width of each strip as you cut it.

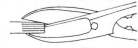
Shears cutting paillons

But when cutting across the strips to make the paillon, the top blade of the shears blocks your view. If left-handed shears are used for this cut, you will be able to see the cutting edge and consequently the size of the paillon as you cut it because the blades of left-handed shears are in the reverse position to right-handed shears. They are, however, not easy to obtain. If the work piece requires a large number of solderings with paillons of the same size, one way of ensuring that the paillons are identical is to make up wire solders into jump rings which, when cut through, will be equally sized units.

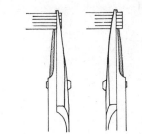
Right-handed and left-handed shears

The paillons are dropped into the already mixed flux in the borax tray and lightly coated on both sides, using a fine sable brush, to be ready for use. Do not, however, leave them there from one job to the next, as you may forget what grade of solder was being used and so inadvertently use hard solder when you meant to use easy solder, or vice versa. Always clean the borax tray and remove any paillons after each job.

Paillons Required

A difficult point for a student to learn is how much solder is needed to join two pieces of metal; only experience can teach you.

As has been explained, the merest film of molten solder is required to flow between the two surfaces to be joined. It is difficult to make a calculation as to the area that a given paillon of solder will cover when it is melted. Too many factors are involved, such as the type of solder being used, its gauge, the type of metal being used and its gauge, the number of solderings to be done, etc.

As the solder is for joining only and as there should be no real gap to fill, the melted solder should flow between the surfaces until it is of almost immeasurable thinness. It will also have slightly penetrated the surfaces, and its bulk will be thereby further diminished. One has therefore to try to calculate what the bulk of a minute paillon of solder will spread to when it is melted. An added difficulty is that solders are available in a variety of thicknesses (or gauges) depending upon whether they are hard, medium or soft.

The diagram demonstrates a very rough visual approximation of the amount of paillons needed to melt and satisfactorily join a given area. In this case, hard silver solder paillons are being used to solder silver.

Solder when heated will run like water; silver solder particularly is remarkably fluid. Therefore, use fewer paillons than may seem necessary and if these are insufficient, extra paillons can be added and resoldered immediately.

An approximation of the proportion of thin paillons needed to solder a given area. If thick paillons were used there would be fewer

If too much solder was used it would overflow the join, and if too little it would not flow over the whole surface. This may be seen as the solder melts, but if it was not evident then, it would become apparent when the work piece was pickled and dried, as gaps would show where the solder had failed to flow to all the edges.

Part of the Hotnitsa Treasure, Bulgaria. Gold medallion of Aeneolithic Age in form of Aen idol. Prior to 3000 BC

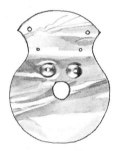

Gold Idol from the Moigrad Treasure. Roumania. Late Neolithic (or even the Chalcolithic). Circa 3000 BC.

Silver pectoral. Chimu. 12th/13th century BC

SOLDERING METHOD

Ensure that everything is absolutely clean and the paillons are cut and fluxed in the borax tray in preparation for soldering. Remember that if the work is not correctly fluxed the solder will not evenly penetrate the area as it should.

To solder

1. The work must be gently warmed before applying the flux.
2. Flux the area where the soldering is to be done. When the flux is brushed on to the warm surface, it should bubble gently and spread evenly, either through a slit or over an area, and this even spreading results in an even soldering. If the flux is applied to cold metal it will dry in a patchy way, which will be uneven and would not penetrate the join. Conversely, if the metal is heated too much the flux will dry immediately on contact and not penetrate evenly or fully, and it is also likely that the brush will stick to the metal.
3. Anneal the work all over to a dull red to relieve any tension that may have been in the metal and to ensure that the flux has evenly covered the area. Examine it to see that no distortion has occurred and, if it has, allow the work to cool, adjust the distortion and reheat. As a rule there is no need to re-flux.
4. The cold wet paillons must be placed in position while the work is hot, taking them from the borax tray with a fine pair of tweezers. Because the paillons are cold fluxed, on contact with the heated flux on the work the fluxes will amalgamate, almost like a glue, and when heat is applied to melt the paillon it will stay exactly where placed.
5. Apply the heat evenly all over the work and the solder will flow correctly.

Only experience will teach a student how to place the paillons so that the solder will flow in the required direction but, for example, in the case of a ring shank, the paillon or paillons should be placed across the join and if the ring is evenly heated all over with the torch, the solder should flow in a liquid state through the join. Immediately the solder flows, remove the flame.

Too fierce a heat concentrated on the solder area, rather than even overall heating, would result in the solder running into little balls and probably dropping off, and the solder would then have to be replaced with new paillons.

Uneven heating, or too much heat on one side only of a join, could result in the solder flowing away from the join to the hotter area, but even heating of the piece will cause the solder to flow into the join. If the solder does flow to one side, stroke it back towards the join with the point of the tweezers, rather like using a brush stroke when painting.

SOLDERING WITH STRIP OR WIRE

If a long join has to be soldered, solder in narrow strip or wire form can be used instead of paillons. This technique requires a lot of practice but will ultimately save the time of paillon cutting and placing. It is not a general practice in jewellery making, but is used in gold- and silver-smithing where long joins will more frequently occur. The technique is to anneal the metal after fluxing, place the point of the strip of solder at the beginning of the join and direct the flame just in front of it. As the point of the solder strip liquifies, move the solder strip and flame along until the join is fully soldered. As previously stated, it takes practice to regulate the flow of the solder evenly, but does save a lot of time.

LEAD SOLDER

In using soft solder, ie lead solder, a minute soft flame or a soldering iron must be used. Lead solder would not be used in making jewellery, but it may be necessary to use it for delicate repairs. For example, should an antique ring with a stone in it require repair there would be a possibility of damaging the stone by removing it. Lead solder should then be used because it will melt much more easily than any other solder. The heat required for any other solder would damage most stones, with the possible exception of a diamond, sapphire and ruby, but it's wise not to take chances with stones where heat is concerned.

Lead solder should only ever be used as a last resort because it can severely damage gold in particular, and silver. It can, in effect, actually eat into gold when the gold is heated.

After using it in the soldering area, make quite sure that all traces of it are swept or cleared away – it is, in fact, preferable to do any work with it on a charcoal block which can be removed and any residue swept off into the dust bin.

Lead solder has its own flux, known as soft soldering flux, in liquid form. Flux for lead solder can be made by putting pieces of zinc in a porcelain bowl containing hydrochloric acid until the acid has dissolved all the zinc. This can then be strained and bottled for future use.

To Remove Lead Solder

Should you have to remove lead solder, scrape off as much as possible with a scraper and then make up a solvent of:

a mixture of 4 parts Ferric Chloride,
$\frac{1}{2}$ part Hydrochloric acid.

Boil, immerse the article (provided it contains no stones, with the exception of a diamond). Remove it occasionally and scrub it lightly until the solder is removed.

Another solution is:

3 parts Glacial Acetic Acid;
1 part Hydrogen Peroxide.

Use warm and treat the article as above. Wash thoroughly and dry in warm sawdust.

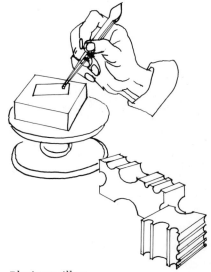

Placing paillons

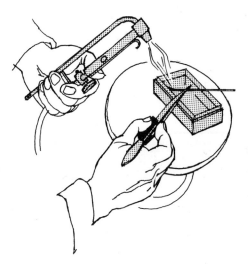

Soldering with strip or wire

53

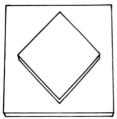

Two squares of metal for a simple soldering exercise

AN EXAMPLE OF SIMPLE SOLDERING

I would suggest that the student begins to practice soldering, using a simple design of one square of metal laid diagonally upon a larger square. Saw the squares out of sheet metal. The piece that is to be the top should have its underside prepared in the usual manner, ie warmed, boraxed, annealed. The solder will have been prepared already, cut into paillons, placed in the borax tray and coated on both sides with borax. While the top piece is still hot, place the paillons at intervals on its surface and then heat until they flow. They will flow into small mounds without flooding the whole surface. If you think you have enough solder on the piece, pickle it. After pickling and drying, take a flat file and file the mounds level. The aim is to retain the solder, so don't file it all away but aim to level it. Slightly bevel the edges on the soldered side of the piece with a flat file, warm, borax and place in borax tray, soldered side down. Now warm, borax and anneal the bottom piece and pick up the cold boraxed piece from the borax tray and place it in position on the hot bottom piece. Because the top piece is cold and wet it will immediately adhere to the hot piece. It is important that the cold piece should be placed in its correct position as it will become 'glued' to the base. If it should have to be repositioned this can be done when you begin heating the two pieces. When you are satisfied that they are correctly in position, apply the heat until the solder flows. You will be able to observe this happening as the top piece slowly subsides onto the bottom piece. As the solder melts it will shine as a bright colour along the joins.

The two pieces are now soldered and can be pickled and finished. In the pickling it will become apparent if the piece has been inadequately soldered as gaps will show along the seam. This will mean that not enough paillons were used.

To add more, warm the whole piece, re-borax all over, anneal and place cold, wet paillons where you think they are necessary. Because they will now be on the outside of the top piece instead of beneath it, they may flow outwards instead of under the piece when soldered. With more experience this fault can be avoided but at this stage the excess solder must simply be filed off after the piece has been pickled. It can then be finished.

This simple piece could be made into a pendant or brooch by the addition of fittings.

Remember the sequence in soldering
1. Warm the metal.
2. Apply borax so that it bubbles on and in.
3. Anneal the metal.
4. Check that no distortion (either expansion or contraction) has taken place.
5. Check that borax has covered the area to be soldered.
6. Place cold, wet paillons in position on heated work.
7. Flow solder.

This example of a more complicated piece of soldering also utilizes saw-piercing, and the use of these two basic techniques in jewellery making will give you some indication of the skills necessary to become a craftsman. The same tools and techniques will be used in almost all the jewellery making processes, and even the more complicated practices and sophisticated tools are based on these simple essentials.

The key pattern design piece is to be soldered to the background piece. For this exercise, use either brass or copper and use silver solder so that the colour differences will expose your mistakes more clearly. As it is merely an exercise in soldering experience, copper or brass will be adequate and will save the expense of silver. Silver solder is a most efficient solder for copper and brass although they each have their own solders, one of which is spelter.

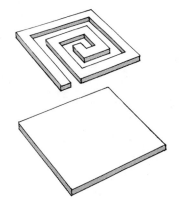

Solder design to backplate

The design can be drawn most simply by using squared paper, and this can then be glued to the metal, or the design could be drawn directly on to the metal.

Saw pierce the design piece. Begin by sawing off the outside edges, keeping the saw frame perpendicular and sawing straight up and down with short strokes. With experience a longer stroke can be made, but in the beginning short strokes provide more security. Now that the square shape of the design piece has been made, the open part of the key pattern is to be sawn out.

Saw along the main band of the design until the corner is reached. The design must then be sawn at right angles. To do this, keep the saw frame moving up and down just before the corner and very carefully cut a minute diagonal across the corner to join the line going at right angles and saw along this. This diagonal can be trued up into a right angle subsequently by careful sawing or filing.

When one is more experienced this right-angled turn can be made by gently sawing up and down on the spot while turning the metal against the saw until the 90° angle has been completed. One will thereby have cut a tiny circular hole, right in the corner, to accommodate the width of the saw blade as it turns, and this will be subsequently trued up with a file. When the design has been sawn out, trim the edges with a file.

Solder does have a tendency to overflow or to flow where it is not wanted. With this design, as any other, a sure way to prevent the solder overflowing or flowing in the wrong direction is to turn the design piece over and lightly file the edges of the back to a slight bevel (or chamfer). Then when the design piece is soldered upon the back plate, any overflow will be concealed beneath the bevels.

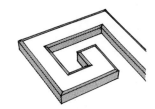

File the edges of the back to a bevel

Prepare the reverse side of the design piece for soldering by warming and applying the borax. Then anneal, and while still hot, take the cold boraxed paillons from the borax tray and lay them on at intervals. As they are wet and cold, the moment they are placed on the hot metal they will stay exactly where positioned. Now apply the flame until the solder flows.

The result will look uneven due to the melting of the paillons. Pickle

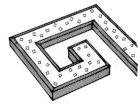

Lay paillons on at intervals

Paillons before flowing

Paillons filed after flowing

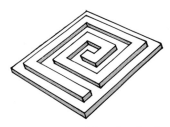

Design piece positioned on back plate

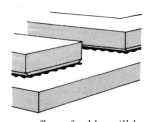

Any overflow of solder will be concealed beneath bevels

Solder on a wig so heat flows evenly all around

and dry, and with a flat file or carborundum stone, level off the unevenness, but not right down to the surface of the design piece, otherwise there will be no solder left. Wash and dry, warm slightly and place in the Borax tray, with the soldered surface downwards.

The design piece and the background plate are now to be soldered together. Warm the background plate gently and apply flux evenly all over and anneal it. While the background plate is still hot, take the design piece from the cold flux and position it as accurately as possible on the background plate. As the design piece is cold and the back plate hot, the two pieces should stay exactly where placed. Apply the flame to solder them. Should the design piece wander in the soldering, gently push it back into position with tweezers. When the pieces are soldered no solder should be visible. If there were to be a slight excess it would be concealed beneath the bevels. Always solder if possible on a pure charcoal block, or on a wig which allows the heat to encircle above and beneath the work.

A less professional, and also more difficult way of soldering this exercise would be to do it without chamfering the edges. The paillons would then have to be placed on the sides of the design piece and in the soldering the tendency would be for the solder to flow down over the background, rather than in and under the design piece. It would have to be filed away and this could be very difficult in the inside corners of the right angles.

For this reason, always try to place the paillons in such a way that, should they flow incorrectly, there will be room for a file to manoeuvre to remove the excess solder with a minimum of damage to the metal's surface.

The earlier example of one square soldered on to another used this method with unchamfered edges for the sake of simplicity, but as soon as some experience of soldering is achieved always use the most professional and craftsmanlike method in preference to what may seem to be the easy solution.

HEAT

A rough general guide to the heating power of the various gases is:
1. Oxygen/Acetylene is the hottest.
In decreasing order . . .
2. Oxygen/hydrogen.
3. Oxygen/propane.
4. Oxygen/coal gas.
5. Compressed air/natural gas or coal gas.
6. Air/propane,
Air/Butane,
Air/Methane.
Any of the methods of heating/soldering/melting could be used on silver or gold, but an intense heat such as that given by the combinations in (1), (2) and (3) would be necessary to solder or melt platinum and some white golds.

Even though one's workspace is equipped with natural gas, I think that a supply of bottled gas and its appliances should also be included in the workshop equipment. Obviously they would be essential if there were some failure of the ordinary gas source, but there would also be instances where it might not be possible to use natural gas, eg in an all electric building or if the expense of connecting gas to the mains was prohibitive.

NATURAL GAS

The coal gas we have been using for domestic and industrial purposes has by now been almost superseded by natural gas. In the fields of metallurgy and gold and silver working, natural gas is superior to coal gas as it is purer, more consistent and almost devoid of undesirable sulphur compounds. All the equipment that used coal gas will have to be converted or replaced to use natural gas.

Natural gas is slightly more difficult to use as it does not function in quite the same way as coal gas, and the jeweller must have the patience to learn to adjust his technique to use this new gas. In general, the volume of gas needed to perform a particular task with natural gas is about half that of coal gas.

Natural gas is hotter than coal gas, and to use it successfully the size of its flame will need to be reduced to compensate for the extra heat given out. If the flame is turned up high and one is using, for instance, a mouth blow torch, it is very difficult to blow hard enough to combine the gas and air in the correct proportion. The gas will have to be turned down until it combines successfully with the air flow to give the type of flame required. You will have to continue to practise and experiment until the correct proportion of air and gas is found. The principle is to turn the gas fully on, then turn it down to almost half. Introduce the air flow gradually and bring them up together until the required flame is reached. The gas will blow out if air is introduced too quickly or too fiercely. Once the correct flame has been obtained, leave it alone. Gentler blowing will give the same size of flame as you are used to with coal gas, but you will find that the flame is not so clearly visible. It is much more neutral in colour, and in daylight can be very hard to see, which increases the risk of over-heating.

Using the flame in a confined space can present difficulties. When the flame is directed, for example, into the hooded crucible used in centrifugal casting to melt the metal, the flame tends to disperse and reflect back from within the confined space. The flame must consequently be turned down until it becomes small enough to be directed accurately without dispersing itself.

It is difficult to judge when the flame will have reached its greatest heat, but as an approximate guide only, this is likely to be when the torch is giving off the fiercest noise, as it was when coal gas was being used.

This governing of the gas/air ratio applies to all natural gas usages and the main point is to start with a small gas flame into which the air source is gradually added and the two brought up together to produce the required flame.

Bottled Gas

If there is no access to coal or natural gas, there are a number of other types of gas that may be used such as Butane, Ronson, Calor, Propane, and others. This type of gas comes in cylinders or bottles, and in some cases the manufacturers supply their own type of soldering torch. With bottled gases tubing of a special composition will be supplied and must be used, as the ordinary gas tubing is not suitable.

If one needs a higher temperature than the gas/air mixture will give, then the combination of either oxygen and gas, or oxygen and hydrogen, or oxygen and acetylene will produce it.

Because of the danger involved in using gas, both ends of the gas tube should be attached with a Jubilee clip where it leaves the gas source and where it is attached to the torch, which will prevent gas leakage.

One of the dangers of using bottled gas is that, should it leak, the gas will lie low on the ground and the chances, therefore, of an accidental explosion are higher than when using coal or natural gas which rises. Therefore when working with bottled gas, make sure that the closing valve is turned off securely after use.

If you are using a gas torch in combination with a compressor, the Gas Board require the fitting of a flow-back cock between the gas meter and the torch, to avoid any likelihood of an explosion.

Incidentally, if you do not have a compressor, the air pipe of the soldering torch can be attached to a pair of foot bellows, to give a greater heat than that you could achieve by mouth blowing.

If, for some reason, it was impossible to use the normal soldering appliances, a blow lamp burning either petrol or paraffin could be used. There are alternative types of burner that use methylated spirits, such as the *Vatlocke* Automatic Blowlamp etc. Even a Bunsen burner could be used for soldering.

SOLDERING TORCHES

The conversion to natural gas will have meant that existing soldering torches would have had to be converted for its use and, of course, a large number of new torches have been specifically designed for natural gas; there will, I imagine, continue to be new torches introduced on to the market for some time. It can therefore be difficult to decide which to acquire. Individual preferences affect the issue, as does the type of work you do and the circumstances in which it is done.

I have now had the opportunity of testing many torches, all of which I can thoroughly recommend. As far as function is concerned, there is nothing to choose between them, as they all perform equally well when correctly used. My students do complain of difficulties in using torches for natural gas, but the fault is not in the torch, but in the usage. Check with the manufacturer if these difficulties continue, as there may be an adjustment required. Otherwise ask his advice on usage and follow the instructions accurately in the realization that you have to adapt your technique to the new torch.

The only drawback to the new torches is that they do not work in exactly the same way as the torch one is used to.

The differences between them, in my opinion, are simply that some are more aesthetically pleasing in appearance, some are better constructed and some are better balanced for handling.

My personal preferences are

1. for use with natural gas, the products made by *Adaptogas* and *Wilkes*,

2. for use with bottled gas, the *Sievert* equipment,

3. for use with oxygen and gas the *Dependox* oxygen and gas torch, in my opinion this is excellently designed and finished and extremely well balanced for handling.

The natural gas torches come in a variety of sizes, most of which would encompass the major part of jewellery soldering. If it was necessary to melt a large amount of metal or to solder larger areas, the bigger torches would have to be used, in conjunction with a compressor.

I must stress that the tools I describe are my personal preferences and in no way reflect disadvantageously on other makes of torch or appliance that I may not have tested.

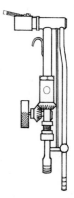

Wilkes natural gas mouth blow pipe

Mouth Blow Pipe Torch

This is a hand-held torch used with coal gas, or natural gas, via a tube from the main gas supply. A second tube of rubber or plastic is attached to the torch, through which you blow air from your mouth. The heat of the gas alone would be insufficient for soldering. The air that you blow combines with the gas in the flame to produce the required stronger heat. The volume of the flame is controlled by a small tap on the torch that regulates the gas, and also by the amount of air blown. To obtain the most efficient heat for a given purpose, the gas and air volume must be adjusted, and with experience you will learn how to govern the blowing and the amount of gas to use. Using the greatest volume of gas and blowing hard does not give the greatest heat nor the most efficient. *Adaptogas* and *Wilkes* and other companies have redesigned their mouth blown torches especially for natural gas. The new equipment allows for great variance in flame and heat, as the torches are available in different sizes, and with interchangeable jets for specific purposes.

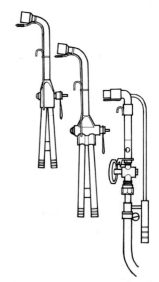

Adaptogas torches for natural gas and air. The third torch can be converted for use with butane and propane

Bench Swivel Torch

The bench swivel torch is also supplied by gas from the mains. It has a gas control tap which is kept full on. The torch will swivel through an arc of 90° and this movement regulates the volume of gas emitted. When the torch is facing away from you, the minimum gas is coming out, which serves as a pilot light. As the torch is swivelled toward you a greater volume of gas comes out and when it is 90° from its original position there will be a full flow of gas.

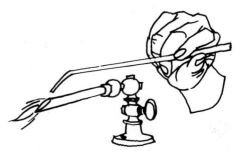

Using the mouth blow torch

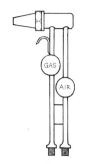

Wilkes needle-valve natural gas blow pipe

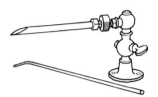

Bench swivel torch converted with aerator unit for natural gas and mouth blow torch

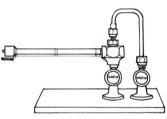

Adaptogas side light for natural gas

Microflame weldmaster torch for use with oxygen or compressed air, and acetylene, butane, propane, natural gas

This flame is directed by a flow of air which is mouth blown via a small tapered metal tube called a mouth blow-pipe. The particular advantage of this type of torch is that it leaves both hands free to work. For all its simplicity, it is still in use among the best craftsmen in the world. *Adaptogas* have introduced an adaptor unit to allow existing equipment to be used with natural gas, and have designed a new model specifically for natural gas.

Birmingham Side Light

The Birmingham side light is the same design as the bench swivel torch except for one detail; instead of using the mouth-blown pipe, air is blown into a rubber or plastic tube connected at the centre of the swivel pipe. This also allows both hands to be free.

Microflame Weldmaster

The Microflame 'Weldmaster' torch for use with Oxygen/Gas was specially designed to produce a minute flame – pencil point or finer. It is only the size of an average fountain pen, but can produce an extremely delicate flame (under 25 mm (1″) in length) or an extremely fierce one simply by changing to a larger size in its range of oxy/gas nozzles. The transition from oxy/gas to air/gas operation is easily achieved by fitting one of the range of four fine air/gas nozzles available. The 'Weldmaster' may be used with either range of nozzles, and either acetylene or the bottled gases, Butane and Propane, or with natural gas.

Economic supplies of oxygen in small volume are not readily available to the small workshop or to the home hobbyist, so the makers, Microflame, market their own, small sets incorporating a refillable oxygen cylinder, hardly larger than the familiar soda-syphon, which will give up to 40 hours continuous burning with the smaller oxy/gas nozzles. Butane is contained in a throw-away container of the aerosol type and combined with oxygen, provides the 'Weldmaster' torch with flame temperatures of some 2,760 degrees Centigrade (5,000°F), more than twice the melting temperature of silver or gold, and beyond the melting temperatures of even Iridium, Palladium, Platinum or Rhodium.

Dependox

British Industrial Gases Ltd make the *Dependox* torch, for use with gas and oxygen. By changing its tube and jet it becomes the *Dependair* torch for natural gas and air.

Flamemaster

The *Flamemaster* (made by Stonechance) uses natural gas and compressed air, and has the advantage of having its own bench clamp, so that it need not be hand-held.

Sievert, Ronson, Super-Nova 11

The *Sievert* equipment, the small *Ronson* cylinder and the *Super-Nova 11*, using bottled gases, would fully cover the average requirements of jewellery making.

60

Micro Weld Micro Flame Gas Generator

It is likely that the most versatile piece of equipment used for soldering is the Micro Weld Micro Flame Gas Generator. This is not a variation on the types of flame already existing, but an entirely new technique.

The essential difference is that this machine produces its own gas. It has been designed specifically to meet all the soldering requirements in jewellery by its capacity to produce a very wide range of flames. All these have the characteristic that they can be very finely adjusted to range from an almost microscopic flame capable of soldering 'one link of the finest necklace chain without, repeat without, discolouring the adjacent links' to a flame which is 'capable of sizing an emerald ring, which is held in one's hand while soldering'.

The use of this accurately controlled flame has made it possible to make work in precious metal of a design that would be technically impracticable, if not impossible, with the normal flames from gas and oxygen. The temperature of the flame is suitable for the full range of solders including platinum. It can also be used to weld platinum (ie join it without the use of solder).

The machine's versatility can be increased by the use of its range of torches, producing flames of differing intensities. The finest of these would be suitable for such difficult work as, for example, soldering the seam of very thin chenier, an application requiring a low-temperature 'bushy' type of flame, as produced by town/natural gas and air.

The machine is simple to use. Having decided on the size of flame required, an appropriate torch tip is selected and attached, and the gas production from the machine will then be automatically controlled. (The torch tips are like hypodermic needles, and the size of each is stamped on its shaft.)

The flame is used in the same way as any other soldering flame, but there is a difference in that the flame is 'needle-like', having no side heat, but with a temperature gradient, so that the flame is hottest at the tip of the blue cone and ranges to a flame that is still hot enough to solder, even beyond the visible part of the flame.

It is in these characteristics that the technique of using this type of flame differs from the usual flame. Someone new to soldering can be trained to produce correct soldering quite quickly. Oddly enough, someone trained in the traditional method of soldering may find it difficult, initially, to accept the differences in the use of the flame.

The technique of the Micro Weld will be explained by the engineer installing the machine, and although it may appear sophisticated, it is in fact one of the simplest machines to use. The Micro Weld produces its own gas from distilled water by electrolysis; the gas produced is hydrogen and oxygen in the ratio $2:1$. As this mixture of hydrogen and oxygen is fast-burning, a device is used to moderate the flame, thereby allowing a greater degree of control.

The solution in the modifying unit is a highly volatile alcohol which mixes with the hydrogen and oxygen as the gases are passed through it. This results in a very clean flame suitable, for example, for welding 18 carat upwards without the use of solder or flux. The solution may be varied to change the flame temperature and its calorific value

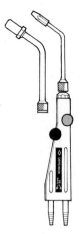

Dependox natural gas and oxygen torch. Alternative tube and tip convert the unit into Dependair torch for natural gas and air

Flame master Stonechance torch for natural gas and air supported in its own bench clamp

Ronson torch with its own butane fuel cylinder

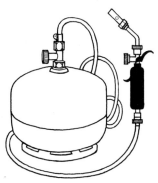

Sievert torch for use with bottled gas (primus)

Approximate flame temperatures

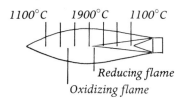

1100°C   1900°C   1100°C

Reducing flame
Oxidizing flame

The flame is hottest about halfway along its length, at the point of the oxidizing flame

It is much easier to hold a large piece of metal while sawing off the narrow band

(amount of heat), but the manufacturers prefer to keep to one solution giving a flame temperature of 1850°C approximately and having a high calorific value, capable of doing larger work. The normal solution will give a flame temperature similar to that of high temperature butane.

For use in large-scale jewellery manufacture, two sizes of machine are available that will cover 85 per cent of soldering requirements, and the larger machines can be made available for use by several operators at one time.

The Flame

Two types of flame are used in jewellery making – the first is a bushy flame that gives a mild, dispersed heat and is less likely therefore to burn or melt work. The second is a short, pointed, fierce flame used for fine work (soldering links or jump rings, etc.) but because of its fierceness great care must be taken to ensure that it doesn't burn or melt the work. To obtain the soft bushy flame the gas volume is turned high and gentle blowing of air is used. The hotter, pointed flame is obtained by turning the gas volume down and blowing harder. In both cases the greatest heat is near the tip of the flame. This heat will be more intense in the fierce pointed flame. The first flame is known as a reducing flame because it reduces the possibility of oxidization taking place and the second is known as an oxidizing flame because it is likely to produce an oxidized surface. For a fully technical explanation of the nature of these flames see E.A. Smith's 'Working in Precious Metals'.

It is worthwhile experimenting on scrap metal and wire in the use of the flame, to become familiar with the amount of air and the amount of heat that will solder, melt or burn. Experiment by placing a paillon of easy silver solder and a paillon of hard silver solder on a piece of silver and apply a flame in an endeavour to melt the easy, but not the hard, solder. This would need a soft bushy flame. Experiment now in melting the hard solder. For this the fiercer flame would be needed, so increase the air pressure and decrease the volume of gas until you can satisfactorily melt the hard solder. Experiment as much as you can to gain knowledge of the use of the torch and flame.

A useful exercise is to make a copper or brass finger ring and solder its join with silver solder. Because of the colour differences in the metals and the solder, it will be immediately apparent whether the soldering has been successful or not. This can also help in determining the amount of paillons necessary for a neat join.

A Simple Ring

One of the earliest forms of personal adornment must surely have been a simple band for the finger, wrist or neck. Prior to the age of metal working, rings were made from stone, bone, wood and even plaited reeds. Their main purpose at that time maybe have been talismanic, hieratic, or a sign of rank, and it was not until many centuries later that the giving of a ring signified betrothal.

The simplest form of ring to make is a perfectly plain band of metal, like a wedding ring. In making it, one will use all the basic techniques in jewellery, and have learnt the procedure for making the shank of all subsequent rings. (A shank is the band that encircles the finger.)

To make a ring, select a piece of metal at least 7·5 cm (3″) long and about 5 cm (2″) wide. Although the ultimate width of the ring may be only 6 mm ($\frac{1}{4}$″) wide, it is much easier to hold a large piece of metal while sawing off the narrow band. Decide on the width of the band required, making sure that one side of the metal is a straight edge, and inscribe the width with a pair of dividers, using one leg of them to run along this straight edge. Begin to saw along the inscribed line, endeavouring to keep evenly on one or the other side of the line. When the piece is cut off, straighten the sawn edge with a flat file.

To ascertain the size of the ring required (and for this exercise it would be simpler if it were for you), try on the set of finger sizes until you find the one that firmly fits your finger. This will correspond to a size on the size stick : let us say it is size M in each case. To find out what length of metal is needed, wind a piece of binding wire around the size stick at size M. Cut the wire and measure its length, and add another 6 mm ($\frac{1}{4}$″) as the binding wire will nearly always be thinner than the metal you are using. With a pair of half-round pliers, holding the strip against the curved inner edge of the pliers, begin to curve one end slightly, then the other one. It is easier to curve the ends when they are apart, then one can gradually turn the two ends to an overlapping position.

Always make the ring as round as possible before proceeding, then with the saw cut through the overlap, which will ensure that both ends will be a replica of each other. Allow the ring to be a little larger than required because it is unlikely that it will be perfectly round. Check again on the size stick and if it is too large, saw out a small piece, keeping it parallel with the first cut. Check again, then with the half-round pliers force the two ends to overlap and then allow them to spring back so that the two ends are pressing against each other. This will give the minimum space in the join. This is a vital point, as the soldering of the ends will not fill a gap, but only join two surfaces together.

To gain experience in making the correct size of a ring, make three bands or wedding rings of varying widths to find out the length required for each width. A narrow ring will slide over the knuckle and fit firmly, but a wide band will have to be made from a slightly longer strip of metal.

Always remember that it is easier to cut a piece out of a ring if it is too large than to put a piece in. Do not leave burrs (from sawing or filing) on the edges when soldering is required, as the solder can build up around the burr and will not flow into the join. Make sure that the join in the ring is opposite the hallmark, otherwise the solder could obliterate the hallmark. As it may be necessary to find the join when resizing a ring, it has become the practice to make the join opposite the hallmark.

It is advisable to have work hallmarked while it is flat, before you have started to shape it, as it is easier for you to stamp your name mark,

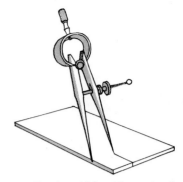

Inscribe the width with a pair of dividers

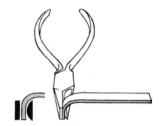

With a pair of $\frac{1}{2}$-round pliers, curve one end slightly

Wind a piece of binding wire around the size stick

Curve one end then the other

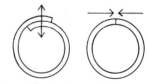

*Saw through the overlap
Overlap the ends and spring them back so that the two ends are forcing against each other*

Make sure that the join is opposite the Hall Mark

Rounding up in swage block

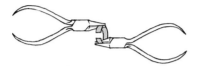

2 pairs of $\frac{1}{2}$-round pliers

Wet solder will adhere on a vertical surface

Solder to be the dimension of area to be soldered

Reverse the ring when tapping on size stick

Rub ring on carborundum stone in figure of eight motion

and for the Assay Office to stamp the hallmark on it at this stage.

If the band you are making is of fairly thick metal, it will need to be rounded up fully before soldering. This can be facilitated by using the swage block and a rod of hardwood (for instance, the stern of a punch is ideal, as it will not mark the metal). Place a piece of cardboard in the curve of the swage block to protect the metal. Place the metal across the curve, and position the wooden rod on the metal. Hammer the rod with a wooden mallet and it will force the metal to take the curve of the swage block. There is a dental product in strip form, known as 'soft metal', which is ideal for this work, instead of cardboard.

The more circular the ring is before soldering, the easier it will be to obtain the correct finger size, as it will fit more easily on the ring stick. Try to make it the correct size before soldering, otherwise (a) it will have to be hammered up to size (which will leave marks that must be removed, or (b) a piece will have to be taken out if too large, or (c) if very much too small, a piece will have to be soldered in.

Bring the ends together with half-round pliers. If the metal is very thick, it may be necessary to use two pairs of pliers.

The ring is now to be soldered. The sequence described in soldering is to be followed:
1. Warm the ring.
2. Borax the ring.
3. Anneal the ring.
4. Check that no distortion has occurred.
5. While hot, place paillon/paillons in position.
6. Apply heat to the ring and flow the solder.

When the solder has flowed, allow the work to cool and place it in hot pickle, using only brass, copper or nickel silver tweezers, until all the oxidization and borax has disappeared. Wash the ring thoroughly and dry it.

Now, file away any residue of solder on the inside with a 20 cm (8″) half-round file, and use a 20 cm (8″) flat file to remove any solder on the outside. Place the ring on the steel ring mandrel and tap firmly to round it with a wooden or leather mallet, which will not leave marks. Tap to the size required, M, checking all the time on the size stick. As the ring stick is tapered in shape, reverse the ring when tapping, otherwise the ring would also become slightly tapered. Emery-paper the outside, the sides and the inside of the ring.

A fine carborundum stone can be used to level the sides which will ensure a very flat surface. Rub the ring on the stone in a figure of eight motion, which ensures that the whole surface is ground evenly by the carborundum. Occasionally place each side of the ring on a flat surface, hold it to the light at eye level to see what high or low spots are present, and keep rubbing down until these irregularities disappear.

If the strip had been filed completely parallel before being turned up into a ring, there will be less work to do after soldering. This approach should be borne in mind with all aspects of jewellery making. Always pre-file, pre-emery and pre-polish whenever possible as work progresses, as it will facilitate the finishing operation. All these pre-finishing techniques result in a higher quality of craftsmanship.

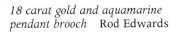
18 carat gold and aquamarine pendant brooch Rod Edwards

A Pendant Brooch

On my first visit to Venice I was very impressed by the magnificence of its architecture, and in particular by the Doge's Palace. The vision of it stayed in my mind, and many years later when I was wondering how to design a pendant for a particularly lovely aquamarine, the memory of it came back and provided the concept of a design based on colonnades reflected in water.

I felt it was necessary for the stone to be held high and as visually free from the base as possible to allow light to penetrate the stone and flow along the base. The design I chose to hold the stone aloft would have to be opened up as much as possible to let light through, and the colonnades of Venice were the main influence here. I wanted to use their decorated pillars to provide a contrast to the clinically smooth reflective surface that I had in mind for the base.

The base began to take shape as a shallow concavity, very highly polished, which by its light would reflect Venice's colonnades and the stone that was the colour of water.

There is a photograph of the final result on this page. This pendant was not intended to be, and of course never could be, a translation of Venice but it does go to show how one's ideas can be influenced by nature, paintings, sculpture, architecture. Each person will find their own stimuli for creative thought – these happen to provide mine. The finished product may differ from the original concept but this evolution of the first idea is the way I arrive at my designs. I drew a rough sketch, and it then occurred to me that, with the correct fittings, it could also be worn as a brooch. The fittings for this will be described later.

I then had to think of the mechanics of the concept. The biggest technical difficulty was to be in attaching the setting for the stone to the base – after both units had been polished. As my intention for the base of the pendant was that it be an extremely highly polished bowl, full of reflections, the difficulty lay in the fact that once it had been polished to the required degree this would have to be preserved and so precluded any subsequent soldering, as the heat would have discoloured it, and it would have been too difficult to re-polish when in one piece.

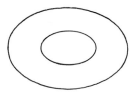
The shapes of the stone and the base

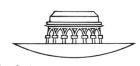
The design

The shape of the bezel and setting

The flat plate of metal, with its centre pierced out to fit the gallery

The shape for the gallery

Colonnades marked on gallery

Detail of the colonnades

The bevelled edge of the plate

Separating an incorrect alignment

Therefore the gallery/colonnades would have to be secured by some means other than soldering (and after all the preliminary soldering had been done).

I devised a solution for this which will be explained. As the piece was to be a brooch as well as a pendant, it had the advantage that when worn as a pendant the brooch pin could secure it on the garment and so prevent the pendant swinging freely and leading thereby, as it so often does, to damage by hitting against something.

In considering the back of the piece, I had to arrange for it to have a brooch pin and catch, as well as a fitting for the pendant and a very small ring to hold a safety chain.

The shape of the stone was an oval and this dictated the echoing shape of the base.

This work was made in 18 carat gold. As a principle, when the shapes of a design have been cut out of the metal it is best to send them for assay while they are still in the flat (including at the same time all the smaller units that may be involved in the job such as wire, catches, joints, etc. There is one exception to this and that is the brooch pin, and the reason for this is explained in hallmarking.)

The work is easier to hallmark in the flat. It is also possible that the work could be bruised by hallmarking and this is easier to eradicate when the work is flat. You can, of course, designate where you wish the hallmark to be placed. Should the metal prove inferior under Assay standard, unlikely as this is, no real work will have been lost while the piece is still in the flat.

I started to make up the design by making a bezel and setting for the stone, using 0·028 metal sheet. If the stone had been an opal or emerald I would have used 0·022 metal as these stones are notably brittle and require a softer or thinner metal to set them safely.

This bezelled setting was to sit on the colonnaded gallery, but sandwiched between them was to be a plate of metal (0·048) slightly larger in diameter, to add to the design. These three components would be assembled after the gallery had been fully completed and polished.

The blank shape of the metal for the gallery (0·048) was turned up and soldered, tapering slightly to the top.

Having decided how many colonnades I required, I marked out their positions. I then saw-pierced between the colonnades and made the necessary adjustments with assorted needle files but mainly with a double half-round needle file. Holes were then drilled between the apexes of the colonnades and these were opened up into triangles with a fine saw.

The setting was now soldered on to the flat plate which had been cut to an oval. Hard solder was used and I was able to use it all through the work. As a principle, always try to use hard solder for as long as you can, as its colour is the closest to that of the metal being soldered and it is, of course, much stronger. The central part of the plate was drilled and pierced out so that its inside edge was nearly level with both setting and gallery, and its outside projecting edge bevelled on both sides.

The plate was now to be soldered to the gallery. To do this, both were warmed, boraxed and annealled. Paillons were placed at regular intervals on the underside of the plate and heated until they flowed. The melted paillons ran into little mounds. They were pickled, washed and dried. The mounds were carefully filed down level. The plate was warmed to ensure that the borax would cover the whole area evenly and put in the borax tray with the soldered surface down.

The gallery was now warmed again. The cold plate was taken from the borax and placed on top of the hot gallery. The two pieces stayed in position because the cold borax met the hot borax and the two amalgamated like a glue. Both units were then heated until the solder flowed. The virtue of this method is that it prevents the pieces wandering or moving while the solder is flowing. However, when you are using this method, if the pieces should wander try to correct this while the solder is molten. If they cannot be correctly positioned then take the plate off and start again. It may be possible, if the solder is still molten, to do this by holding the gallery steady with locking tweezers and giving the top unit a quick flip with tweezers to free it. If they have joined, however, they can be separated by tying a four-stranded binding wire around the circumference of the top piece and another around two or three of the legs of the gallery. Turn the wires to face in opposite directions, reheat and while the solder flows, very gently pull the units apart (like a tug of war.) It helps to have someone pull in one direction while you are heating and pulling the opposite way, but if you have to do it alone, one set of binding wires can be held in locking tweezers and anchored.

Clean the work if you have had to separate them and start again. If you find my method of aligning by borax too difficult, an alternative is to tie the two units together with binding wire to hold them in position while you solder. This is one of the advantages of using a Birmingham side light – it allows you to have both hands free, as does the Stonechance torch which can be held in a clamp especially designed for it.

My design included the use of round and square wires. The round wire was used to surround the base of the setting. It was cut to size with a saw for a clean join and soldered, then shaped with half-round pliers to fit very tightly onto the setting, having almost to be force-fitted so that it would touch both plate and setting. Paillons were placed on the plate and the wire was soldered onto it.

The square wire was used to make a decorative cross bar on the colonnades. Before it could be put on, however, the inside walls of the colonnades had to be fully finished and highly polished because the area between them would be inaccessible for polishing once the cross bars were soldered on. Soldering the bars on discolours the walls a little but they can be finally string finished (as described in the section on polishing).

For the cross bars the process of cutting and joining the square wire was repeated. The wire was placed in position as a force-fit and a paillon of solder placed on the underside of the wire where it crossed each colonnade and soldered.

If some paillons failed to flow under the wire, they were gently stroked into position with the tip of the tweezers until they did. The wire was then sawn through between the colonnades to give the cross bar effect I wanted.

Round and square wires used for decoration

Paillons placed under cross-bar

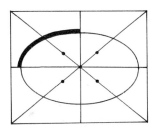

Tracing one segment of an oval on paper

Colonnade legs with chenier

Colonnade legs drilled and tapped for screws

Colonnade legs with half round wires

Pattern for loop

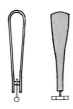

Profile and front view of loop, rod, hook and chenier

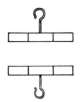

The revolving middle chenier has a hook to attach it to the loop

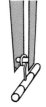

Rod, hook and chenier

The domed oval for the base of the pendant/brooch was the next step. The assayed metal had been previously roughly cut to size but now the oval had to be drawn or scribed on it.

There is a relatively easy way of obtaining an oval even if you cannot draw. On tracing paper rule vertical and horizontal lines at right angles to each other and roughly mark out the size and proportion of the oval you want around these. Now complete one quadrant of the curve as accurately as possible. By folding the paper on the horizontal line this curve can be traced through to the opposite quadrant and similarly by folding vertically and tracing through, the oval can be completed. By drawing diagonal lines through at a 45° angle and measuring equal lengths along them, the inaccuracies can be corrected.

I have yet to explain how the colonnaded structure was attached to the base, but for the moment I need only say there were four alignment points on the base and they lay on the diagonal lines. By estimating the length and width of the gallery their position was approximated. This was checked as the work proceeded for accuracy was essential.

The paper pattern was glued to the back of the metal. As it was the back of the piece, light markings could be made on it, so with a blunt point the centre and marks for the vertical, horizontal and diagonal lines were gently 'dimpled' onto the metal. (The latter were kept just within the edge as they needed to be visible after filing for subsequent accurate alignment.) The colonnade was pressed down onto the paper so that the locating legs could be marked where they lay along the diagonal. (Depending on the number of colonnades in another design they may lie on a diagonal other than the 45° one.) The oval was then pierced out and trued up with a file.

The oval was now domed and I ensured that it was free of all marks before doming was started on it. I removed all extraneous marks (except the 'dimpling') by using emery sticks, beginning with medium and working through the grades to fine emery paper, ending with Water of Ayr stone.

The doming block and punch is described in the section on tools, but in brief, the flat metal is placed over a concave shape and beaten down into it until it follows the concave form. The doming blocks which one can buy have varied sizes of semi-spheres, but should you need a doming hollow that is not circular you will have to make it or have it made.

Lead/tin alloys, wood or metallic putties are the most useful materials for making moulds for doming blocks. I made a lead doming block for the oval shape I wanted, and domed it up, using wooden doming punches. Because both the wood and lead are softer than the metal, they won't mark it. I checked that no flakes of lead were left on the metal before annealing or soldering. If thin paper is laid between the metal and the lead cake there is less risk of lead contaminating the metal.

In doming, the metal takes up the shape of the form it is in remarkably well, without crinkles at the edge, and the metal can be formed evenly and smoothly.

If you were making a piece of jewellery that included an unusual domed shape, while a steel stake may have the sort of form you want, do not use it for this type of work because, in the forming, its hardness may bruise the metal.

When I had completed the doming all the components of the design had been made – the setting plus gallery and the bowl in which they were to sit.

I planned to attach the gallery to the bowl by making tiny screws that went from the back of the bowl through it and up into four of the legs of the colonnade. I used this method as opposed to soldering to avoid interfering with the highly polished surfaces. The four legs of the gallery were located on the back of the bowl along the diagonal lines and at these points holes were drilled through the bowl.

Using the doming die

I then carefully drilled up into the legs and tapped them. Four matching screws were made (as described in the uses of taps and dies). The screws were made from wire and a circular head with a slot in it was soldered on. The holes in the back of the bowl were counter sunk to take the head of the screws and they were screwed through into the legs.

There are alternative ways of securing the gallery to the bowl. One is to solder round or square cheniers on to the ends of the four locating legs to give additional length. These are passed through the locating holes and sawn off, but leaving them projecting slightly. The ends of the chenier are then spread and opened out with a tapered punch (round or square, whichever is applicable), thereby turning them into rivets and so securing the gallery to the bowl.

Loop and bar

Another way is to lengthen the four legs and treat them as a claw setting by soldering round or half-round wires to their ends which can then be bent over and flattened against the back of the base. Taper their points beforehand. The reason for using half round wire is that its flat side can then be pressed up against the base. If round wire is to be used; engrave a shallow channel in which the round wire will lie, slightly proud of the surface.

The next stage was to make the joint, catch and pin for the brooch. The section on Findings will describe how these are made. I soldered the joint and catch to the back, placing them approximately a quarter of the way down from the top, as this prevents the brooch from becoming top heavy and falling forward. A little ring to hold a safety chain was soldered on near the joint.

I had devised a pendant fitting that would be unobtrusive when the piece was worn as a brooch. It was a detachable loop for the pendant chain. The important point was that this fitting should be small, strong and inconspicuous. A device to hold this loop was made as a hook, and soldered to a small length of chenier. The principle is the same as that of making a joint as described in the section on Findings, ie three pieces of chenier are used, two are soldered to a small base plate and the middle one is not soldered but held between the two by a rivet that goes through all three cheniers. I then soldered the hook to the middle chenier so that it could be moved up to hold the loop, or folded down flat against the back of the pendant/brooch when not in use. This fitting was placed near the top of the piece so that the hook, when up and in use, still lay just below the edge.

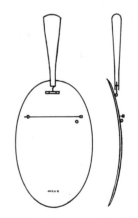

Back of pendant.   *Profile*

Next was the loop. It was shaped as the pattern in the diagram, based

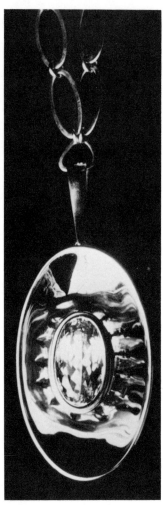

18 carat gold and aquamarine pendant/brooch and chain Rod Edwards

on a curve that was similar to the curve of the bowl, using metal of 0·028 gauge. I domed it in a swage block and turned it up with half-round pliers until the two ends met. I then forced them slightly apart and inserted a piece of round wire, about 0·7 mm ($\frac{1}{32}''$) long, between them and soldered this little bridge in. The loop could then be attached by sliding the hook over the bridge. The whole unit was neat and inconspicuous but still strong enough to carry the quite considerable weight of the pendant.

I made a chain of 0·048 round wire, of links that followed the shape of the bowl, and soldered and polished the links except for the last one. The chain was then threaded through the loop and the last link soldered and polished. Despite the work on the back of the bowl it required only a minimum of polishing and the piece was then complete.

Polishing

Polishing is the final stage in bringing a piece of jewellery to completion by imparting to the metal its characteristic patina. If stones are included in the work, however, the setting would be done after polishing to avoid any damage to the stones. Pre-polishing may have been done in the earlier stages to complete a section that would be inaccessible when the work was complete. Keep the polishing area as clean as possible (as with all working areas) because as the work progresses to a finer and finer degree of polishing, even a tiny scrap of foreign matter can be caught up in the polishing materials and thereby score the metal's surface.

POLISHING WHEELS

Work can, of course, be wholly polished by hand but this is very arduous and polishing is usually done by polishing wheels, ie mops and brushes of varying degrees of abrasion, used on the spindle of a polishing motor.

The most abrasive is the tripoli mop, a hard fabric mop on which one uses the polishing compounds tripoli or crocus. The black bristle brush is next in abrasion, using the same compounds. There follow in diminishing order of abrasion felt bobs using tripoli, fabric mops using rouge (or a chamois mop using rouge for larger surfaces). The last mop is a lambswool mop using whiting powder.

The inside of ring shanks are polished with tapered felt cones, one using tripoli and another using rouge. For polishing delicate work, a hand-held flexible shaft with miniature versions of the same brushes and mops is used, with the same compounds. Dental polishing brushes can be used with the flexible shaft and are excellent for very fine work.

On a large smooth surface a felt wheel can be used after the bristle brush and prior to the rouge. This mop does not require dressing. It is particularly useful for domed surfaces, and has the further advantage

that it can be shaped to fit specific concavities. It is a tough material
but it is possible to shape it – probably the simplest way is to pare it
down with a coarse file or carborundum stone while it is revolving on
the polishing spindle.

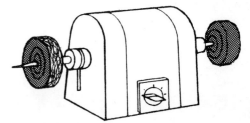

Polishing motor

DRESSING MOPS

Before you begin to use a new mop it has to be 'dressed'. The threads
are of different lengths and while they look even when you buy the
mop, when you put it on to polish the loose threads will soon make an
appearance. These loose threads can be brought out to their full length
by holding a coarse file, like a wood file, against the mops as they
revolve until the loose and long threads are exposed. I find the best
method is to buy a cheap cheese grater and hold this against the mops.
Even the teeth of a broken hacksaw could be used. The long threads
left can be burnt off by slowly turning the shaft of the polishing
machine by hand and holding a match to the threads. Or they can be
cut off with scissors. These long threads must be removed as they could
become very abrasive, even grooving the metal.

Polishing mops

The mops are made of cloth – linen for tripoli and muslin for rouge
and 'swansdown' (a fluffy wool) for the very soft mop which gives a
final polish. There are also chamois and leather mops. Other types of
polishing aids are felt wheels or felt bobs. Another polishing aid is the
emery impregnated rubber wheel. They are of various grades from
rough to very smooth and, used carefully, the smooth ones can take the
place of emery paper, although they cannot replace flour emery, Water
of Ayr stone, felt dobs or the final polishing by hand.

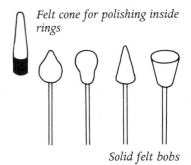

Felt cone for polishing inside rings

Solid felt bobs

THE CORRECT PLACING OF MOPS ON SPINDLES

I use only tripoli mops on the left-hand side of my polishing machine,
and keep all rouge polishing to the right-hand side. This is to prevent
mops becoming mixed up, either with the wrong polishing compounds
or by being put on the wrong end of the spindle. The tapered spindles
on the polishing motor are different on either side – the thread on one
side is left-hand thread and on the other a right-hand thread. If tripoli
and rouge mops were to be alternated on these threads the central holes
in the mops would soon lose their 'grip' and become insecure. The point
of the alternate threads is that while the machine is in motion the mops
are being forced onto the threads in the opposite direction. This is what
keeps them on the spindle, and why it is important to stick to one or
the other side.

  Polishing mops are made of many discs of cloth that are held together
by a leather washer on either side, and secured by three flat-headed
nails. These are hammered through the washers and cloth and the points
bent over on the other side. This can be a guide to putting the mops on
the same way each time you use them. Decide which side (ie the side
with the head of the nail or the side with the point) is to go against the
spindle and always use it this way, so that the centre hole does not lose
its grip on the spindle. Mops could be marked to show which is to be

71

the spindle side. I usually put the cloth mop with the side that has the turned-over nail point against the spindle.

APPLYING POLISHING COMPOUNDS

To apply the polishing compound in block form to the brush, put the brush on the spindle and start the motor. Then press the compound firmly against the surface of the brush to give an even but not too thick layer of compound. Too thick a layer will cake the surface of the brush and scratch the work. When polishing, keep the brush or mop continually charged with compound – failure to do this will result in the work being scratched rather than polished. Keep the work on the mop to ensure an even polish, and maintain a steady but not severe pressure against the mop.

If the compounds stay on the work it means you are not polishing firmly enough or moving it about sufficiently.

After the use of tripoli, wash the piece out with hot water, detergent and a drop of ammonia, and dry in hot sawdust before using the rouge mop. The work should be cleaned after using any compound and before using another, so that one compound is not carried on to the next brush. It is particularly important that the rouge mop does not become dirtied by other polishing compounds, as its characteristic bright polish would be diminished.

Polishing compounds in paste form can be applied to the mop most easily by making a substitute for a brush by binding a piece of cloth around the end of a flattish stick, and coating the paste onto the revolving mop with this.

POLISHING COMPOUNDS

These are available in block form or powder. They are of varying grades of abrasion: in order these are crocus, tripoli, rouge and whiting. For platinum and some types of white gold a green rouge is used.

Pumice powder is a strong abrasive, but is not for polishing jewellery. It is used in enamelling to level off the enamel prior to the final firing.

The compounds in powder form are usually mixed with methylated spirits, white spirit or turpentine. Polishing compounds in powder form are more efficient than the block ones, but they have the decided disadvantage that they disperse into the atmosphere and then settle on workroom surfaces. This is unhealthy and obviously a great nuisance when cleanliness is of the utmost importance. An extractor fan will help draw off some of it, and the rest is best taken up by a vacuum cleaner. Use protective clothing and a head covering.

Many people wear gloves while they polish to protect their hands. I strongly discourage this practice as I feel it is highly dangerous – a glove can get caught up in the mop or spindle. It is far better to use a barrier cream if you are worried about the condition of your hands.

Useful accessories for polishing broad, flat surfaces are disposable abrasive bands. They are narrow strips of abrasive paper, twill-backed and turned into a circle and glued. They are used in conjunction with a rubber cylinder on the end of a steel shaft. This shaft must be gripped by a chuck, which in turn is held in a polishing machine/drilling machine flexible shaft or a lathe. The abrasive band is slipped over the rubber cylinder and fits neatly. A hexagonal nut on the shaft is then tightened. This expands the rubber cylinder which then holds the abrasive band securely. When the abrasive band is worn out or a different grade of abrasive is required, undo the nut, slip off the worn band and replace with a new one.

For polishing awkward curves, emery paper can be used by gluing it onto balsa wood. As the polishing progresses, the balsa wood adapts to the shape of the curve. A hard but pliable rubber can also be used. There is an architect's flexible ruler which is excellent for getting to difficult curves, which consists of a core of a lead/tin pliable composition and a strip of tempered steel on either side, the whole surrounded by rubber. These can be bought in good art shops in 30 cm (12″) or 38 cm (15″) lengths and it can be made to conform to any shape you choose to set it in.

The teeth of a tortoiseshell comb, quills, sharpened sticks of lignum or boxwood can be most useful for polishing in otherwise inaccessible places, as they can be used as burnishers. They can be filed to fit a tiny space if necessary, and their flexibility and 'give' is invaluable.

You can file Water of Ayr stone to the shape you require. Occasionally you may find a piece of grit in the stone, in which case file the stone down and try it on a piece of waste metal to make sure the grit has disappeared. If not, repeat the process but if it still persists discard the stone, as it is no doubt a rogue piece, and begin again with a fresh stone.

FELT TAPERS

These tapered felt bobs are ideal for polishing the inside of ring shanks. If they do not fit easily onto the spindle of your polisher, it is worth taking a little trouble to see that they do. If it is a reasonably good fit, the wooden core will take up the thread on a tapered spindle. If it does not fit well, drill the core a little deeper and try it on the spindle. It may well now fit. If it does not, then widen the circumference of the entrance. If it still does not fit, it will have to be drilled in steps.

Choose a twist drill slightly smaller than the entrance and drill in a little way – then repeat the process with diminishing drills to make steps within the core. Now fit the stepped core onto the spindle and the steps should grip. If you start off by putting this tapered bob on the right-hand spindle of the polisher, remember always to use that side for that bob because the wooden core will have taken the thread of that side. Were you to use it on the opposite side, you would strip the thread.

STRINGING

There may be parts of the design where the tripoli and rouge mops cannot penetrate, such as the well-nigh inaccessible areas in a coronet setting. String can be used to polish here. Hanks of a special type of string can be purchased in three grades, coarse, medium and fine. Ordinary string is not strong enough.

Depending upon the size of the aperture, thread as many strings as possible through it, twisting them slightly. Secure one end of the strings by knotting them over a nail or something similar. Hold them taut and charge them with the polishing compound (and if you change the compound, change the strings). Shuttle the piece back and forth along the strings until polished. Wash and dry in the usual manner. When stringing, great care must be taken as they have a highly abrasive quality. Used in a bundle of three or four, their impact is softened but one string used strenuously can quite easily cut a groove in metal.

POLISHING MOTORS

To get the polish required for highly finished work, a polishing motor is an essential. An inexpensive or second-hand machine can be suitable provided that:

1. It is capable of at least 2000 rev/min. A lower speed, say 1 300 rev/min could be used when polishing chains or drilling some stones, but as will be explained, is too slow for general polishing.

2. It can be adapted to take a tapered spindle if it does not already have one. (Most polishing brushes and mops are designed for a tapered spindle.) Recognized trade names in this field are *De Soutter*, *Wolfe*, and *Black and Decker*.

3. A flexible shaft can be fitted. This will be necessary for fine work and is usually part of the pendant drill, but for economy you could buy the flexible shaft alone, and drive it by the polishing motor instead of the pendant drill motor.

I use a *Jugodent* motor. This is a two-speed, 1 300/2 750 rev/min induction motor. It is made in Yugoslavia and is available from Porro Dental Suppliers and others. This is not normally used in jewellery – it is a piece of dental equipment, used by dentists to polish, drill or grind. I decided to use it as a polishing motor for several reasons:

1. It is fast. Obviously this saves you time, but also fast polishing, ie 2750 rev/min, is considered to be the best speed for polishing jewellery. It may seem odd that speed of polishing can affect the result, but slow polishing is inclined to drag the surface of the work. (Viewed microscopically, tiny grooves would show.) Fast polishing passes over the surface too quickly to drag at it.

2. It is quiet. Because it is normally used by dentists, it has been designed to keep noise to an absolute minimum. It gives off only a quiet hum.

3. The motor is completely enclosed. None of the fine polishing dust can penetrate into the working mechanism and it does not need oiling or greasing because the whole motor is a sealed unit.

4. A flexible shaft can be attached to it.

5. It will accommodate an arbour for emery wheels.

PENDANT DRILL

While the ordinary brushes and mops used on the polishing machine allow one to bring the work to a high degree of finish, it may not be possible to reach all the delicate undercut parts of the work in this way. One may need, therefore to complete these areas by hand, using very fine burnishers or scrapers.

However, the pendant drill with its flexible shaft can be a valuable asset here. Firstly, because of the freedom of movement it allows and secondly, because with it one can use many small implements that would normally be used by dentists, die-sinkers, toolmakers and precision engineers. While these tools will be similar to a jeweller's, they will be in miniature and can be used to reach difficult areas and do small work with greater ease.

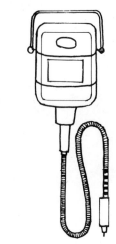

Pendant drill

The pendant drill has, as well, a set of its own specific jeweller's tools for polishing. These are scratch brush mops, tripoli mops, rouge mops, black bristle brush mops, felt mops, etc – a repetition of those used on the polishing machine but in miniature. They usually have three sizes of shaft, 2·4 mm ($\frac{3}{32}$″) in diameter, 1·6 mm ($\frac{1}{16}$″) and 3·2 mm ($\frac{1}{8}$″). There is also a shaft on its own called a mandrel, 1·6 mm ($\frac{1}{16}$″) in diameter, onto which different heads can be screwed. There is quite an advantage in this because when the head is worn out, it can be discarded.

To use the mandrel it is inserted in the chuck of the hand piece, the screw in the centre of the mandrel is taken out and put through the centre of the unit to be used, and the unit screwed back onto the mandrel. The wheels for the mandrel come in various diameters, thicknesses and abrasive grades. There is one particular wheel made of rubber impregnated with fine emery powder. It is a most useful wheel, and can in fact replace emery papering. It removes file marks, scratches, extraneous solder, etc, and is ideal for polishing the inside of ring shanks. When the rubber wears down, the wheel can be unscrewed and replaced with a new one.

As well as these polishing heads, there are grinding wheels, ruby crystal wheels, diamond-impregnated wheels and grinders, and pumice wheels to smooth off roughness, dents and chipped edges. The other heads for use on the mandrel are: muslin buffs (for rouge), felt polishing wheels (both flat-edged and knife-edged) and abrasive bands.

SCRATCH BRUSH

The hand scratch brush is made of very fine brass threads set into wood, rather like a toothbrush. Its purpose is to brighten metal after it has been pickled or plated. It must be used with water, keeping the brush and the work wet as you rub, as this renders it less likely to make marks on the metal. If detergent is added to the water, it will soften it. On the other hand, it may be used dry to give a satin finish to the surface of metal.

Scratch brushing is done professionally and the work may warrant using this specialist service, which gives a very attractive soft sheen to the polishing, and a better and more even finish than can be achieved by hand scratch brushing.

This is another method of producing a very fine texture on metal. It gives a uniform matt finish (rather like frosted glass) that would be very hard to achieve by either hand or machine texturing.

The principle is to mix a jet of air with sand of varying abrasive grades, and to blast the sand at the object. Contrasting effects can be obtained if the surface of the object is pre-polished, a design or shape masked off, and the object then exposed to sand blasting. Sand blasting as a technique is best given out to specialist workers.

First Aid

Accidents do happen. Be prepared for them.

In jewellery making they will usually be of a minor nature, but there is always the risk of a major accident.

EVERYBODY WORKING WITH TOOLS OF ANY SORT SHOULD HAVE TETANUS PROTECTION, with a booster injection every five years.

You can deal with minor injuries yourself, following advice, using your own commonsense. Anything about which you are doubtful, or an obviously major injury, needs attention from a doctor AT ONCE.

Have a First Aid box handy. As well as the usual contents, it should specifically contain:

Gold figure – Quimbaya (Cauca) 1400–1000 BC.

Melolin Dressings (sterile dressings that are non-adherent) for any wounds.

Two or three Cotton Bandages.

wow (white open wove) Bandages for applying dressings, and possibly one 7·5 cm (3″) crepe or elastic bandage.

Savlon liquid to wash dirty injuries.

Acriflavin for slight burns.

ACCIDENT

In any serious accident, call a doctor or if necessary an ambulance, meanwhile reassuring the patient. Check if you can on whether the patient may have a disability (eg diabetes) or is on a course of drugs (eg anti-depressants) or has allergies or penicillin reaction (by asking or looking in wallet or purse). If you are working in a school or factory, notify a senior member of the staff. Display a notice of the 'phone numbers of the nearest doctors and Casualty Department. A copy of the Factories Act which describes the need to use the protective covers on machinery should also be displayed.

If you are working alone, make sure that you have some means of attracting attention other than the telephone.

ACID

Gold zoomorphic figure

Acids can splash as work is put in and taken out, or could be spilt. Sulphuric, which will be the most commonly used, will usually have been diluted, but none the less can be dangerous, particularly if it splashes in the eyes. Acids must be washed off immediately with plenty of running water under the tap particularly if it splashes in the eyes. If, after thorough irrigation, there is pain or obvious injury, see a doctor. This applies also to alkalis (potash of soda, etc.).

CARE AND HANDLING OF ACIDS

All acids should be kept securely corked and when in use put in a lead bath or pyrex bowl, standing on asbestos. NEVER ADD WATER TO ACID, ALWAYS ACID TO WATER (think of it alphabetically as adding A (acid) to W (water). Do not pick up bottles by the neck or with one hand. If it spills, quickly throw carbonate of soda over and around the area. This neutralizer should always be kept close to acid work area and always kept covered.

It is advisable to wear protective goggles to prevent any direct acid splash – or even ordinary glasses with plain glass lenses, or a face shield. The best types are those which completely cover the face. They are made of plastic and are very light. These are also useful when polishing, grinding etc.

BURNS

A burn from soldering can be either a minor or a major burn, but a burn from molten metal is very serious and must be treated as a major burn.

Minor burns can be coated with *Acriflavin*, then covered with a dry sterile dressing until you can see your doctor, but if the burn is quite large or appears deep, cover it with the dry dressing and see your doctor or casualty department at once. Always work carefully when using heating or melting equipment or moving machinery and remember to keep long hair or loose clothing fastened back out of the way.

BLEEDING

In most cases bleeding can be controlled at the site of bleeding by applying local pressure with a pad or sterile dressing. But in any cut where the blood spurts out in regular, pumping gushes it is an extremely serious situation. See the doctor or casualty at once.

CUTS

Everyone working with tools of any sort should have tetanus protection.

When filing the most common accident occurs if the file is being used without a handle. The tang of the file could slip and penetrate the palm of the hand as you are working. Avoid this possibility by always using a file in its handle. This type of stab injury particularly calls for tetanus protection.

When saw piercing, cuts can often happen because the blade breaks. Should it penetrate the hand or finger nail obviously one should try to

Gold mask. Chimu. 12th or 13th AD

Order of the Tress, Austrian, c.1400.

Pre-Columbian Peruvian gold

*Colombian gold figure,
AD 1000–1500.*

pull it out. If unable to do this go to a casualty department. Even though a cut is small it may still bleed freely, so to reduce this apply a Band-Aid or sterile dressing using a tight bandage to stop the bleeding. Any cut more than about 1 cm ($\frac{1}{2}$″) long is likely to need a stitch as it will heal more quickly and neatly.

POLISHING

When polishing with an electric motor it is important to be careful, particularly when polishing, for instance, a chain or open ended pieces, eg bracelets. They could become caught on the mop, the mop will spin the chain or workpiece in an arc and it could twist itself around your hand or fingers, cutting and bruising them or even dragging your hand against the mop or spindle.

Remember when working with polishers, lathes, power drills, soldering flames, etc not to wear a garment where the sleeves or some part of it could become entangled with the equipment. The damage caused by a sleeve becoming caught in a lathe can be imagined. For this reason guards should always be kept on mechanical parts, even when they are not in use. Remember again, loose-fitting clothes should be tied back, and long hair tied or preferably put in a net. If it is possible, always position the OFF switch to be within reach when using moving machinery. Never use machinery if working alone unless you can reach the OFF switch.

PROTECTIVE GOGGLES

When using any electric machinery – polishers, grinders, drills, lathes, etc., protective goggles or at least glasses must be worn. One of the most common of eye injuries is caused by a fragment of metal thrown up by moving machinery. Endeavour to wash anything out of the eye immediately.

*Gold mask of the God Xipe Totec
Mixteca – Pueblo Culture.*

Shock

In any accident shock may well occur as it is a nervous reaction. It may well appear out of proportion to the actual injury, eg a small cut, bleeding freely and not painful, may be followed by a 'faint' ten minutes later – this is an aspect of shock.

Should shock occur, reassure the patient. Lie them down. If it appears that the person is in a bad way, call an ambulance. If they are apparently recovering, as would be the case usually, either spirits or tea could be given provided you are pretty certain the person is on the mend.

Electric Shock

Do not use any electrical equipment with damp or wet hands.

Do not attempt to do any electrical repairs unless the current has been switched off at the master switch.

If someone has been injured do not touch them until you have switched the electricity off.

Call an ambulance immediately and begin artificial respiration if necessary.

II METALS

Properties of Metals

The physical and mechanical properties of gold, silver and platinum are such that they can be worked upon by bending, stretching, hammering, and pressing or stamping into steel dies. The qualities that allow this to happen are ductility, malleability and tenacity (or tensile strength).

Ductility, Malleability, Tenacity
Ductility is the property that allows the metal to be stretched or drawn, as when wire is pulled through a draw plate. Malleability allows metal to be extended in every direction at the same time, as when it is hammered, stamped or pressed, and extends outwards, upwards or downwards simultaneously. Pure gold is unsurpassed for this characteristic, to the point where it can be beaten thin enough to use as gold leaf or even thinner. Tenacity is the attribute whereby the metals can resist being torn asunder or fractured under a stretching force.

Ductility and malleability are often overlapping qualities, but the ductile properties of a metal can be adversely affected by its tenacity. For example, in wire drawing, a great strain is put upon the structure of the metal, but its ductility and malleability allow for this. But in the process of drawing, its ductility will have decreased and its tensile strength will have increased, causing it to harden. At this stage, it must be carefully annealed.

79

A gold ingot of the present day

Roman gold bar stamped by the mint of Sirmium, late 4th century AD.

Typical structure of fine silver ingot. Longitudinal section

Typical structure of alloyed gold ingot. Longitudinal section

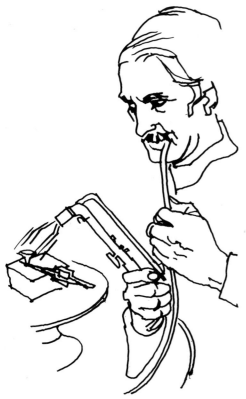

Alloy

Precious metals in their pure state can be worked very easily because of their relative softness, but equally they are more vulnerable to abrasion and wear. For this reason they are hardened by combining with another metal. This combination of two or more metals melted together to form a homogeneous mass is called an alloy.

Annealing

Annealing is the process of restoring a metal to its soft state by heat after it has been made hard by working it, ie rolling, hammering. The metal is softened by heat, generally to a dull or cherry red colour, which is sufficient, as overheating can result in upsetting the molecular structure and the metal may become brittle and crack or break on further working. Overheating can result in the surface beginning to resemble the pitted texture of orange skin (in fact, the surface of the metal is beginning to melt at this point) which again upsets the crystalline structure of the metal.

In large workshops, heating can be controlled efficiently with modern annealing equipment, such as a heat-controlled furnace with pyrometer and rheostat. The advantage of this is that the work can be annealed in a virtually oxygen-free atmosphere, thus preventing unnecessary oxidization (or fire stain) in silver. The craftsman lacking these facilities will usually anneal by using a torch to heat the work. The work would be placed upon a wig or a charcoal block to allow the heat to circulate. It obviously requires less effort if the torch can be attached to foot bellows or a compressor. Oxidization or fire stain may result from annealing in the open air whereas annealing in a furnace would reduce this. This oxidization (or fire stain) must be removed, as will be described. A study of E. A. Smith's book, *Working in Precious Metals*, and various articles written by P. E. Gainsbury, F.I.M., will give a clear picture and understanding of the heat treatment of metals.

There is another method of annealing called 'salt bath furnace annealing', that also has the advantage of protecting the work from the oxygen in the atmosphere. To the best of my knowledge, a small furnace, such as is required for this work is not available on the market at present, but if the craftsman is prepared to make his own, which would cost very little, P. E. Gainsbury's TAC Project No 17 Report No. 17/2 September 1968 gives the explanation and diagrams of how to make one. It would be a decided advantage for a craftsman to have a salt bath furnace, as it greatly reduces the risk of fire stain in silver, and gives better temperature control in annealing.

Advantages of Melting and Rolling Equipment

Apart from the gold alloys subsequently listed, there are many more which fulfil the need for colour variation in gold and for varying degrees of hardness and softness.

From a craftsman's point of view, it is essential to know how to alloy, melt and roll metal and solders. It is ultimately cheaper to make and roll your own alloys if you can afford the initial cost of melting apparatus and a rolling mill. With this equipment one can experiment with alloying coloured golds, blue, green and other colours, apart from the usual warm coloured golds. These coloured golds can be expensive if ordered from the bullion merchant, as they are seldom in stock, and may have to be made up to order. Also when you are buying metal, some bullion merchants will only accept an order of a fairly substantial amount. This can be uneconomical if you require less than this amount and you may then have to sell the remainder back to them at scrap prices. For example, when buying gold one pays the fluctuating daily price, but when selling even clean left-over pieces (or scrap) back to them, you will only receive about three-quarters or less of the price per ounce you paid. So you lose on this transaction. As mentioned earlier, save all the filings (or lemel) as well as the scrap, and if you have not the equipment to melt and roll them they will have to be sent to the bullion merchant for refining. Their charge for refining accounts for the difference in price between buying new metal and selling back scrap metal.

Melting

When melting your own scrap and lemel, you must make certain that it is free from all extraneous matter, such as emery paper dust, iron or steel which may have come from files or binding wire, and which could be removed by a magnet, and in particular lead or lead solder which would render the alloy totally unworkable, and this can only be remedied by sending the metal for refining.

When the alloy has been melted, it must be cast into an ingot mould. Depending on the shape of the mould, this will result in a flat piece or a squarish rod shape. The former will be rolled in the flat rolling mills into sheet. The latter will be rolled into wire in the square rolling mills in preparation for pulling through draw plates, of which there are many basic shapes, and variations.

If you intend to make your own alloys, buy the pure metals in granulated form, as they will more easily melt together in a homogeneous mass. However, should you wish to granulate solid pure metal for yourself, prepare a bucket of cold water about 45 cm (18") deep, melt the metal in a crucible and when molten pour from a height of about 1 metre (3') into the water. This will result in the metal separating in its fall and on hitting the water these pieces solidify into granules. Incidentally, these granules can make a very decorative shape and may well be used as part of a design.

It is advisable when alloying gold or sterling silver, to add a few more grains of pure gold to the gold alloy and pure silver to the silver alloy, to ensure that the quality will be fractionally higher than necessary for Assay.

When making an alloy the metal that is hardest to melt (ie, has the highest melting point) is melted first, then the metal that will melt a little more easily is added, and finally the most easily melted metal. By following this order of diminishing melting points the metal will combine in a homogeneous mass. For example, in making a gold alloy using copper, gold and silver, the metals would be melted in that order, as copper melts at 1083°C, gold at 1063°C and silver at 960·5°C.

To melt up to about 90 g (3 oz) may be done in an open crucible, using a blow torch assisted by a compressor or foot bellows. A mouth blow torch alone will never give the degree of heat required. To melt a larger quantity, it would have to be done in a furnace.

When the metal is molten it will resemble the yolk of a fried egg, in that the particles adhere together in a roundish shape of a bright yellow. At this point it will spin. Sprinkle pure powdered charcoal mixed with a little powdered borax on the molten metal. This will move any impurities to the edge of the crucible, where they can be gently lifted off with a carbon rod before pouring.

Before pouring, the crucible should be shaken gently or stirred to make certain the alloy has mixed into a homogeneous mass. The inside of the ingot mould should have been heated, and either slightly oiled, or smoked with the flame of a candle, both of which ensure that the molten metal will flow more smoothly when poured into the mould.

The temperature of the ingot mould is important. The molten metal should flow evenly into the mould, and while it may not fill it, should produce a regular block of metal. A mould that is too hot or too cold will result in an uneven shape, which will need re-melting and re-pouring. Only experience will establish the correct heat for the mould, but a rough general rule is that it should be a little hotter than is comfortable to touch. This heat, however, will vary depending on many factors, such as the alloy used, the weight of it and the size of the ingot mould.

While pouring from an open crucible, keep the flame playing upon the crucible, because the metal will cool incredibly quickly, and even leaving the flame off momentarily allows a crust to form.

When the metal is poured into the ingot, it sets immediately. Take it from the mould, allow it to cool a little and quench it in pickle, to remove any residue of charcoal or borax. The whole process of melting, pouring and quenching is aimed to produce an alloy that, on solidification, is a homogeneous crystalline structure, and the quenching aspect can affect this greatly. If the alloy is quenched correctly, the desired crystalline structure will be obtained, and result in ductility, malleability and tenacity. If incorrectly quenched, the result could be brittleness and cracking, and could lead to a tendency to harden.

As a general rule, most alloys can be quenched, after allowing them to cool slightly, so that red-hot metal is not being plunged into pickle. Because of the many factors liable to affect an alloy that you have melted yourself, alternative methods of quenching, that allow for rapid or slow cooling, should be tried to see which offers the best result.

Bullion merchants will offer advice on the annealing and quenching of their particular products. One company, Johnson and Mathey, in their catalogue, in an article on carat golds, list 31 gold alloys of which 8 can be quenched immediately, 20 must be allowed to cool until dull in colour before quenching, and 3 must be allowed to cool slowly in air before quenching, so it is evident that it is important to quench correctly for the particular alloy involved.

To melt a silver alloy, follow the same basic procedure, but it is recommended to put on a thicker layer of charcoal powder before pouring, to help prevent oxidization; and not to keep the crucible at too great a temperature for too long before pouring. Silver can be quenched immediately after taking it from the ingot mould.

Fire Stain

Frequently after annealing or soldering silver, patchy stains of blackish-grey appear on its surface. This is known as 'fire-stain' and is caused by the oxygen in the flame attacking the copper in the alloy on the surface of the metal which results in patches of copper oxide forming. This may be avoided when annealing is done in a furnace or a salt bath, because of the oxygen-free atmosphere. There are products to alleviate this recurring and irritating problem, *Argo-tect* and others. A solution for the prevention of Fire Stain was devised by the Royal College of Art, as follows:

Anti-Fire Stain Solution for Silver
Heat 1420 millilitres (50 fluid ozs) of distilled water in a Pyrex bowl and stir in the following salts until dissolved:

Borax	80 grammes (2·6 ozs Troy)
Monobasic sodium orthophosphate	80 grammes (2·6 ozs Troy)
Boric acid	120 grammes (3·8 ozs Troy)

Keep in a stoppered bottle. Crystals may be deposited if left standing and should be re-dissolved by warming before use. Wetting of metal surfaces is facilitated by the addition of about 2 per cent liquid wetting agent such as Shell *Teepol* or I.C.I. *Lissapol*.

To apply, gently heat the work and spray with the solution which forms a white film. Alternatively, the warm work may be dipped into the solution ensuring that the whole surface is wetted.

After annealing or brazing, the residual film may be removed in the normal sulphuric acid pickle.

However, as far as I know there is nothing that can completely prevent fire stain. Overheating or prolonged heating is a contributory factor but if you have avoided this and fire-stain still occurs, the only way of removing it, in my experience, is by polishing it out. Start with emery paper and if this does not remove it, then polish it with the black bristle brush and tripoli. If the fire-stain is still there, wash and dry to remove tripoli, and rub while wet with Water of Ayr stone. This will ultimately remove the fire-stain but can be a long and tedious job. The advantage of the Water of Ayr stone is that using it will not dull the sharp edges of the work. The disadvantage of prolonged polishing with the black bristle brush is that it will blunt sharp edges, and may interfere with the design.

Titanium

Titanium is a metal that is basically used in industry and aircraft production, because of its lightness and strength. It is now being used in making jewellery because of the range of colour it gives. Although alloys of gold will give a certain degree of colour range (white gold, yellow gold, pink gold, blue gold) it is a very limited and subtle range. Titanium, on the other hand, under heat treatment gives a degree of colour range that is surprising in a metal. When oxidized it will produce a range of quite definite colours – pinks, browns, blues, greys. The degree of heat needed to produce a particular colour will have to be found by experimentation – a lot will depend on the method of oxidization.

The simplest way of heating to colour the metal is by using a soldering torch. To colour an area or to draw a colour pattern on the titanium, a heated needle can be used. For instance, a darning needle held in a heat resistant handle can be heated and kept at a steady temperature when in contact with the metal by using a battery (eg a car battery).

To do this, attach the anode wire to the metal (with metal clips) and the cathode wire to the needle (also with clips). This completes an electrical circuit. Because the metal is then charged, the needle heats on contacting it.

Prior to heating, the metal must be absolutely free of grease, and kept clean in handling and annealling by using tweezers.

Intense colours can be obtained if the metal has been highly polished. Overheating can be ruinous and prevent the colours from appearing. If you heat to cherry red you will have overheated it. As far as I can ascertain at present the colours are 'fast'.

The disadvantages of titanium as a metal for jewellery are: it is limited by its considerable hardness. It is very difficult to bend, hammer, drill, file, saw, stretch or roll as wire. It is worse than stainless steel in these aspects. Special saws, files and drills are needed to work it, although it is suitable for lathe work.

It cannot be soldered. It has to be fused in a vacuum, using a piece of titanium as 'solder', and this is not always successful. It will often give the appearance of having joined successfully, but on further working the join may break.

It is apparent therefore that in designing for titanium it is far better that it be riveted, screwed, bent and fitted to join it. This may well be an instance where metal bonding adhesives solve a problem well.

It is slightly cheaper than silver and attractive jewellery can certainly be produced from it, but it is best suited for jewellery in which the components can be fitted or slotted together without subsequent work on them.

The following table shows a comparison with fine silver for melting point and weight.

	Melting Point	Specific Gravity	Atomic Weight
Titanium	3035°F 1668°C	4·51	49·70
Fine silver	1728·9°F 961°C	10·70	107·88

Platinum

Platinum is the most expensive of the precious metals, and therefore its use may not often come within the range of a craftsman/jeweller. However the extension of hallmarking to include platinum as from January 1, 1975 will have caused considerable interest in its qualities.

Platinum is an element, as are gold and silver, ie it is one of a number of substances that cannot be destroyed. Metal elements are distinguished from other solid elements by several important aspects. They often have

high tensile strength
ductility
malleability
lustre – in the sense of the capacity to be polished
good conductivity of heat
good conductivity of electricity

Pure platinum has a higher density than pure gold or silver. (It is 11 per cent heavier than pure gold and more than 100 per cent heavier than pure silver.) While it has a similar tensile strength (ie: tensile strength is the measure of the stress required to 'break' the metal under a tensile load) as these metals, it has a very much higher melting point and greater 'elasticity'.

The greatest differences in working platinum and working gold or silver lie in the fields of annealing, soldering and casting, where the intense heat required for platinum could present difficulties.

Platinum has an extremely high melting point, ie 1773·5°C whereas gold melts at 1063° and silver at 960·5°C therefore platinum requires almost twice the amount of heat required to melt silver.

Even annealing platinum requires the same greater degree of heat (for example, about 1000°C whereas carat gold and silver alloys can be annealed in the range of 600°C to 750°C).

Soldering platinum presents the same difficulty of the use of intense heat.

From this it will be obvious that it is a difficult metal to work, as well as possessing its own idiosyncrasies, and, in all, does require a high degree of accomplishment and skill. For this reason I would consider it beyond the range of any but the most experienced craftsman.

Hallmarking and Assaying

Great Britain is unique in its approach to the inherent hazards of making and trading in precious metals: no other country has such a thorough system to ensure that the true quality of the metal content is stamped on articles made of precious metal. This system – compulsory hallmarking – began in 1300 and has remained as a symbol of integrity and a means of providing a unique protection for the purchaser of platinum, gold and silver articles.

The Hallmark

In brief, a hallmark certifies that an article has been assayed (accurately tested) at one of the official Assay Offices in the United Kingdom and that the platinum, gold or silver content is up to one of the legal standards. As well as providing a purchaser with an absolute assurance that the precious metal content is as stated, the hallmark also shows the maker's name (or that of the firm responsible for the work), the Assay Office where the work was tested and marked, and the year in which it was assayed.

The word hallmark is derived from Goldsmiths Hall, the headquarters of the Company. Today there are Assay Offices in Birmingham, Sheffield and Edinburgh as well, and all platinum, gold and silver articles made or sold in Britain must by law be sent to one of these four offices for assay and hallmarking, before being offered for sale. They therefore carry a guarantee that is quite independent of the manufacturer.

Rod Edwards' hallmark shows these series of symbols which denote:

1. The maker responsible for submitting the article to the Assay Office.
2. The standard of the precious metal.
3. The Assay Office at which the article was assayed.
4. The year in which it was assayed.

The Rod Edwards Hallmark

The Makers Mark

When hallmarking began in 1300 the leopard's head was the only mark required, but in 1363 the addition of a maker's mark become compulsory. At that time a maker's mark would have been a decorative device such as a fish or a fleur-de-lys, but now it will be the initials of the maker or of the firm concerned with production of the article.

MAKERS MARK

The Standard Mark

Gold and silver as pure metals are too soft to be used to make jewellery, and a certain quantity of base metal must be alloyed with the precious metal to harden it. Various legal standards regulate the amount which can be added.

The present standards showing the minimum silver or gold contents are

Gold   *9 carat*

Silver	– Sterling	92·5 per cent
	– Britannia	95·84 per cent
Gold	– 22 carat	91·66 per cent
	– 18 carat	75·0 per cent
	– 14 carat	58·5 per cent
	– 9 carat	37·5 per cent

From January 1, 1975, the hallmarking of platinum became a legal requirement.

Britannia Silver   *Sterling Silver*

Carat

In metals, a carat is one 24th part of the whole. Therefore 18 carat gold means that 18/24ths of the alloy is pure gold and the remainder a baser metal or combination of metals.

Platinum

STANDARD MARK

The Date Mark

This was introduced in 1478 and its purpose was then to be able to identify the official responsible for the assay. The mark took the form of a letter of the alphabet, enclosed in a shield. The letter was changed annually and at completion of an alphabetical cycle, the style of letter and shape of shield were altered. It is therefore possible to date any hallmarked article exactly.

DATE MARK

87

London Gold and Silver

Birmingham Gold   *Silver*

Sheffield Gold and Silver

Edinburgh Gold and Silver

Duty marks used between 1784 and 1890

Assay Office Mark

Today there are four Assay Offices in Britain – London, Birmingham, Sheffield, Edinburgh – but there were also other offices at various times. Each of the four offices used a different cycle of letters, and it was necessary in attempting to date an article to identify the Assay Office involved, and then a list of its relevant letters could be consulted.

This system was changed on January 1, 1975, and from that time the four Assay Offices use the same alphabetical letter and shield, which is changed annually on January 1 of each year.

The Duty Mark

A further mark was used between 1784 and 1890. This was the duty mark which was in the form of the reigning sovereign's head. It signified that the duty that was then levied on gold and silver articles had been paid. This was collected by the Assay Offices on behalf of the government, but was abolished in 1890.

Hallmarking Act 1973

This Act became effective from January 1, 1975 and it differs in a number of respects from the preceding hallmarking Act, including the different system for changing the date letter, and the introduction of the hallmarking of platinum. Details of the law are obtainable from Assay Offices, and it is now required that a copy of an official notice showing the marks be prominently displayed by a dealer/retailer/wholesaler.

Method of Assaying

Every piece of platinum, gold or silver jewellery must be sent for assaying. The articles must be complete, but they can be sent in the flat state and certainly prior to the final polishing. Every part of every article is sampled, where practicable, to be sure that the whole will come up to standard.

The assay is made by examining a minute piece of the article that has been scraped off, but so delicately done that it does not damage the article. Its equivalent in metal is returned with the hallmarked goods.

Gold scrapings are assayed by the 'cupellation' method, and silver by the 'volumetric' method. Details of these techniques are available from the Assay Office, but for my purposes it is sufficient to say that the methods are complex but extremely accurate, to the point where precious metal content can be established to the nearest 0·01 per cent.

Hallmarking Metals of Different Quality

With all hallmarking, there is a difficulty if two or more metals of different quality are to be combined. The workpiece will be given a hallmark stamp for the lower quality only, and the fact that a higher quality metal is included will not be taken into account. For example, if a brooch was made in 22 carat gold its fittings of joint and catch would have to be made of 18 carat gold or lower, as the 22 carat would be too soft a metal to carry the wear and stress put upon these fittings. The hallmark stamp would then be '18 carat gold'.

There are a few exceptions. The pins for brooches and the metal used for springs can be exempt from this ruling, as they will need to be made from the strongest metal, sometimes even steel. On a larger piece of work such as a trophy, that may have to be assembled from a number of pieces, an exception would be made for the assembly units, such as screws, or the nuts for screws provided they were made of plastic and could therefore cause no confusion regarding metal content.

Very fine work such as the links of delicate chains could be impossible to hallmark as the link would not be large enough for the mark to be stamped on it, and similar exemptions would be made where it is not possible to fit the mark on the article as in for instance, filigree work. Generally, however, every link of a chain will be assayed and hall-marked.

Assay of Lemel or Scrap

If you decide to melt your lemel and scrap for re-use, it is possible that, unless it was perfectly clean before melting, it may come out slightly under standard. It is for this reason that the earlier mentioned addition of the extra 2 grains of silver or gold ensures that it is still above standard.

If the quality of sterling silver is not up to Assay standard, the Assay Office will have to deface the work so as to render it unusable, to protect and maintain the high standards of metal quality demanded in Britain. For this reason, send work for Assay while it is in the early stages, rather than take it to an advanced stage and find that it fails to meet the Assay standard. Should this happen with silver (sterling), the Assay Office will return it to you after defacing it.

Should 22 carat gold be under standard, the Assay Office will ask your permission to hallmark it 18 carat, and the same principle will follow with 18 carat, 14 carat, and then to 9 carat. Should 9 carat fail Assay, they will treat it in the same manner as silver. If you buy metal directly from a bullion merchant, it will almost undoubtedly meet the Assay requirements.

STANDARD MARK		ON BRITISH ARTICLES	ON IMPORTED ARTICLES
GOLD	22 CARAT	👑 916	916
	18 CARAT	👑 750	750
	14 CARAT	👑 585	585
	9 CARAT	👑 375	375

Gold, Silver, Platinum and Solder Alloys

Carat, in this connotation, denotes the quality of gold. For example 22 carat is of a higher quality than 18 carat, because it contains a greater quantity of pure gold.

It is not to be confused with the use of the word 'carat' in relation to stones. Carat in that connotation, denotes a measurement of weight and has nothing to do with quality.

1 ounce = 20 pennyweights	*Abbreviations*
1 pennyweight = 24 grains	ct = carat
	oz = ounce
	dwts = pennyweights
	grns = grains

Gold Alloys

	oz	*TROY* *dwts*	*grns*	*METRIC* *Decimals*
To make 22 carat				
Fine Gold	0	18	10	0·920
,, Silver	0	0	19	0·040
,, Copper	0	0	19	0·040
Total	1 oz			1·000
To make 18 carat				
Fine Gold	0	15	0	0·750
,, Silver	0	2	12	0·125
,, Copper	0	2	12	0·125
Total	1 oz			1·000

Gold masks from Mycenae.

To make 18 carat

	oz	dwt	gr	
Fine Gold	0	15	0	0·750
,, Silver	0	3	12	0·150
,, Copper	0	1	12	0·100
Total	1 oz			1·000

To make 14 carat

	oz	dwt	gr	
Fine Gold	0	12	0	0·600
,, Silver	0	3	0	0·150
,, Copper	0	5	0	0·250
Total	1 oz			1·000

To make 9 carat

	oz	dwt	gr	
Fine Gold	0	7	12	0·375
,, Silver	0	7	0	0·350
,, Copper	0	5	12	0·275
Total	1 oz			1·000

Gold stag, 37 cm long, Scythian, found at Kostromskaya Stanitsa, 6th–5th century BC. The bevelled edges suggest this style was developed in a carved base like wood or stone.

Silver Alloys

Pure silver is, in general, too soft to be used in making jewellery. To make it harder, pure copper is added and the proportions result in sterling (or 'Standard') silver. Two alloys which give this result are:

	oz	dwt	gr	
1. Pure Silver	0	18	14	0·929
,, Copper	0	1	10	0·075
Total	1 oz			1·000

	oz	dwt	gr	
2. Pure Silver	0	18	12	0·925
,, Copper	0	1	12	0·075
Total	1 oz			1·000

Persia. Gold cup decorated with 3 lions. The bodies in profile are embossed, the heads are in the round. From Kalardasht (Mazanderan) 9th century BC

The latter alloy makes certain that there will be no problems when the article is assayed for hallmarking, as the extra two grains of silver and deleted two grains of copper puts the alloy slightly above the quality demanded by the Assay Office. I think it is advisable to do this with alloys, as a couple of grains towards a better quality will ensure the correct assay.

Gold open-work dagger handle. Chinese 4th century BC. Late Chou Dynasty.

Gold Solder Alloys

14 carat Gold	TROY oz	dwts	grns	METRIC Decimals
Fine Gold	1	0	0	1·000
,, Silver	0	2	12	0·150
,, Copper	0	9	0	0·450
*Composition	0	2	18	0·105
Total	1 oz	14	6	1·705
14 carat Gold				
Fine Gold	1	0	0	1·000
,, Copper	0	12	6	0·605
Pure Spelter	0	2	0	0·100
Total	1 oz	14	6	1·705

Oxidized silver pendant with glass and pearl, Rene Lalique, c. 1900

Silver Solder Alloys

Solder (Hard)	oz	dwts	grns	Decimals
Fine Silver	1	0	0	1·000
,, Copper	0	5	0	0·250
Total	1 oz	5	0	1·250
1. Solder (Medium)				
Fine Silver	0	15	0	0·750
,, Copper	0	4	0	0·200
Zinc	0	1	0	0·050
Total	1 oz			1·000
2. Solder (Medium)				
Fine Silver	0	14	0	0·700
,, Copper	0	4	12	0·225
Zinc	0	1	12	0·075
Total	1 oz			1·000
Solder (Hard)				
Fine Silver	0	16	0	0·800
,, Copper	0	3	12	0·150
,, Zinc	0	0	12	0·050
Total	1 oz	0	0	1·000

Gold torc found near Belfast, Ireland, date uncertain, possibly c. 700 BC

1. *Solder (Easy)*

Fine Silver	0	12	12	0·625
,, Copper	0	6	0	0·300
Zinc	0	1	12	0·075
Total	1 oz			1·000

2. *Solder (Easy)*

Fine Silver	0	12	12	0·620
,, Copper	0	5	12	0·270
Zinc	0	2	0	0·110
Total	1 oz			1·000

Gold armlet from Oxus Treasure, Persia, 400 BC.

Gold and Silver Alloys for Enamelling Solders

12 carat Gold Solder	TROY			METRIC
	oz	dwts	grns	Decimals
Fine Gold	0	10	0	0·500
,, Silver	0	5	0	0·250
,, Copper	0	5	0	0·250
Total	1 oz	0	0	1·000

(The above solder could be used for all gold soldering in enamelling, but a colour difference will become apparent when it is used on the higher carats.)

18 carat Gold Solder

Fine Gold	1	0	0	1·000
,, Silver	0	6	0	0·300
,, Copper	0	4	0	0·200
Total	1 oz	10	0	1·500

Persia. Solid gold rhyton. From Hamadan. Archaemid period (539–331 BC)

(The above solder should be used on 18 carat when a solder join will be visible.)

Hard Silver Solder Alloys

1. Fine Silver	0	14	12	0·725
,, Copper	0	5	12	0·275
Total	1 oz			1·000

2. Fine Silver	0	16	0	0·800
,, Copper	1	3	12	0·175
Zinc	0	0	12	0·025
Total	1 oz			1·000

Colombian gold figure

To Improve or Reduce the Quality of Golds

To improve 1 oz (20 dwts) of 9 carat to 14 carat (in TROY):

1 oz (20 dwts)   20 × 14 = 280 (14 carat quality required)
20 × 9 = 180 (9 carat quality to be improved)
= 280 — 180
= 100 ÷ 10 (10 being the difference between 14 carat and 24 carat)
= 10 dwts of Fine gold to be added to the 9 carat.

To improve 1 oz (20 dwts) of 9 carat to 18 carat:

1 oz (20 dwts)   20 × 18 = 360 (18 carat quality required)
20 × 9 = 180 (9 carat quality to be improved)
= 360 — 180
= 180 ÷ 6 (6 being the difference between 18 carat and 24 carat)
= 30 dwts (1 oz 10 dwts = 1·500) of Fine (pure) gold to be added.

To reduce 18 carat to 9 carat:

1 oz (20 dwts)   20 × 18 = 360 (18 carat quality to be reduced)
20 × 9 = 180 (9 carat quality required)
= 360 — 180
= 180 ÷ 9 (9 being the difference between 9 carat and 18 carat)
= 20 dwts (1 oz) of alloy (silver and copper) to be added.

To reduce pure Fine silver (this would be reduced to sterling silver for Assay and hallmarking):

	TROY	METRIC Decimals
1. Fine Silver	18½ dwts	0·925
,, Copper	1½ dwts	0·075
	20 dwts =	1·000 oz

Gold Solders

18 carat	oz	TROY dwts	grns	METRIC Decimal
Fine Gold	0	15	0	0·750
,, Silver	0	3	12	0·170
,, Copper	0	1	12	0·080
Total	1 oz			1·000

9 carat	oz	TROY dwts	grns	METRIC Decimal
Fine Gold	0	7	12	0·750
,, Silver	0	6	6	0·125
,, Copper	0	6	6	0·125
Total	1 oz			1·000

For more detailed information regarding working in precious metals and alloys for gold and silver, and gold and silver solders, I recommend *Working in Precious Metals* by E. A. Smith, and *Preparation of Precious Metals for Enamelling* by H. de Koningh.

Platinum Alloys

		TROY			METRIC
		oz	dwts	grns	Decimal
1.	Platinum	0	15	0	0·750
	Palladium	0	5	0	0·250
	Total	1 oz			1·000
2.	Platinum	0	19	0	0·950
	Iridium	0	1	0	0·050
	Total	1 oz			1·000

NB   Rhodium can also be alloyed with platinum as can gold and silver.

Platinum Solder

	oz	dwts	grns	Decimal
Gold	0	16	0	0·800
Palladium	0	4	0	0·200
Total	1 oz			1·000

NB   Ternary alloys of platinum/gold/silver/ or palladium/silver/gold can also be used as solders.

DESIGN AND RESEARCH CENTRE

In the United Kingdom the Design and Research Centre exists to encourage and promote high quality design in the gold and silver industries in combination with technical research.

The Centre will provide technical assistance not only in respect of processes but in the fields of metallurgy and other materials. In this respect the Technical Advisory Committee of the Worshipful Company of Goldsmiths works in association with the Design and Research Centre for the Gold, Silver and Jewellery Industries.

At the time of writing the current research includes investigations into the tarnishing of silver with a view to controlling this; another area of research involves establishing a formula for Niello in an attempt to make this a marketable product for use by jewellers and silversmiths. Discoloration of the skin in a number of people after wearing gold is also under investigation.

Membership of the Centre is essential if a service of technical assistance and information is required, including bulletins published from time to time.

Gold and garnet bracelet with Heracles Knot, Eretria Greece, c. 300 BC

Gold bracelet, Roman 1st century BC/AD

Electrum Torc from the Snettisham Treasure, 1st century BC, diameter 7.75 in, Early Iron Age British Museum

Testing the Quality of
Precious Metals

Touchstone

One of the oldest and most reliable ways of testing precious metal quality uses a touchstone and acids. A touchstone is a hard ceramic slab used for 'streaking'. In use, a piece of metal of known quality is rubbed along the touchstone, leaving a streak of metal behind, and the metal of unknown quality is streaked alongside this. A drop of acid is then put on both streaks and this will cause a colour change. If the colours match, then it is most likely that both metals are the same quality. If they do not match, the stone must be cleaned and further tests made, using the other metals of known quality until finally a match will be found. If a match is not found, the unknown metal is base metal or too low a quality to be used for jewellery.

For the streaking, make a rod of each metal, roughly 2 mm ($\frac{1}{12}$″) square and 25 mm (1″) in length, on which the quality is clearly marked. Solder a ring on the end of each streaking 'needle' and they can then all be attached to a larger ring for easy handling.

The acid solutions and their proportions may vary from jeweller to jeweller, but nitric acid is the most commonly used. Its action is slow on golds over 9 carat quality, and for these a mixture of 1 part nitric and 3 parts hydrochloric acid is used, or a mixture of 2 parts nitric acid, 1 part distilled water and 10 parts of common salt saturated in distilled water.

Rolled gold is difficult to test accurately because it is made of a base metal core encased in a thin layer of 9 carat gold (it is seldom made in higher carats) and subsequently gold-plated, which can give it the appearance of anything from 18 carat to pure gold. As the surface streak would be deceptive, you must find out if it has a core to establish if it is rolled gold. If it is a made-up piece of jewellery, the core must be exposed as inconspicuously as possible. This could be done with a saw or a knife edge needle file, making only a small nick, but sufficient to show how thick the casing is, so that you will have a rough idea of the gold content of the casing. Very lightly emery paper the surface to remove the plating, if any, and streak to establish if it is a gold alloy.

Bridal crown of Princess Blanche, daughter of Henri IV, c.1402.

Acid Tests

The acids used for testing precious metals are:
1. *Gold below 9 carat*
   1 part Nitric acid
   1 part distilled water
2. *Gold from 9 carat to 14 carat*
   3 parts Hydrochloric acid (Sulphuric can be used in place of Hydrochloric)
   1 part Nitric acid
3. *Gold from 14 carat to 18 carat*
   2 parts Nitric acid
   1 part distilled water
   10 drops of common salt saturated with distilled water
4. *Gold from 18 carat to 24 carat*
   2 parts Nitric acid
   1 part Hydrochloric acid
   (This is Aqua Regia and will have no effect in testing on golds of 18 carat or better, but will discolour golds of lower quality. However, this is the only solution that would dissolve gold if the gold were left in it for a period of time.)
5. *Rolled Gold or Gold in doubt*
   1 drop of Nitric acid on the touchstone, and then add a drop of Hydrochloric to this.
6. *Platinum and Palladium*
   1 part Hydrochloric acid
   $\frac{1}{3}$ part Nitric acid
   $\frac{1}{6}$ part distilled water
   $\frac{1}{3}$ part Ammonium crystals
7. *Silver*
   1 part Chromic acid
   6 parts Nitric acid
   2 parts distilled water

As you gain experience with handling metals, you may be able to judge by the colour and the weight of the metal in your hand what its quality is likely to be.

Crown of the Holy Roman Empire, also known as the German Imperial Crown

Crown of Stephan Bocskay (Austria), 1605

III BASIC TECHNIQUES

Chain Making

Gold necklace with emeralds and mother of pearl beads, Roman, from Pompeii, 1st century BC/AD.

Chains can be used extensively in jewellery, both for practical and decorative purposes. Their obvious advantage is their flexibility – the fluidity with which they will conform to a desired contour that would otherwise have had to be formed out of solid metal, as for instance in a bracelet or necklet, or as in medieval times following the contours of the body in chain mail.

There are very many variations of links that can be made for chains, beginning with simple forms made out of round or square wire and other simple shapes of wire, extending into more complicated forms using twisted wires and links that have been modelled or cast.

Round Link Chain

To make a simple chain of round links using round wire, decide on the gauge of wire and the size of link required. To establish the length of wire required for a link, the basic principle is that the circumference of the circular link is $3\frac{1}{7}$ times the diameter of the link. This will vary slightly according to whether the wire is thick or thin.

Always take the precaution of annealing the wire. To do this, wind the wire into a fairly tight coil (perhaps 5 cm (2") or 7·5 cm (3") in diameter), anneal the wire on a wig, then reverse it and anneal the other side, as it is vital that wire used in making links is evenly annealed. Pickle, wash and dry it. Always apply this principle when making links or twisted wire. The wire should then be straightened. This is usually done by securing one end in a bench vise, and holding the other end with a pair of draw tongs or strong, all-purpose pliers and gently stretching the wire, thereby straightening it. Do not stretch it too much or in its softened state it may extend to a thinner gauge. While the wire is held taut, run fine emery paper along it, then follow this with cloth impregnated with tripoli, and finally a cloth with rouge. Despite the bending and soldering that will follow, this pre-polishing facilitates the final finishing.

Simple link made of round wire

To start to make the links, the wire must be coiled onto a rod of the required dimension, preferably steel or a metal of similar hard nature. This rod is known as a spit. In every other shape of link-making, the spit must be covered with paper, but in making a round link this is not necessary. The paper is coiled onto the spit with as slight an overlap as possible too much overlap could result in some rings being larger than others. The best type of paper to use is a magazine cover, as the paper should not be too thin. After coiling the links they are annealed while still on the rod, the paper burns away allowing the links to be easily withdrawn from the rod. In the case of links other than round the join is always on the narrow bend so that when they are joined the join does not show.

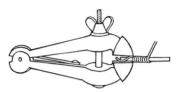

Spit and coiled wire held in hand vise

There are many ways of coiling wire onto the spit. One of the simplest ways when making small links is to secure the spit and one end of the wire in a hand vise, and holding the wire taut in the other hand, keep an even tension (which ensures that the links will all be the same size) and twist the hand vise, coiling the wire onto the spit. When all the wire is coiled on the spit, it is very important to unwind the hand vise several turns (ie wind it the opposite way) as the winding has virtually made the coil into a spring and the sudden release of its end would cause it to spring back and hit the hand or face. Always remember this point, and of course it is even more dangerous in the case of thicker wire. The reverse winding releases the tension built up by the wire hardening as it is coiled.

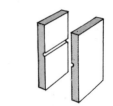

Wood grooved to hold wire

When using thicker wire, it can be easier to use a bench vise to hold the wire as this leaves both hands free to twist the hand vise.

For this method of coiling, two strips of wood are used to hold and protect the wire. They are placed face to face with the wire between them, and the faces will have previously been grooved to hold the wire firmly as it is being pulled through and wound onto the spit. Clamp the wood enclosing the wire in the bench vise. Clamp the required size of spit in the hand vise, and having twisted the wire end around the spit to secure it, you can now use both hands to coil the wire onto the spit, pulling the wire through the wood and keeping an even tension.

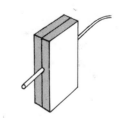

Wood enclosing wire

Other ways of making round links include securing the spit and one end of the wire in the jaws of a lathe or the chuck of a hand drill to hold it while you turn the lathe head or the drill by hand to wind the wire on the spit. When a large number of links are needed the bench drill or the lathe can be run at their lowest speed while the wire is being wound, but if this mechanical method of winding is used it is advisable to work in conjunction with a colleague who will turn the power off

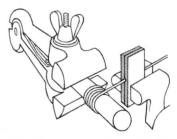

Wind the wire onto the spit held in a hand vise as it comes through the wood held in the bench vise

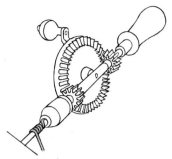

Secure the spit in the chuck of a hand drill

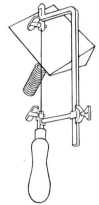

Hold coil just under edge of bench peg and saw through

The link will be asymmetrical

With two pairs of flat pliers twist the link to align it

A cutting punch has a hollow at one end

Position this over the open link to align and level it

when the wire winding is almost completed as the wire could fly out and cause damage. Remember to reverse the machine after it has been switched off, to relieve the tension built up in the coil.

Because of the potential danger of spring wire, always try to avoid standing directly in front of the spit (specially if you are using a lathe) – endeavour to stand to the side of it while working in case you accidentally release the wire and it recoils; you should then be out of range of the end that whips free. Slide the coil off the spit, anneal it, pickle, wash and dry it. (Additional polishing can be done at this stage if desired, by replacing the coil on the spit, for it is easier to polish one larger unit than individual links. After polishing, wash thoroughly and dry.)

The coil can now be sawn into separate links. Always saw, do not use shears or cutters as these would distort the cut ends. Hold the coils by pushing it just under against the edge of the filing peg and as you saw through, the links will drop off.

If there is any burr on the cut edges, remove it with a very fine file, but this will be unnecessary if a very fine saw blade has been used to cut through the links.

When the link has been cut through, it will be apparent that the two cut edges are not aligned. To align them for soldering, hold the link near its ends with two pairs of flat pliers and gently turn the ends until they meet. There is an alternative way of doing this by using a cutting punch. (This is a steel rod with a hemispherical hollow at one end.) These punches come in a variety of sizes. Select one into which the link will only just fit, so that a fraction of the link shows above the edge of the punch. What you are going to do is to close and level the link in one operation. Place the link on a wooden block or piece of thick brass or copper. A lead block can be used but it is advisable to place a piece of paper beneath the link, in this case, to prevent any likelihood of a flake of lead penetrating the join of the link as this would make soldering impossible. Position the cutting punch over the link and tap it sharply with a hammer. The blow will force the open link to contract and the ends to meet evenly within the concavity of the punch, and the force at the same time will level the link.

In the other method of aligning the ends, the levelling of the links must be done after soldering, by putting the link between two sheets of brass or copper (approximately 3 mm ($\frac{1}{8}$″) thick) or two blocks of hard wood, and tapping the top sheet. This will level the link, removing any twist left from the coiling process.

The links are now ready for soldering. Two of the simplest ways of placing the links for soldering are by resting them on a charcoal block with the join slightly overlapping the block, or by fixing a doubled steel wire to the bench, from which the links will hang with the joins at the base, and bending the wire up away from the bench so that the flame doesn't scorch it.

Because it is easier to solder individual links or a limited number of links at a time, link the chain in the following way: of the unsoldered links, put aside some for the final linking, and onto the others put two soldered links. (Opening the link to thread the others on it will not cause it to come out of alignment.) Close it and continue to thread up the

EMERALD   CITRINE   ZIRCON

RUBY   DIAMOND

SAPPHIRE   OPAL   SPINEL

GARNET   TOURMALINE

AQUAMARINE   TOPAZ   AMETHYST

Above: *18 carat gold, diamond and emerald necklace*
John Donald

Below: *18 carat gold bracelet*
David Thomas

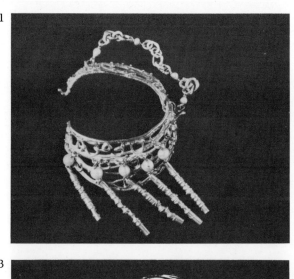

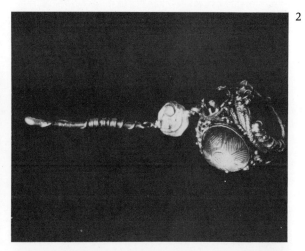

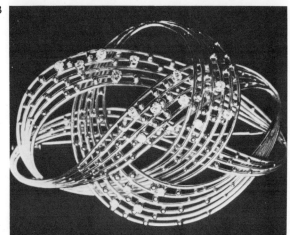

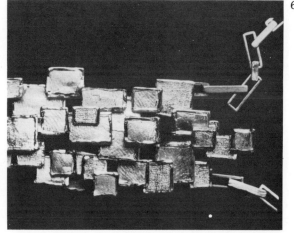

1   *Bracelet of silver with cultured pearls*   Gerda Flockinger

2   *Bracelet of 18 carat gold and silver with cultured pearls, moonstone and engraved topaz*   Gerda Flockinger

3   *18 carat gold brooch with diamonds*   David Thomas

4   *18 carat gold ring with square diamond*   Jocelyn Kingsley

5   *18 carat gold ring with square diamond*   Jocelyn Kingsley

6   *18 carat gold pendant with crystal quartz*   Jocelyn Kingsley

7

8

9

10

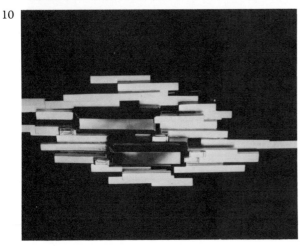

11

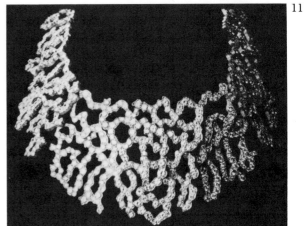

7 *18 carat gold ring with white gold encircling four diamonds, and 18 carat gold ring with tanzanite* Gillian Packard

8 *Two 18 carat gold rings with diamonds* Gillian Packard

9 *18 carat gold ring with tourmaline and diamonds* Andrew Grima

10 *18 carat gold brooch with tourmalines and diamonds* Andrew Grima

11 *18 carat gold and diamond necklace* Andrew Grima

soldered links in this way. When all the soldered rings are linked on, the open links can then be soldered.

One of the problems in link soldering is to prevent the solder flowing from the already soldered link while you are working on the new one. To prevent this happening, coat the already soldered link with a creamy mixture of powdered rouge and methylated spirits on its join. This will stop the solder from flowing out. At the same time place the rings so that their joins are as far apart as possible. Pickle, wash and dry to clean off borax and rouge, and polish. If the solder flows inaccurately (perhaps because too much flux has been used) the links may become accidentally joined. They can be separated by holding one link firmly in locking tweezers, reheating, and when the solder flows again, gently prising them apart with another pair of tweezers. Generally this will not affect the soldered rings, and the excess solder can be filed and emery papered away, but if too much damage has been done to the link it may have to be replaced with a new one.

Place the links on a charcoal block to solder them

or suspend them from a double wire

Oval, Rectangular, Navette Links

From this basic principle of making a simple chain, one can progress to more complicated shapes and designs for links, but the following description of how to make oval and rectangular links gives the technique necessary for making any other more complicated shape of link.

Links of any shape can be made provided you have the suitably shaped spit, or can devise one. For instance, a spit for a long oval link could be improvized by binding two steel rods together to give sufficient length. Similarly, a long rectangular link can be shaped around two pieces of square or rectangular steel.

A variation on an oval link is one with pointed ends (gem stones of this shape are called navette shaped). To improvize a spit for this, use two pieces of steel that have a flat base and a shallow curved top, shallower than half round. Bind them with the two flat faces together to give the pointed oval shape.

In making links other than a round it is essential that a strip of paper be spiralled around the spit. Allow only a minimum overlap, as too much overlap would mean that the rings turned onto this section would be slightly larger than the rings in between the overlaps. This strip of paper could be approximately 19 mm ($\frac{3}{4}$″) wide and must be of a fairly substantial nature, certainly thicker than newspaper. A heavy quality writing paper or magazine cover is about the right thickness.

The purpose of the paper is to stop the sharp edges of the spit biting into the metal thereby making it impossible to withdraw the spit from the coil. With any sharp-edged spit, such as a rectangular one, it always facilitates removal if the edges are very slightly blunted with emery paper before wrapping the paper around it. However when annealing it the paper will be burnt away and the coil will slip easily off the spit.

If the spit has had to be improvized by using two pieces of metal, overlap their ends before binding them together, so that if there is still difficulty in getting the coil off after the paper has been burnt, one piece can be held in the bench vise and the other gripped and gently pulled

Place the rings so that their joins are as far apart as possible

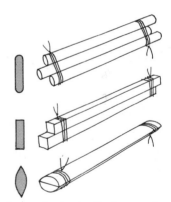

Improvized spits for long oval link; rectangular link, and navette shaped link

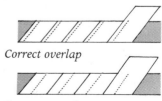

Correct overlap

Incorrect overlap

Blunted edges allow easy removal of spit

Sharp edged spit will prevent link removal

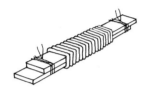

Overlap the ends of an improvised split

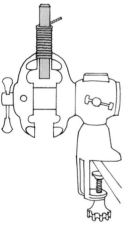

The spit can be hammered out of a coil through the jaws of a vise

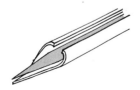

Iron wire is laid within chenier strip to make a hollow link

out. Alternatively, the spit can be hammered out of the coil. Rest the coil on the jaws of a vise which are just sufficiently open to allow the spit to drop through as it is hammered out.

When the coil is removed from the spit, follow the processes for soldering and polishing as for round rings, except that levelling can not be done with a cutting punch but must be done between the two sheets of metal or using two pairs of flat pliers as described. With rectangular, oval or irregularly shaped links saw the coil through at one of the narrow ends as here it will be hidden by the interlocking link.

Curb Chain

A curb chain link is a variation on the simple round link. To make a round link curb chain hook one end of the chain over a strong steel rod secured firmly in a bench vise. Put another steel rod through the other end of the chain, pulling it taut, twist the chain, keeping an even tension. Two things to bear in mind are: (1) to position the joins beneath the interlocking links (2) the chain will be subjected to great stress when being twisted. The strain put upon the link by twisting will break open an inadequately soldered join.

When using a very thick wire, it will be necessary to anneal the chain several times in the process of twisting it. Despite the degree of curve in each link the chain, when finished, should lie flat. To test this suspend it and see if the whole chain hangs with all the links facing in the same direction. If the chain itself twists it means that the links have not been twisted enough. Continue to twist the chain until it does hang properly. Allow for the fact that twisting will reduce the length of the chain, and the two end links will be misshapen and unusable. The chain must now be flattened with a hide mallet to indent one link upon the other.

Curb chains can also be made from oval links. A band can be added across the short axis of the link to add decoration. In all chain making, the variations on the basic principle are numerous.

It may sometimes be advisable to make a hollow link instead of a solid one – for instance – a long chain of large solid links would use a great deal more gold than its counterpart with hollow links, and the weight of it may also be a consideration. A hollow link is made by inserting into chenier a core of iron, copper or steel wire to maintain the shape of the chenier while it is being coiled, and this core is subsequently dissolved out by acid.

For this purpose, iron, copper or steel wire of the chosen gauge is laid within the partially closed chenier strip and then is drawn through the draw plate, until the chenier almost closes on the wire. It is important to keep the chenier seam in a straight line, but do not fully close the chenier as the iron wire is going to be eaten out through this gap.

The coiling and levelling of the links follows the usual practice in link making, but ensure that the seam is always on the inside of the coil. The links are soldered at their join, but not along the seam, as you assemble them. For a hollow curb chain link, twist the wire as you would in a solid curb chain, keeping the join beneath the overlapping link.

When the chain has been completely linked up, the iron or steel must be eaten out by pickling the links in a stronger solution of sulphuric acid and water than the ordinary pickle. There will be a constant stream of bubbles rising to the surface as the acid dissolves the iron or steel and when this ceases the filling will have been eaten out of the chenier through the seam. The acid should now be thrown out as it would discolour any further work. The new hollow rings must be thoroughly boiled in water with a little ammonia added, and then re-boiled in clear water and allowed to dry thoroughly.

Remember if you have to open the links for a repair, for instance, that their hollowness makes them that much more susceptible to distortion. Gentle handling is needed and an added precaution is to glue chamois leather over the jaws of the pliers being used, or wrap a strip of lead around them as a protection. In the finished chain the seam should not be apparent provided the links have been coiled with the seam on the inside.

Loop in Loop Chain

The simplest chain, of one link threaded onto another link, has been used from the most ancient times. A development of this, called 'loop in loop' chain, is found from B.C. 2 500 in work from Ur and Mochlos.

A round link is narrowed into an oval, and this is turned up into a U-shape. The second link, when formed in the same way, is slipped over the ends of the first link, and the process continued until the chain is complete. More complex chains are made by slipping two or more links onto the first link (a double or triple 'loop in loop' chain), and continuing from there the variations of linking can be made to produce a great variety of chains.

Curb chain of round links

Curb chain of oval links

A loop in loop chain

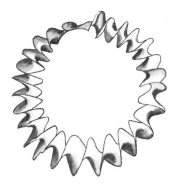

Gold torc, found near Belfast, Ireland, c. 700 BC.

Twisted Wires

The Loch Buy Brooch, silver with rock crystal and river pearls, Scottish, c.1500. This was made by a tinker; twisted wires are used extensively both for decoration and to delineate the form.

Twisted wire can be a very attractive form of decoration on all types of jewellery, and on larger work such as boxes, frames, trophies, chalices, handles, etc., the possibilities are unlimited. It is interesting to find their equivalents in architecture – the decorated columns of Renaissance Italy and Baroque Spain show beautiful examples of the richness of twisted forms. Orvieto Cathedral alone has over twenty different patterns in the twists of its columns. When using twisted wires a remarkably effective decoration is achieved both simply and inexpensively. Even an inexperienced student can achieve attractive results with the simpler twists. Any shape of wire can be used, by itself or in combination with other shapes. A single square wire twisted gives a satisfyingly three-dimensional shape with the minimum of work, and the combinations of forms are endless. If decoration is needed, even the simplest piece of jewellery can be given an added quality of finish and craftsmanship by the detail of twisted wires.

Wire can be bought ready made in a large variety of shapes and gauges, or it can be hand made by the craftsman to his own specification, using draw plates. Wire can be drawn thinner on the draw bench, or rolled to a shape in the rolling mills. The wire is generally twisted by clamping one end in a bench vise and holding the other end in a hand vise or strong pair of pliers and twisting manually.

As no filing or subsequent finishing is required there is very little

Gold Saxon ring with twisted wire borders, 9–10th century AD

wastage in this form of decoration. Herbert Maryon, author of *Metal-work and Enamelling*, explored the possibilities of twisted wires very thoroughly and made up seventy-two different designs from them. This is the most comprehensive range that I have ever seen and I know of no better way of illustrating the subject than by showing them here.

To Make Twisted Wires

The two essentials in making these are that they must be fully and evenly annealed, and that the wire must be absolutely straight before starting to twist.

The most effective way of annealing the wire is to make it into a tight coil, anneal it and then turn it over and anneal the other side. This ensures that the whole coil will be evenly annealed. Allow the wire to cool, undo the coil, put one end of the wire in a vise, and holding the other end with draw tongs, gently pull the wire out into a straight line. Do not pull too hard, or it could be accidentally pulled to a thinner gauge. Insufficient annealing or inadequate straightening of the wire will always produce an irregular, uneven twist.

To make a simple two-stranded wire twist, it is more efficient to double one long wire than to work with two separate ones. Place the loop of the wire in a hook (such as a cup hook), the shaft of which is held in the chuck of a hand drill. The two free ends of the wire are held side by side, touching, in a bench vise.

Start to twist the wire by turning the handle on the hand drill. If the annealing and straightening of the wire has been correctly done, the wires will twist evenly, but there is a limit to the amount of twisting that can be done before re-annealing. The more it is twisted, the harder it becomes and it could be stressed to the point of breaking.

Release it from the vise and the hook to anneal it, and do so on a perfectly flat surface. Allow it to cool, then replace in position and continue twisting. When the wire is first twisted, it will form naturally into a long, easy twist.

Further twisting will bring the strands closer and tighter, producing a shorter twist. Twisting does not alter the gauge of the wire, but it obviously shortens the original length. If a length of twist of 30 cm (12″) is required, the length of the straight wire would have to be at least 4 or 5 cm (2″) longer, as this is taken up in the twisting.

Most twisted wires can also be used to make links for necklaces and bracelets, on the same principle as link-making in plain wire. In a round link of twisted wire the join may be obtrusive because the continuity of the twist has been broken, but by filing the faces back to the point where they do match and soldering them here, the continuity will be restored. If this has caused the link to become slightly smaller than the diameter required, it can be stretched on a mandrel by tapping lightly with a hide mallet.

When making a link of any shape other than round, it is possible for the join to be concealed. As described in chain-making, on an oval link, for instance, the join should be made on the end where it will be hidden by the overlapping link. In the same way a coil of, for example, oval

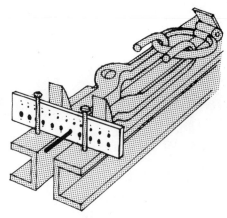

The draw plate in position on the draw bench

105

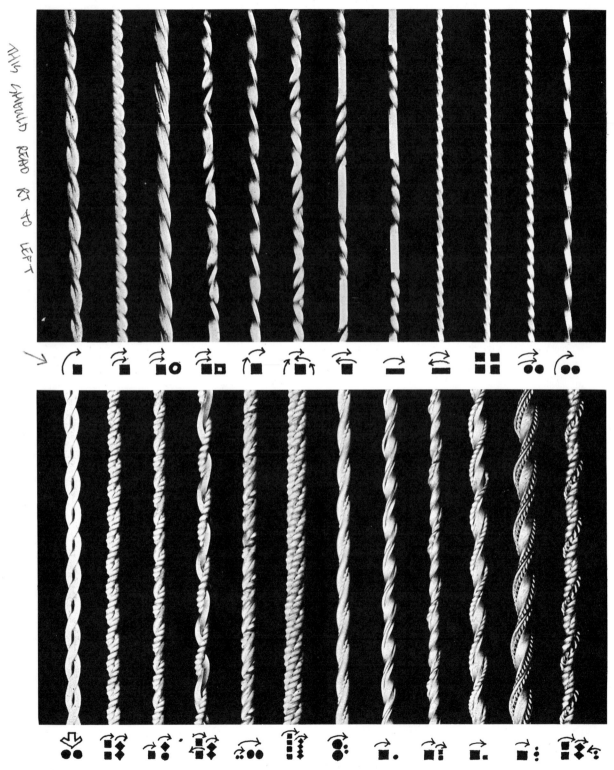

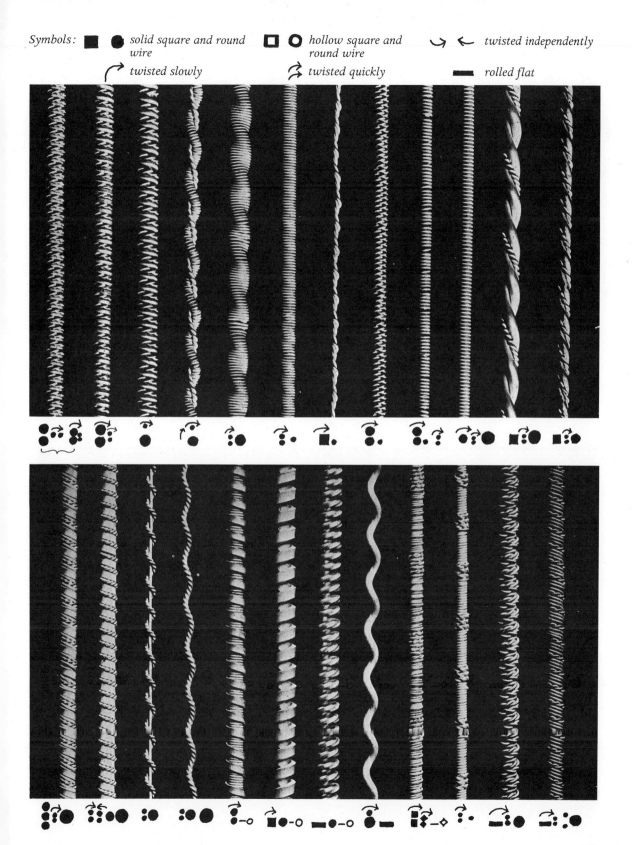

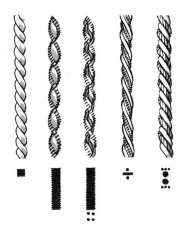

Square wire twisted

A threaded wire rolled flat and twisted (No 5 in text)

A threaded wire rolled flat with two fine twisted wires on either side of it and twisted (No 4 in text)

A threaded wire with a round wire on either side of it and twisted (No 1 in text)

Two round wires twisted, then two strands of three twisted wires twisted around them

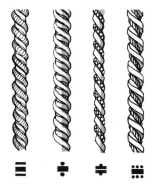

A flat wire with threaded wire on either side and twisted (No 2 in text)

A flat wire with a round wire on either side and twisted

Two strips of machine-made wire, which has a pattern of dots on it, soldered back to back and twisted

A flat wire with two strands of three stranded twisted wire on either side and twisted

twisted wires should be cut through in the same place. Even though the join will not be visible beneath the next link, it should nonetheless be filed, finished and the continuity of pattern restored.

The range of pattern possibilities in twisted wires is large, and variations can be added to even the simplest twist by rolling it lightly through the flat rolls of the rolling mill, or drawing it through a square drawplate, both of which will add decorative 'flats' to the twists. I have designed a number of twisted wire variations, some of which use threaded wire, this is made by putting a thread on a round wire and rolling it flat in the rolling mills. This produces a flat strip with a serrated edge, which looks very decorative when twisted.

1. Thread a piece of round wire, then lay on either side of it a rod of round wire, slightly less in diameter than the flattened wire. Bind the wires together and twist them as described.
2. Two lengths of round threaded wire are placed on either side of a flat strip of wire, bound and twisted.
3. Two lengths of round threaded wire are rolled flat and placed on either side of a piece of square wire, bound and twisted.
4. A threaded wire is rolled flat and two fine twisted wires are placed on either side, bound and twisted.
5. A round, threaded wire is rolled flat and twisted.
6. Two V-shaped strips are soldered together along their apex and two fine round wires are laid in the corners opposite each other; then two threaded round wires laid in the other two corners, bound and twisted.
7. One V-shaped strip with a straight strip soldered along its apex, and a threaded wire laid in each of the three corners.
8. A threaded wire rolled flat and one round wire laid along the centre of it, bound and twisted.

Some patterned wires can be bought from Johnson & Matthew, and would lend themselves to being twisted, or if they are very narrow and thin, two could be soldered back to back, for thickness, and then twisted.

Chenier

In jewellery, the very fine hollow metal tubing from which hinges and similar items are made is traditionally referred to as chenier. A craftsman will need to acquire the technique of hand making chenier as it has so many uses. Seamless tubing similar to chenier of different shapes and sizes in precious metals can be ordered or brought from the bullion merchant. It is, however, expensive and one may only need a short length, and as certain bullion merchants will not sell under a minimum length, its cost may outweigh its usefulness. It would be impracticable to try and make seamless chenier oneself, with the exception of a round chenier. (A seamless round chenier could be produced by drilling down through a piece of round wire, but its length would be governed by the length of the drill.)

Chenier can be made in most of the simple shapes – round, half round, oval, square, rectangular, triangular, etc and while it is mainly used for functional purposes it can be made up as it is, into simple jewellery. In the case of a bracelet, for instance, chenier would be very light as it is hollow and one could perhaps afford to use 18 carat gold, whereas a solid bracelet of 18 carat may be prohibitively expensive.

Despite the fact that chenier is hollow and light, it is strong by the nature of its construction. (It is, for instance, much more difficult to bend hollow tube than solid tube.)

Taper one end of strip

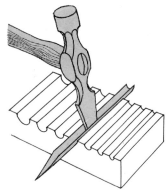
Curve the strip in a swage block with a cross pein hammer

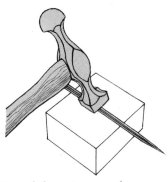
Round the strip as much as possible with a planishing hammer

Mark the seam with fine saw strokes

ROUND CHENIER

The simplest chenier to make, and probably the most frequently used, is round chenier. Assuming one wants to make a chenier of 4 mm ($\frac{1}{16}$") outside diameter, one would start with a flat strip of metal of the required length (ensuring that its sides are absolutely parallel) and with a width of the required 4 mm ($\frac{1}{16}$") diameter multiplied by $3\frac{1}{7}$; this will give the circumference of the chenier. This width may need to be increased depending upon the gauge of metal being used. The formula of $3\frac{1}{7} \times 4$ mm ($\frac{1}{16}$") would be suitable for thin metal but as the thickness of the metal increases so the width must be increased. The difference may be fractional, but only the making of a chenier will establish the correct width for a particular gauge of metal. The inside diameter is relatively unimportant, unless one requires the inside of the chenier to be threaded to take a tap (see Taps and Dies) or to be used as a setting.

TO MAKE CHENIER

In starting to make the chenier, double check that the sides of the strip are completely parallel and free from burrs. Emery paper both sides, anneal it and taper one end. Place it in the half-round channel of a swage block most closely matching its width and gently tap it down into the curve with a cross pein hammer, or a creasing hammer. If one had steel doming punches with cylindrical shafts, these could be placed along the strip and tapped with a hide mallet to help force the metal down into the curve.

Having curved the strip as much as possible in that channel, it is taken down to a size smaller channel and gently tapped to take up that curve, and so down through the graduated channels, resulting in a half round strip. Keep the metal well annealled in this process.

The half-round strip is to be rounded as much as possible by planishing before being pulled through a draw plate to close it. Lay it on its side on a steel block and carefully planish along the top to bring the edges towards each other. Do not hit too hard or the chenier will become distorted. Endeavour to close fully the tapered ends.

Anneal the metal and before it cools, coat it with beeswax. After cooling, pull it down through the draw plates with draw tongs until the chenier has just closed. There may be difficulty in keeping the seam straight in the drawing down. If there is, counteract it by inserting the point of a penknife blade in the seam of the chenier where it goes into the back of the drawplate. Keep the blade upright and draw the chenier through. This will have kept the seam in a straight line and it will generally not distort in subsequent drawing down.

When the edges of the seam are just touching, anneal and pickle the chenier and run the point of a scraper lightly along the seam to make a slight V-shaped channel. The seam is then to be carefully soldered, and the V-shaped channel will allow the solder to flow more readily. Lightly file the seam to smooth it, emery paper it, and anneal and beeswax it again. One then has a hollow tube very close to the required diameter

110

but it is extremely difficult to be totally accurate on such a small scale and the chenier may need to be drawn down further, and then annealed and pickled.

Left: Place the seam of chenier against object
Right: Unsoldered chenier would weaken with use

THE CHENIER SEAM

It will be necessary to find where the seam is when soldering the chenier on to an object, and as it may have become almost invisible, mark it after drawing it down. With a very fine saw, make very short light strokes all across the seam.

When the chenier is placed in position it must be soldered with the seam against the object for strength and neatness. If an unsoldered chenier were used and not accurately soldered with the seam against the object, the seam would be left open and at the subsequent stage of inserting a rivet the chenier would not function properly. The seam would continue to open with wear and it would look wrong, showing poor craftsmanship.

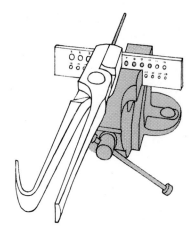

Pull chenier down through drawplate to close it

SQUARE CHENIER

If settings are required for a number of square stones of similar size, it would be more practical to make a length of square chenier and cut it to the required height of the setting than to make each setting separately. This would apply to any of the simple shapes of setting. The bearing would have to be inserted subsequently, or if the chenier was thick enough, a bearing could be carved out of it.

Square chenier is made similarly to round chenier, but is drawn through the drawplate on a metal core.

When the chenier is to be made for stone settings, the inside diameter is important. Establish this by choosing a piece of square copper wire of the same size as the stones. The chenier will be drawn around this copper rod. In this instance a bearing would be inserted later, which could itself be made of smaller square chenier. If it is intended to carve a bearing out, the square copper wire must be smaller than the stones and the metal of an adequate gauge for both the setting and the bearing to be cut out. Measure a side of the rod, multiply it by four and add a little extra for the corners. Cut a strip of metal to this width and of the required length. The desired square shape cannot be hammered up, so the chenier must be made up as round chenier and then drawn into square chenier. Follow the process of making it into round chenier until it is of a size that will just take the square wire. Slightly taper one end of the wire, cut it considerably longer than the chenier, cut a long taper on the chenier, and slide the wire into the chenier. Close the taper of the chenier onto the taper of the core so that both can be inserted through the hole of the drawplate and gripped together by the draw tongs.

Now draw the chenier and wire down through successive sizes of the square drawplate until the chenier almost closes onto the wire.

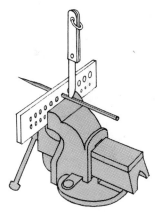

Keep the seam straight by inserting a pen knife in it

Left: Make round chenier of a size that will just take the square wire
Right: Square chenier can be used to make square settings

Wire tapered, inserted into chenier, and the long taper of the chenier wrapped around it

There are instances when the wire would be left in the chenier, as when making square links, or any small item where the square shape must be retained during another forming process. The wire can later be eaten out by acid.

In this case, in using chenier for settings the wire must be removed. Cut the chenier into the required lengths and the wire can usually be pushed out quite easily.

If the length of chenier had been shaped in any way there would be difficulty in removing the wire. There are two ways of removing it:

1. is to immerse it in acid which will slowly eat the wire out,
2. is by stretching the copper wire core. To do this, carefully saw the tapered end of the chenier off without cutting the wire. Remove the chenier taper and anneal the chenier and wire. After it has cooled, secure the tapered end of the copper wire in a vise and grip the other end with a pair of draw tongs or strong pliers and pull, stretching the wire. The chenier should then slide off easily. If it doesn't, re-anneal it and stretch it again.

This principle of making square chenier is used in the making of any of the other shapes of chenier. Copper, steel and iron are the best metals to use for cores as the acid will attack them more readily than other metals.

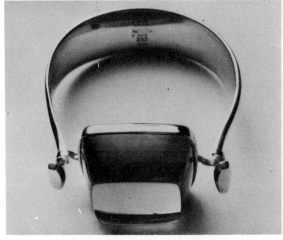

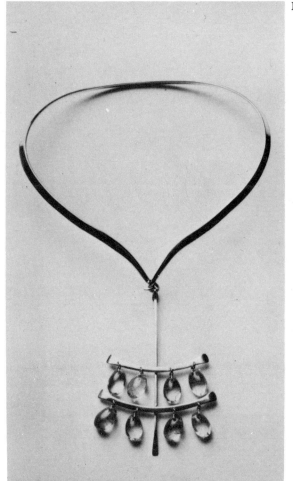

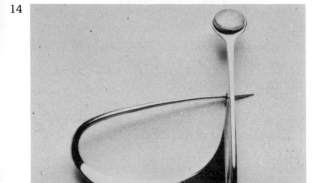

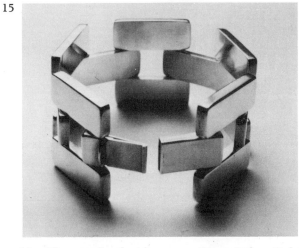

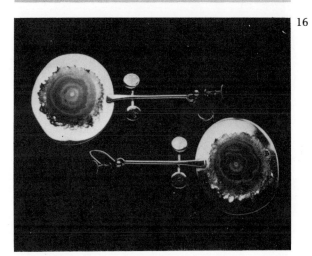

12 *Silver armband with quartz*   Torun Bulow-Hube   15 *Silver bracelet*   Astrid Fog
13 *Silver neckband with rutile quartz*   Torun   16 *18 carat gold earrings with crystal/moss agate slices*
    Bulow-Hube   Barbara Cartlidge
14 *Silver brooch with moonstone*   Torun Bulow-Hube

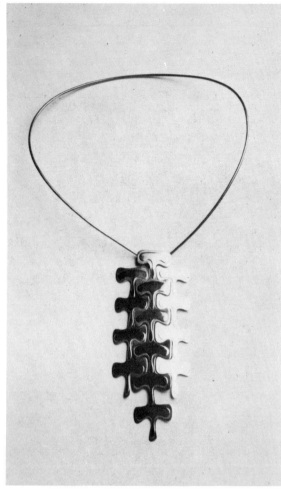

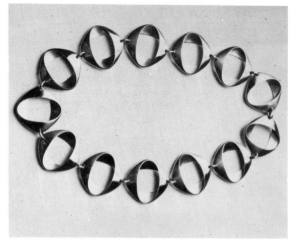

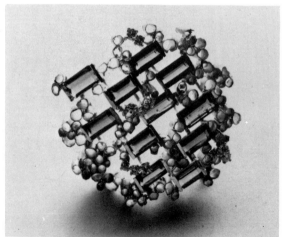

17 *Silver pendant, with 18 carat gold design overlaid*
    Helga Zahn
18 *Silver necklace* Henning Koppel
19 *18 carat gold bracelet* Arno Malinowski

20 *Brooch with tourmalines and 22 carat gold scrolls*
    Geoffrey Turk
21 *18 carat gold pendant/brooch with cabochon blue
    sapphire* Rod Edwards

Findings and Fittings

Jeweller's findings is the name given to the components and appendages used in jewellery that hold it in position or make it possible for it to be worn, eg the fitting for a cuff link, the clip for an earring, the joint, catch and pin for a brooch. There is a very wide range of findings for all purposes. They are machine made, mass produced, and vary subtly from country to country. It is likely that they may need some hand work on them to ensure that they function correctly. When buying findings, do check that they function correctly before taking them away from the suppliers.

Machine made findings include brooch pins, joints, catches, safety catches, bolt rings, jump rings, screw snaps for necklaces, earring screws and wires, earclips, cufflink connections, safety chains, stone settings, bezels, wedding and signet ring blanks, patterned wires and similar items.

I would like to make a purely personal distinction here between *findings* and *fittings*. A finding is a mass produced article, and for my purposes a fitting is the term that will be applied to an equivalent article that has been hand made. In my terms of reference here, a bought ear-clip is a finding and a hand-made ear-clip is a fitting.

Making findings is extremely delicate work. One is working, in the main, on tiny complicated units whose total size may be as small as 5 mm and under. It is possibly the need for such precision and patience that causes many jewellers to use machine made findings. They are, of

One of the earliest types of pin or brooch, made from one wire, formed concentrically, which produces the requisite spring

A gold fibula (brooch), Ruvo di Puglia, 6th century BC National Museum, Taranto

113

Gold earrings with quadriga (four-horsed chariot) Greek 4th century BC
Boston Museum of Fine Arts

course, time saving. However, I have a very strong belief that findings must be hand-made as a correctly made handcrafted piece will be of superior quality to a mass produced piece. If one has the creativity to design a piece and the craftsmanship to execute it, that piece is an entity, and the hallmark says 'I made this'. If I made it, I made it all (with the obvious exceptions of lapidary work, etc.). There is a pleasure in good craftsmanship – in the correct handling of good materials to give an aesthetically pleasing coherent whole. It does seem to be a waste of work if the piece of jewellery ends as a facade or a compromise – the back of the piece and its detail should be pleasing too, because of the sheer quality of craftsmanship that has gone into it. This sort of compromise is evident if a machine made chain is used on a hand-made pendant – the whole just does not look 'right'.

I particularly advise hand-making the safety type of findings, such as catches and pins, so that you can be sure that there is no chance of error in their functioning.

Buying Findings

I have recommended making fittings and findings by hand, but there are exceptions, particularly if one is working on one's own.

The complexity of hand-making some of the fittings may take such an amount of time that it could become uneconomic if one were self-employed. As a manufacturer, it would be viable as the work would be carried out by mechanical means and/or by employees, and the cost thereby absorbed. For the craftsman/jeweller, however, the ultimate price for the work may not compensate for the expenditure of time.

I recommend buying any finding that involves the use of a spring made of a different metal, such as steel, as the working of this combination presents many difficulties. For example:

1. Gold and silver bolt rings. A bolt ring is a circular fastening. It consists of a hollow tube containing a steel spring and this is attached to a projecting tongue. The tongue can be drawn back, with a knob which slides along a slot in the tube, and so opens a gap in the bolt ring to allow a link to be threaded onto it. The steel spring will have been compressed by this drawing back, and when released the tongue slides forward to close the gap.

2. The cuff link finding illustrated is made of square rod, containing two steel or bronze strips which act as springs.

3. The spring ear clip illustrated is made of 18 carat gold with a spring of 18 carat hard white gold. Its particular advantage is that the small central ring pivots to fit the plane of the ear smoothly.

4. Scarf or tie pin safety devices are slipped over the pointed end of the pin to prevent it coming out. The device is spring-loaded and consequently grips the pin firmly. To release it, its two components are compressed, and this forces the pin from the spring mechanism.

5. A 'Swivel' catch is used as the connecting unit for heavy chain, in the same way as a bolt ring or jump ring would be used to connect fine chain. Its most popular use would have been in the reign of Queen Victoria, when it would have been used to connect, say, a fob watch to

A bolt ring

Cuff link finding

Spring ear clips

Pin with safety guard

114

one end of an Albert, and a seal, sovereign, keys, or a simiar item to the other end. (An Albert, named after the Prince Consort, is a watch chain, usually heavy, often tapered, that was threaded through a gentleman's waistcoat buttonhole, and the watch, or items on the other end, lodged in his waistcoat pockets.)

Swivel

The swivel action of this catch allowed free movement of the chain so that it hung correctly and did not twist. A similar version of the catch is available for linking heavy units, but without the swivel action. (The securing device on a dog chain and collar follow exactly the same principle as the jewellery swivel catch.)

A locket catch

6. A 'Heart-shaped' locket catch was frequently used in Victorian bracelets and necklaces, and has a pleasingly traditional appearance which may complement the jewellery on which it is to be used. Its catch functions on the same principle as that of a box snap.

7. Safety chains and their pins are of such a delicate nature that I recommend that they be bought. They will have an open jump ring at one end and this is threaded through a closed jump ring on the article of jewellery, and soldered.

A safety chain

8. The fitting of a ring with a wide shank can sometimes present difficulties, however accurately the sizing was done. Fingers do alter in size, heat and cold can affect this and, of course, the shape of the finger can make fitting difficult. For example, after the ring has cleared the knuckle it may be too large on the finger. One solution is to use a ring clip, a simple device in the form of a band of metal which is placed inside the ring shank and hooked over the sides, to keep it on the shank but allow a degree of movement. As the ring is passed over the knuckle, the band is pushed flat against the shank, and when the ring reaches the narrower part of the finger, the band springs back to take up the space between finger and ring.

A ring clip

Earring Findings and Fittings

If earrings of value, either intrinsic or monetary, are to be worn the only absolutely safe way of wearing them is through pierced ears. If this is not an acceptable idea, there are many alternative types of earring findings for unpierced ears. Someone with very thin lobes to the ear may however find that these findings do not grip with sufficient security. If one does have one's ears pierced, a small round earring, called a sleeper, must be worn for some time to prevent the hole closing, and the sleeper must be made of silver or gold and not a base metal.

THE SIMPLEST EARRING FITTING FOR PIERCED EARS

This is a smooth round wire bent into roughly the shape of a shepherd's crook, and predominantly used for suspended or drop earrings. The length of the stem helps to counterbalance the weight of the earring.

It should be made of round wire, approximately 30/32 mm (1–1¼″) in length and 0·022 diameter. Curve it into shape with round nose and half-round pliers, and file a gentle taper on the long end of the crook.

Turn up a tiny U shape and solder a ball onto the end

Close the U shape

The wire is extended to make a locking device

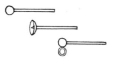

The shaft of wire could have a ball on the end, a cup for a pearl, or a ball and jump ring

An earring with butterfly attachment

The rod has a thread on it and the disc screws onto this

The other end is turned up on itself into a tiny U-shape and a ball is soldered on its end. The earring is subsequently fitted into the U-shape, which is then pinched together with round nose pliers to close it, leaving the earring to swing free.

An alternative form of fitting, with added security, incorporates a simple locking device. A longer wire 44/45 mm ($1\frac{3}{4}''$) in length is used to turn up the shepherd's crook shape, and when this shape has been made the wire is turned into a small loop from which the earring may be suspended, and then continues as a straight wire to hook around the tapered end of the shepherd's crook. The straight shaft and hook should be made so that they do not quite reach the tapered end of the crook, which will therefore have to be compressed slightly to slip into the hook and lock there.

The ball is placed above the loop but in this case is purely decorative. A setting and stone could be used in place of the ball. In either case the ball or setting should be soldered on before the wire is bent, or the wire will lose its tension.

AN EARRING FITTING WITH A BUTTERFLY ATTACHMENT (FOR PIERCED EARS)

This is made from a straight piece of round wire, approximately 12 mm long and 0·022 diameter. At one end there is a ball, or this could be a setting for a stone. Directly behind this a small jump ring is soldered on, from which the earring can be suspended. Alternatively, the rod can be soldered directly onto the back of an earring.

When the rod is fitted through the pierced ear, it is secured in position by a butterfly clip. This is a strip of metal approximately 3 mm ($\frac{1}{8}''$) wide, 18/19 mm ($\frac{3}{4}''$) long and 0·020 gauge, with a hole the diameter of the rod drilled in its centre and its ends turned up into scrolls which meet. (The scroll shapes suggested the name 'butterfly'.) In use, the butterfly is pushed onto the rod, up against the back of the ear, and as the rod will be forcing the scrolls apart they will grip it tightly. The end of the rod is to be gently tapered, and a shallow groove made with a fine round needle file, or a gapping file, all around the rod and about 2 mm from the end. If the butterfly were to become loose due to wear, and slide towards the back, it would automatically spring into this groove and not fall off.

AN EARRING FITTING WITH A THREAD AND SCREW (FOR PIERCED EARS)

This fitting is a refinement of the butterfly attachment. It is unavailable as a finding and would have to be hand-made, but its superiority warrants its use on the highest quality jewellery.

Its principle is like the butterfly fitting, with the advantage that it is almost impossible for this fitting to work itself loose, and it is therefore undoubtedly the safest fitting for pierced ears. The rod can either be soldered on to the back of an earring, or be made to hold a drop earring as with the other fittings.

The essential difference is that the rod is made with a very fine thread on it, and a disc is screwed along this as a fastening (so that they function as a nut and bolt). As the disc will need to be relatively light in weight, it will not be thick enough to contain an adequate thread. In place of thickness it will be given length by the addition of a piece of chenier, soldered centrally. The inside of the chenier is given a thread that corresponds to the thread on the rod. To facilitate the handling of the disc in use by providing a larger area to hold, a small jump ring is soldered on either side of the chenier.

The disc is given length by a chenier

Jump rings are soldered on to provide a larger holding area

Taps and Dies

Making this fitting will demonstrate the use of taps and dies, and/or taps and screwplates. To make the rod, use a piece of wire 0·020 gauge. Although its ultimate length is to be approximately 18/20 mm ($\frac{3}{4}$″), one can as easily thread 80 mm (3″), and thereby have enough threaded wire for two pairs of fittings.

The wire is held in a pair of pin tongs, allowing only about 15 mm ($\frac{5}{8}$″) to project, and the end is to be slightly tapered. The die is secured in a die holder. Insert the point of the wire into the front of the die and, holding the wire still, turn the die by its holder in a clockwise direction. As the die rotates, it cuts a thread onto the wire. If the wire seems unduly difficult to cut, add a drop of oil at the entry point of the die, or the wire may break. As a rule, it is better that the wire remains hard, as long as it is kept lubricated.

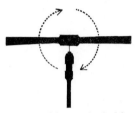

The die is held in a die holder and pin tongs hold the wire

As the die progresses along the wire and approaches the jaws of the pin tongs, these must be undone and a further length of the wire pulled out and the pin tongs tightened again. Cutting with the die then proceeds but always only on these small lengths. Apart from using a drop of oil occasionally to ease the cutting, reversing the die by a couple of turns will also help, by clearing away the swarfage (ie lemel). Continue cutting until the wire is completely threaded, cut the wire to the required length, 18/20 mm ($\frac{3}{4}$″), and solder it to, in this case, the back of the earring.

The fastening (the nut for the bolt) is made from a disc about 8 mm ($\frac{1}{3}$″) in diameter and a 0·028 gauge. Solder a piece of chenier approximately 4/5 mm ($\frac{1}{5}$″) in length to the centre of the disc. Now solder a jump ring on either side of the chenier. If it is too difficult to place them freehand, hold them in position with locking tweezers. Drill through the disc via the chenier, using a drill of a size that corresponds to the tap to be used.

The die will cut a thread on the wire

The tap, of the die size used, is secured in the tap holder, inserted in the chenier and turned in a clockwise direction. This will cut the thread on the inside of the chenier and through the disc. Continue tapping for about another 5 mm to make sure the thread is even all the way through, as the point of the tap is slightly tapered. Wind the disc off the tap.

The tap is inserted into the chenier to make a thread

Provided that the tap, die and drill corresponded in size, the disc should screw perfectly along the rod. If it is difficult to screw on, this may mean that too small a tap was used – if it screws on too loosely, too small a die was used on the rod or too big a tap was used in the disc.

The disc can be decorated by doming, or fluting, and the edges can be scalloped, knurled or mill-grained. Decoration would be done prior to soldering and tapping.

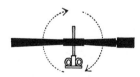

The tap is secured in the tap holder

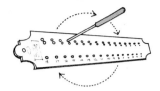

The screwplate, with corresponding tap, puts a thread on wire

Taps and Screwplate

The same process of making a thread and a nut can be done by using a screwplate and the corresponding tap, instead of a die and tap. The screwplate is a steel plate with a number of graduated threaded holes, and the corresponding taps for these holes are bought with the plate. It has the advantage of being more compact insofar as it is one unit with varying sizes on it, as opposed to the series of dies needed for the same range of sizes.

The principle is the same as using the die. The screwplate is screwed onto the tapered end of the wire in a clockwise direction. The making of the fitting is completed in the same way as when using a die.

Take care of this equipment as it is delicate and expensive. After use, smear it with *Vaseline* to protect it from rust.

EAR SCREW FITTING

This is the most commonly used type of finding for unpierced ears. Such fittings are readily available as findings, and can be used in a variety of ways: by being soldered directly onto the back of an earring, by the addition of a claw setting for a stone or a cup for a pearl, or by adding a jump ring for a drop earring.

The fitting to be described will be soldered directly onto the back of an earring.

A tapped chenier is soldered to the wire

As this does not go through the ear, a slightly thicker wire may be used. To make the fitting take a length of round wire about 25 mm (1″) in length and 0·0709 diameter. A piece of chenier approximately 3 mm ($\frac{1}{8}$″) in length with an inside diameter of 0·0503 is soldered to one end at right angles. This chenier is then tapped to make an inside thread. Prepare another wire, approx. 8 mm ($\frac{1}{3}$″) in length of 0·0551 diameter, by putting an outside thread on it using the die. As described before, while threading these wires one might as well make enough for several fittings, so double or quadruple the length of the wire as required. The chenier cannot be threaded in any considerable length as its thread is limited by the length of the tap, and this may not be longer than 15 mm ($\frac{3}{5}$″).

A threaded wire is inserted in the chenier

Make a small domed disc 4 to 5 mm ($\frac{1}{5}$″) in diameter and of about 0·028 gauge, and solder one end of the threaded wire inside the dome. This is the part of the earring that will fit up against the back of the ear. Now thread the wire through the chenier almost to its extremity.

A disc is now to be made and soldered onto the other end of the threaded wire, to enable one to turn the screw up against the ear. The disc should be slightly domed and can be decorated, by fluting it, or by scalloping, serrating or knurling the edge. Make the disc about 5 to 7 mm ($\frac{1}{5}$″) in diameter and from 0·028 gauge.

Bear in mind that the work will have to be hallmarked, either on the earring itself or on the fitting. If the hallmark cannot be stamped onto the earring due to the delicacy of the work or for some other reason, it may have to be stamped on the fitting and an area must be allowed for

The long wire is turned up into a U shape

this. The most suitable place will usually be on the thumbscrew disc. For this reason, send the components for Assay before the disc is soldered on, so that it can be hallmarked without damage to the ear screw fitting.

When it is to be soldered on, protect the thread and previously soldered areas by coating them with a mixture of methylated spirits and rouge powder. Make sure that the end onto which the disc is to be soldered is perfectly clean.

The easiest way of positioning the wire accurately on the disc for soldering is by placing the disc on the charcoal block, running a little solder on the back of it, and while the solder is molten gently bring the threaded wire onto the molten solder in the centre of the disc. Conversely, the disc could have a hole drilled in its centre, and this could be tapped and a threaded wire could be screwed in and soldered.

The other end of the long round wire is gently hammered and spread fractionally, and soldered onto the back of the earring. Polish the work and then with half round pliers, turn the long wire up into a U shape. Heat will have had some softening effect on the wire, and this will be counteracted by bending, and thereby hardening the wire after all the soldering has been done.

A CHAIN CUFF LINK FITTING

One of the oldest ways of joining two components and allowing flexibility was by the use of chain, and one of the traditional cufflink fittings utilizes this concept. It consists of five oval links, each end of which is linked to jump rings (or half jump rings) that have been soldered onto the back of the cuff link and the back of the bar that goes through a buttonhole. The distance between the cuff link and the bar is usually about 15 mm ($\frac{3}{5}$"). As this is such a fine chain it will have to be soldered very carefully to avoid solder running where it was not intended to. Make the five oval links and link them, but leave the first and fifth ones open.

A chain cuff link connection

It requires skill and patience to solder a jump ring onto a surface at right angles. Obviously, it will not balance, but if a flat is filed across it, it will stand on this flat, or at least can be held there with locking tweezers. File the flat across the join of the jump ring, for if it had been inadequately soldered in the first place, this second soldering would seal it. However, provided an adequate 'flat' has been made, an unsoldered jump ring can be joined and soldered to the back of the cuff link in one soldering.

There is an advantage in using a half jump ring as it takes up less space between the cuff link and the bar and consequently a thicker, more durable wire can be used. Saw a jump ring in half, true up the ends and the jump ring will stand upright while being soldered.

The chain is now to be linked to the jump rings, but as it has already had a number of solderings over its very small area, these must be carefully protected by brushing on a rouge and methylated spirit paste. Link the open first and fifth links through the jump rings and solder them.

A CUFF LINK FITTING ('S' SHAPED)

'S' shaped cuff link fitting

This cuff link connection would have to be hand made, as I believe they cannot be bought. It is agreeably simple to make and produces an elegant curved shape, almost a cross between an 'S' shape and a figure of 8. It is made from a strip of metal approximately 2 to 3 mm ($\frac{1}{8}$") wide, 0·028 gauge and 40 mm ($1\frac{5}{8}$") in length, and turned into shape, using fine half-round pliers, or round-nose pliers. Finish the ends by rounding them. This connection is well suited for use with 'double' cuff links (ie those in which there is a decorative unit at each end of the link instead of one decorative unit and a bar). In cases like this the decorative unit will usually be too big to go through the buttonhole, and this connection allows for one unit to be threaded on, the connection is then passed through the buttonholes and the second decorative unit threaded on.

Solder a jump ring or half ring on each cuff link.

In the bending of the metal a spring-like effect is achieved and when the connector is threaded on to the cuff link, via the jump ring, it does have to be forced through the aperture of the connector, causing it to spring closed again securing the cuff link.

CUFF LINK FITTING WITH INBUILT SPRING

Cuff link fitting with inbuilt spring

This fitting is also constructed from strip metal 2 to 3 mm ($\frac{1}{8}$"), 0·028 gauge but 30 mm ($1\frac{1}{5}$") in length. This is turned up into a narrow elongated oval and the ends are overlapped and bevelled to a finer shape, fitting lightly against each other. The principle is the same as in the previous connection: the bending causes a springing tension so that the ends are forced apart by the insertion of the cuff link units and then spring together, locking in the units.

EARRING FITTING

Turn the ends back on themselves

Planish and groove the top of the earring

Particularly efficient earring fittings are those known as Spring Clips. Such a fitting is very light and very strong, but cannot be made in silver, which is too soft. It must be made in one of the harder alloys such as 14 carat hard yellow gold, or 18 carat hard white gold. It is a beautifully designed thing because not only is it aesthetically pleasing but this attractive shape comes from its functionalism, ie it is a very simply shaped springing device.

To make it, take a piece of round wire gauge 0·050, approximately 40 mm ($1\frac{5}{8}$") long which, when turned into a circle, will give a diameter of approximately 13 mm ($\frac{1}{2}$").

File each end to a taper, approximately 5 mm ($\frac{1}{5}$") long. Turn the wire up into a circle and then turn the tapered ends back on themselves, which leaves an opening. The ends are turned down at an angle of approximately 45° and this lower part bent as illustrated. Cut a piece of metal 0·048 gauge into a rectangle 6 mm ($\frac{1}{4}$") long by 5 mm ($\frac{1}{5}$") wide for the earring base.

18 carat gold ring with green
cat's eye sapphire
Rod Edwards

Above: *Silver necklace with
18 carat gold detail, with
quartz, aquamarine,
tourmalines, cultured pearls,
amethyst and garnet*
Gerda Flockinger

Below: *18 carat gold ring
with diamonds*
David Thomas

Slightly groove one of the long edges with a gapping file and fit into it a piece of chenier of the same length 6 mm ($\frac{1}{4}$"). The chenier is of 0·028 gauge; solder it in position. Ultimately the tapered ends of the circle will fit into this chenier. Cut out the centre of the chenier, taking away approximately 4 mm ($\frac{1}{6}$"), which will leave 2 mm ($\frac{1}{12}$") at either end.

For both functional and decorative effect the top third of the circle should now be lightly planished to flatten it slightly and at the same time this will make it harder and more springy. With a small three-cornered file make a series of shallow grooves across this area which allows it to grip the ear more firmly and gives in itself a decorative effect.

What now has to happen is that the springy tapered ends of the circle have to be fitted into the cheniers where they will remain securely held due solely to the springiness of the round wire.

If they were put into the cheniers as they now are, they would be held quite firmly and the round wire could be moved backwards and forwards quite easily, but at an equal tension through its circle of movement. However, to cause the clip to snap onto the ear, an unequal tension is required. This means a stronger tension is needed where the circle leaves the cheniers. To get this, a degree of force, however slight, must be used as the circle moves in the cheniers. This is achieved by forcing the ends of the circle to compress as they run over a projection. To make this projection, use a round needle file to shape out a groove in the centre of the cheniers. This is smoothed off. Then, when the circle is forced to ride over the projection and into the gap, the greater degree of tension required is achieved.

Solder the rectangular base to the earring itself before fitting the tapered ends of the circle into the cheniers, so that the soldering heat cannot diminish the hardness of the circle.

Safety Catch

The type of safety catch that is useful if you have only a thin narrow section to solder on is the 'pull out' type of catch. The principle of this type is similar to the revolving one (as are most other safety catches) in that two pieces of chenier are used and the inner one moves within the outer. In this case, it doesn't revolve but slides in and out of the outer chenier.

To make it, take two pieces of chenier – one to fit closely within the other as before, but in this case the chenier is much longer. While the chenier in the revolving catch would have been about 4 mm ($\frac{1}{6}$") long, for this catch the whole unit is longer – the outer chenier 7 mm long and the inner 10 mm ($\frac{2}{5}$") long, the outer chenier to be 0·022 gauge and the inner of 0·020. Cut a piece of metal of 0·048 gauge to the length of the short chenier and about 4 mm ($\frac{1}{6}$") deep. This will serve as a base for the fitting, supporting it above the work piece, so the catch can be manipulated. Solder this to the outside chenier.

With a fine saw cut a slot along the side of the chenier, starting from the right and stopping short of the other end. The slot should be the width of the brooch pin that will finally be inserted.

File one end of the inside chenier at an oblique angle.

The tapered ends are inserted into the cheniers

The centre of the chenier is cut away

The shaping of a groove into the cheniers leaves a projection over which the circle must ride

Profile and $\frac{3}{4}$ view of the shape into which the circle must be bent

Position of spring ear clip

Solder the base strip to the outer chenier

Cut a fine slot along the side

File the inner chenier at an oblique angle

The 'stop' and thumbpiece are soldered on the chenier

When the thumbpiece is drawn back the brooch pin can be inserted

Bend the strip into the shape of a question mark

Divide the strip into 3 bands

Solder a square peg on as a thumbpiece

Saw a gap in the inner chenier

The purpose of this fitting is that the brooch pin is inserted through the slot in the outer chenier, and the inner chenier slides up over it to lock the pin in. This is why there is the difference in length between the two cheniers. To achieve this, the inner chenier will have to have a knob (or thumb piece) on one end so it can be pushed and pulled, and on the other end a tiny projection to stop it being pulled right through the outer chenier. So slide the inner chenier into the outer one until their two flat ends are level. The projection, which will be a little knob, is to be soldered on where the inner chenier starts to protrude. Take the inner chenier out and solder the knob on. You now have the 'stop' on the inner chenier. Slide the chenier back into the outer one, turn it until the little knob lines up with the slot, now push the little knob along the slot until it stops. The thumb piece can now be soldered on the projecting end.

The thumb piece could be a flat disc with a knurled edge, or a slightly domed disc that has been fluted with a fine file, or could also be a plain sphere. The thumb piece will be bigger than the cheniers but ensure that it has adequate clearance from the back of the brooch.

Pull the thumbpiece back and the brooch pin can be inserted through the slot into the cavity of the inside chenier. Push the thumbpiece forward, the inner chenier will slide over the pin, and then turn the thumbpiece to move the stopping knob around away from the slot.

There are a number of alternative versions of the two types of catch I have described, but the principle is the same although there may be slight differences in design.

The Revolver Type of Safety Catch

This is one of the best types of safety catch for brooches. The principle is that the brooch pin is locked into a tube.

To make this tube cut out a strip of metal about 4 mm wide by 13 mm long of 0·048 gauge. Bend this in the shape of a question mark so that the circle at the top is about 4 mm wide (but not fully closed). Divide the circular band into three sections, stopping short at the open end and before the upright bar.

Saw pierce out the centre band. File the outside edges of the curve into a gentle rounded shape. This unit is the outer shape of the fitting.

For the inner fitting, cut a piece of chenier 4 mm long. This should fit firmly inside the circle of the 'question mark'. Having ensured that it fits, withdraw it and solder a square peg centrally on the outside. This peg will become the thumbpiece for opening and closing the mechanism.

Return now to the outer casing. The central band or slot has to be opened up to allow the chenier and thumbpiece to be fitted in with the thumbpiece projecting up through the slot. Having done this now close the outer casing around the inside chenier to its original position with a pair of strong flat pliers. You will see that by moving the thumbpiece backwards and forwards the inside chenier will revolve within the slot. The unit now has to be made ready to take the pin. As the outer casing (the 'question mark') has an opening the inner casing must be sawn through to provide an identical opening. Push the thumbpiece to the back of the slot as far as it will go, and then saw a gap through the exposed part of the inner chenier. It will be evident that by moving the thumbpiece forward to the front, the gap in the chenier moves around in the casing, closing off the entrance. Once the pin is clipped into the aperture, the chenier is revolved to close the entry point, and the pin locked in.

The thumbpiece is revolved to the front and the pin locked in

Joint, Pin and Catch

The finding used to fasten a brooch to a garment is comprised of three units, a joint, a pin and a catch. The ancient form of garment fastening took the form of a fibula, and this would have evolved towards a safety pin type of fastening, and ultimately to the refinement and security of the joint, pin and catch.

The joint is soldered to the back of the brooch, and made as a hinge, holding the pin. The pin is tapered to pass easily through cloth, and secured at the other end by inserting it into the catch, which is also soldered to the brooch.

The joint can be made in two basic forms.

A joint, pin and catch

1. The Ball Joint

This is made from a strip of metal, gauge 0·035, about 3 mm ($\frac{1}{8}''$) wide. Inscribe three circles of 3 mm ($\frac{1}{8}''$) diameter, in a line and slightly over-lapping. Drill a hole in the centre of the two outside circles and saw pierce out the shape. Stop a little before the intersection of the circles and allow enough metal to remain joining them to provide the strength that will be subsequently needed.

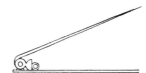

A joint and pin mounted

Now bend the piece into a U-shape, curving across the axis of the centre circle. Ensure that the outside discs remain parallel, with a clear opening between them. Soften the outside rims of the circles with a file, to round and smooth them.

Inscribe 3 overlapping circles

The placement of a joint, catch and pin on a brooch should be above halfway. If not placed in this way, the brooch will be top-heavy and fall forward. The joint is usually on the right-hand side of the brooch back, and the catch on the left.

Place the joint in position for soldering, standing upright with its spine facing the catch and the open-ended U-shape facing outwards (ie to the right). It must be very carefully soldered as the area of contact is minimal, where the arcs of the fitting sit on the brooch. Place a small paillon where each arc touches the brooch and solder, but make sure that solder does not flood into the U-shape, or it would prevent correct functioning of the pin.

Drill a central hole in the 2 outside circles and pierce the shape out

The catch is now to be soldered on, in line with the joint. Make the distance between them generous, but not too close to the edges of the brooch, keeping them 3 to 4 mm ($\frac{1}{6}''$) from the periphery. Either the revolver or the pull-out catch can be used.

Bend into a U shape and round the edges

Make the pin from 0·040 gauge metal. Make it long enough to pro-trude beyond the catch by approximately 3 mm ($\frac{1}{8}''$) and taper this end. Keep the taper short, as a long taper will be weak and inclined to bend.

The units ready for assembly

The pin should touch on the highest point of the joint

At the other end of the pin a unit will be soldered on, known as the 'heel'. Select a piece of metal of the same gauge as the space inside the U-shape. File it round so that it will fit into this space (applying the same principle as in cheniers for a hinge).

Prior to the ultimate fitting, drill a hole through its centre to be in line with the two holes in the sides of the joint. Solder the pin, slightly before its end, onto the rim of the heel and file it down to blend in with the shape.

A rivet is made and tapered and inserted through the three holes. Saw off the extraneous length of the rivet but leave a short piece projecting on either side. Remove any burr. Place the thick end of the rivet on a steel block, and lightly tap the other end with a slightly domed hammer. This will spread the head of the rivet so that it cannot slide out through the holes. Now reverse the fitting and tap the other end of the rivet to spread it.

The rivet should always be inserted from the top of the brooch. If it did tend to become loose with wear, and had been inserted from the bottom, its taper might allow it to drop out, releasing the pin, and perhaps the brooch. An added safety measure for brooches is a small safety chain and pin attached to a jump ring soldered in the vicinity of the joint.

As the pin revolves in the joint, towards the catch, it should touch upon the highest point of the joint. It will then be put into tension as it needs to be depressed slightly for insertion into the catch. This tension will force the tapered end of the pin up into the roof of the catch, providing added safety. To test before completion whether the pin has sufficient tension, press its tapered end down onto the brooch and release it. If it springs back in an arc, the tension is adequate. If there is a lack of tension, which could be due to soldering the heel on, the pin must be lightly planished on a steel block to harden it, and emery-papered.

A more elegant way of making a rivet for this particular type of joint is to broacher the three holes from the top and then from the bottom, which ensures that the three holes are exactly the same size. (Drilling alone does not ensure this.) Draw a piece of round wire that will fit firmly through the three holes, and use it to rivet, cutting the ends off as before. Now take the rivet out and file a blunt taper on each end of it. Re-insert the rivet through the joint and heel.

Instead of merely spreading the ends with a hammer, they will be finished with a beading tool, which produces a little dome, which not only holds the rivet in position, but gives a much more professional finish to the work. To do this, use two beading tools slightly larger in diameter than the rivet, and insert one in a vise. Place the rivet end in the hollow of the beading tool in the vise, and with the other beader press down, in a circular motion, to make a bead on the rivet. Now reverse the process, beading the other end of the rivet.

2. The Flat Joint

Whereas the ball joint, because of its narrowness, is suitable for use on delicate work such as a bar brooch, the flat joint is wider, will carry more weight, and is therefore suited for use on larger work.

A square of metal 0·028 gauge, 6 mm ($\frac{1}{4}''$) × 6 mm ($\frac{1}{4}''$), is bent across its centre to form a right angle. This will be the base and front of the catch. Round the four corners. In the centre of the rim of the front, make a small half-round groove using a round needle file. When finished, the riveted end of the pin lies in this groove under slight pressure, which puts the pin into tension.

Cut two pieces of chenier 2 mm ($\frac{1}{12}''$) in length and approximately 2 mm outside diameter. These are soldered into the right-angle of the base and front, leaving a 2 mm ($\frac{1}{12}''$) gap between them. Make the pin wire from 0·040 gauge metal. Take a piece of the same chenier and solder the pin on top of it at right-angles, leaving a little of the pin projecting. File the chenier to accurately fit into the space between the other two cheniers (the hinge principle). The three cheniers are now broachered out, from one end and then the other as before. The rivet wire is now inserted through all three cheniers, and spread as in the ball joint.

Having established the length of the pin, taper it. As with the ball joint, this joint can be used with either the revolver or pull-out type of catch.

An added refinement to the joint would be to flatten the end of the pin prior to soldering, then shape and file it, as shown, into a decorative fork shape, and one can devise variations on this.

Similarly decoration can be added by using an alternative to chenier in the form of jump rings soldered together. Having made a coil of jump rings, leave them as a coil and solder it to join the rings, so that it becomes a decorative chenier. It is then treated as ordinary chenier.

Another variation is to use chenier which has a wall thick enough to allow for the two ends of the chenier to be filed to a taper, giving a blunt torpedo shape. The same effect can be achieved by using a piece of thick wire, drilling a hole through its centre to take the rivet, tapering the two ends and then cutting the wire into three cheniers.

Two cheniers are soldered into the rightangle

The pin is soldered onto the third chenier

The end could be flattened and filed to a decorative finish.

Brooch Pins

A brooch pin consists of the pin itself, made from round wire, a joint which will be soldered on to the piece of jewellery, and a unit that allows the pin to open and close. This is soldered to the end of the pin.

There are two forms this unit can take

1. The unit is a piece of chenier which is to be fitted in between matching cheniers on a joint plate. All three cheniers are secured by a rivet, and thereby become a hinge.
2. In this case the unit is a flat disc with a hole through its centre which fits into a ball joint. The ball joint has a central hole in its sides and a rivet is again used to secure the disc in position. The ball joint itself will have been soldered to the back of the jewellery.

Having established the length of the pin, its point must be tapered but not made too long or sharp or the point will have a tendency to bend.

Gold brooch, enamelled, with pearls, Burgundian or Dutch, c.1430–40.

One of the drawbacks in making these types of brooch pins is that in soldering the unit to the end of the pin, the pin will become softened by the heat. It must be rehardened by planishing on a steel block.

Findings with Springs

Some ready-made findings, eg cuff link findings and bolt rings, have internal springs. If any soldering is required on these fittings the springs must be removed, as the heat would destroy the tension in the spring. As many springs are made from steel they should not be put in pickle as the acid would eat into the steel, and were they put into water and not fully dried out in hot sawdust they would rust and lose their tension.

Springs can also be made from bronze or hard gold alloys. The latter can be pickled but not heated as the tension would be destroyed. Gold and silver can be made sufficiently hard to be used for springs by rolling or planishing (hammering) but must then never be annealed.

Steel or other base metal is used for springs or brooch pins because of its hardness, and this is one of the few instances in which it is permissible, from the Assay point of view, to combine a base metal and a precious metal. The springs or pins themselves are exempted from hallmarking.

A Box Snap

A Box Snap

Of the many ways of fastening bracelets or necklets, the box snap is probably the safest method and would be used on quality jewellery. Most other types of fastening for bracelets or necklets are a derivation of this principle. Watch bracelets usually have a fastening of similar type but hinged.

While this snap may be available as a finding, there will always be the difficulty of matching it, in the limited range of sizes of findings, to the size of the piece of jewellery, so the snap would probably need to be hand-made. It is in very common use in the costume jewellery industry, made of base metal, as there the jewellery will be calibrated to match a commercially available finding.

These snaps are difficult to make, and require considerable patience to fit onto the jewellery – they can be exasperating to handle because of the precision required, and I recommend that a student make two trial snaps, one flat and one curved, before attempting a finished one, and in the construction of these the difficulties and the solutions to them will become apparent.

FLAT BOX SNAP

To make a box snap 15 mm ($\frac{5}{8}''$) long, 8 mm ($\frac{3}{8}''$) wide and 4 mm ($\frac{3}{16}''$) deep, one needs three pieces of metal, approximately 0·028 gauge. One piece, which will form the walls, is to be a strip 46 mm ($1\frac{7}{8}''$) long by

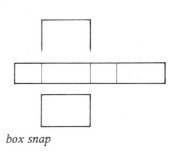

box snap

The Lyte Jewel. Gold locket, enamelled, and set with diamonds with portrait miniature of King James I. Attributed to Nicholas Hilliard. English 1610. British Museum

Drill a fine hole in one corner

The face plate with the keyways pierced out

The box is to be cut into $\frac{1}{3}$rd and $\frac{2}{3}$rds

The U shape is fitted into the gap

Saw the box in two

4 mm wide. The other two pieces, the top and bottom, are to be 15 mm long by 9 or 10 mm ($\frac{3}{8}''$) wide. The strip is marked into four lengths, the first being 8 mm ($\frac{3}{8}''$), the second 15 mm ($\frac{5}{8}''$), the third 8 mm ($\frac{3}{8}''$) and the fourth 15 mm ($\frac{5}{8}''$). Make a light saw cut into the divisions, and with a fine needle file open the divisions into a shallow V-cut. Chamfer the two ends of the strip, and with a pair of flat pliers proceed to turn this up into the walls of the box, and solder the chamfered ends. Solder the bottom on and drill a fine hole close to one corner. Now solder the top on.

There is quite an important point involved in making any hollow work. In the course of construction the work will be pickled, and if it had been imperfectly soldered, leaving even a minute hole, pickle and water could seep into it. If this happened, when heat was subsequently applied, it would cause the acid/water to turn to steam, which builds up a very high pressure. The steam may not be able to escape quickly enough through the minute hole and could literally burst the box apart. The explosion could be highly dangerous, and the box would be beyond repair. Therefore always allow some means for moisture to escape. This is the reason for drilling the small hole in the bottom of the box snap.

Trim the slight overlap of the top and bottom of the box so that they match the sides. The box is now ready to be made into a box snap. At a later stage it will be cut into two unequal lengths, across its width, giving two open-fronted boxes. The smaller box will have a tongue soldered to it, which will fit into the larger box, and lock there. Both boxes need a face plate.

To make the face plates, use metal of gauge 0·028, approximately 9 to 10 mm ($\frac{3}{8}''$) in both width and length. Mark it in half. A keyway for the tongue is pierced out on both halves, but of slightly differing dimensions. The metal is then bent along the marked line into a narrow U-shape. Before bringing it fully to the narrow U, coat the inside area with a rouge and methylated spirits mixture.

The box is to be cut into $\frac{1}{3}$ and $\frac{2}{3}$. Saw it, but not fully through, only down to the beginning of the base plate. This cut is then opened up, using the saw and flat needle files, into a straight-sided channel just large enough to take the inverted U-shape. Fit the U-shape firmly and centrally, and as it is slightly wider than the box, file the overlaps off level with the box. The top of the U will also project. Saw and file it off flush with the top of the box. Place the saw in the gap and saw through the bottom of the box, separating it into two. Each will now have a faceplate with its individual keyway.

A tongue is now to be made. Use a strip of metal 0·025 gauge, 6 mm ($\frac{1}{4}''$) wide and approximately 20 mm ($\frac{4}{5}''$) in length. One end is inserted through the keyway on the faceplate of the smaller box, to a length of about 1 mm ($\frac{1}{25}''$), and soldered there. Although the paillons have to be placed on the outside of the box, on the back of the strip, the solder will run through to the inside of the box when heated.

Take a piece of metal sheet 0·048 gauge and make a 3 mm ($\frac{1}{8}''$) square. Turn the box upside down and solder the square at the other end of the strip. Place it centrally, and so that half of it overlaps the edge. This, at a later stage, will be filed into a thumb piece.

Turn the strip right side up again and mark a line across it 10 mm ($\frac{3}{8}$") from where it is soldered to the box. Hold the strip with a pair of flat pliers and bend it back upon itself on this line at an angle. The thumbpiece will now be close to the top of the box. This bent strip is now the tongue. Where the metal is bent, it becomes very strong and springy, and should only be bent after all soldering has been done, or the soldering heat would, in effect, anneal it and destroy the tension.

The keyways will now have to be adapted to allow for insertion of the thumbpiece. They are already open to the top of the boxes, but this space must now be extended, with fine needle files, to make a very small slot towards the back of the boxes. The thumbpiece slides firmly into this and stands clear of the surface when the snap has been closed. The slot must be made only fractionally wider than the thumbpiece to guarantee the firmness of the fit.

In closing the snap, the tongue is inserted into the larger box and pushed home by compressing the angle of the tongue through the keyway. When it is fully inserted it will spring up behind the faceplate, locking itself in, and the thumbpiece will again stand clear. To undo the snap, the thumbpiece must be depressed to reduce the angle of the tongue and allow it to be withdrawn. The top of the thumbpiece is usually slightly serrated, both for decoration and to give additional purchase for one's thumbnail when depressing it.

From the measurements given for the width of box and tongue, it is evident that the tongue will fit firmly in the box, and this is important, as any lateral movement between the two lessens the strength of the snap. For the most expensive type of jewellery, the inside of the larger box would have channels for each side of the tongue to run along, making lateral movement impossible.

If the box snap should at some time need repair, the heat used would cause it to lose its spring, but this can be restored by planishing the bend. Fortunately one can now buy hardened silver that does not lose its hardness after annealing or soldering, and this is ideal for use in instances where spring is required.

A CURVED BOX SNAP

I have recommended making a curved box snap also, for practice, and it follows exactly the same procedure except in one respect: the strip for the walls will have to be deeper. There are two ways of making a curved snap, but the first is preferable as it is easier. In this case the walls are made as before, but the added depth allows for the edges of the long sides to be filed into matching curves.

File along the rim from the centre of the curve out towards each end. When filing the top of the walls use a flat file that is wide enough to cover the whole of the box, so that the extra metal on the ends is removed at the same time. Use a broad half round file across the bottom rim to give it the concave curve.

The top and bottom plates are curved to fit the sides, either in a swage block or with half round pliers, and soldered in position. From this point on the procedure is exactly the same as for the flat box snap.

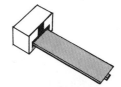

Insert tongue in keyway

Bend the tongue back upon itself

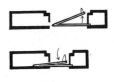

This illustrates the action of the tongue in the box snap. It is compressed to enter the keyway, and springs open within the box

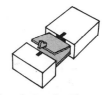

The thumbpiece has been serrated and keyways extended

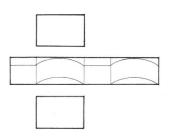

A curved box snap is most easily made by turning it up as an ordinary box and then filing it to a curve

Use a broad file that will cover the whole box to remove excess metal

The more difficult way is to saw out the shape and then make the rightangles

The second way of making the snap is slightly more complicated. It consists of sawing the walls to the required pattern first of all. The same broad strip is necessary, and the plan of the curved sides and the straight ends is marked out on it. When the shape has been sawn out, it is turned up at right angles and soldered, and from then on made as the flat box snap was, except that the top and base are curved to fit the sides. The difficulty lies in fitting the top and bottom on to the sides on such a tiny unit, whereas the first way of doing it makes the whole thing easier to handle.

Reliquary, Rheims, 9th century

Hinges

Hinges are used in jewellery in many ways – on bracelets, watch bands, watch cases, clasps, snaps, lockets, boxes, etc. The method remains the same in each case, and if the work is being made in precious metals the jeweller will have to hand-make the hinge.

Hinges are made from an uneven number of hollow tubes, ie cheniers, held together by a rivet. Each alternate tube is soldered to the side of the work piece, the other tubes to the lid of the piece and they revolve around the rivet.

A Hinge for a Square Box

As an example I will describe how to put a hinge on a square box. The tubes for the hinge are lengths of chenier. Cut a rod of chenier into three, five, or seven equal lengths. If only three cheniers are being used, it is advisable to make the middle one slightly longer to strengthen the hinge. To cut the chenier into equal lengths, use the jointing tool. Let us assume we are using five cheniers on a small box : two are to be soldered to the lid and three are to be soldered to the side of the box. The hinge is to be the same length as the side of the box.

Make a narrow cut with a back saw where the lid meets the side of the box, to open up this area fractionally. It is not to be a V cut but a straight cut taking off a fraction of the lid and a fraction of the side to make space for the hinge. Be careful in making this cut not to cut

A watch ring with an alarm mechanism, Augsberg c. 1580

A miniature case, c. 1610 enamelled, with rubies and diamonds.

131

Three cheniers are soldered to the work piece and two cheniers are soldered to the lid

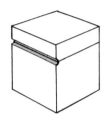

File out a groove that will hold the cheniers at their diameter

A broacher

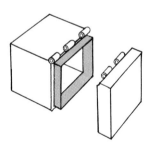

Solder the cheniers on the lid first

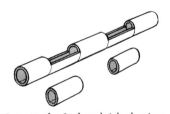

Cut out the 2nd and 4th cheniers

through the bearing. Now open up the area with a gapping file of the same diameter as the cheniers, which will give you a groove, into which the cheniers will ultimately sit. File the groove out as a half-round channel until it will hold the cheniers at their diameter, ie half in and half out of the box. They are to be soldered in this position. Before soldering them, very gently bevel the ends of each piece of chenier. This will help to cause the solder to run under each chenier and not flood across onto the next one. (This same principle was shown in the early exercise of soldering a key pattern to a base plate and bevelling the edges to assist the direction of the solder's flow.)

Solder the two cheniers on the lid first, having protected the other three with a mixture of methylated spirits and rouge powder. This mixture is used merely to dirty the surfaces and thereby prevent solder flowing there (and incidentally demonstrates an excellent example of how essential utter cleanliness is when soldering).

Pickle, wash and dry the box and cheniers. The three cheniers on the side are now soldered, having coated the others with the rouge mixture to dirty them and protect them from solder. Pickle, wash and dry again.

Even with the most carefully made chenier one cannot be sure that the inside of the chenier is completely round. This must now be rounded, using a broacher (rather like a long darning needle with five cutting edges). Insert it into the chenier and rotate it to round off any projections. As the broacher is slightly tapered it may not have fully reached the further end, and must be taken out and inserted in the other end and rotated again to complete the rounding of the inside of the chenier.

The cheniers are now to be held together by a rivet. A rivet in this case is a piece of round wire of the same diameter as the inside of the chenier, but slightly longer. It is to be pushed through the cheniers, but may need to be eased off slightly with a file or emery paper until it fits, and then lubricated with beeswax or oil. It must be a firm fit to prevent any lateral play between box and lid. Provided it fits correctly and firmly it will not need to be secured at its ends. Saw off and trim up the projecting ends, and the hinge is now complete.

I have chosen to describe this method of hinge making because it explains the principle as simply as possible. There is, however, another method that I use. It involves using one piece of chenier only as opposed to five pieces and I recommend it because I find it easier and more accurate. Cut the chenier to the length of the side of the box and mark it into five equal parts. Saw through the divisions 1/6th of the way down on either side of the seam on the chenier, ie 1/3rd of the way in all. On the second and fourth areas cut across with the saw to take out this area, leaving the first, third and fifth areas intact. Now place the length of chenier in the groove between lid and box, with the seam facing the centre of the groove.

Areas one, three and five are to be soldered to the side of the box. When this is done the 2nd and 4th pieces are sawn out completely, leaving three cheniers accurately positioned on the side of the box. Cheniers two and four now have to be replaced. Cut them from the same size of chenier and file them to slot down into the vacant places accurately as a tight fit. It is not necessary to champher the edges in this case, but remember to coat the three soldered cheniers with the rouge mixture. The lid will be put in position and the two new cheniers fitted in place and soldered onto the lid. The rivet pin is then fitted after broaching has been done.

With cheniers used in this way the lid of the box will open fully, ie to 180° or beyond, which may present a hazard if it were to be enamelled, decorated or set with stones. It could fall back, overbalancing the box, and the constant wear could cause damage. I recommended setting the cheniers halfway in and halfway out of the box to facilitate their handling, but once this technique is mastered it can be taken one stage further to prevent the lid falling back. The cheniers must be set deeper into the groove, three-quarters of the way in, and then when the lid is opened to about 90° its edge will touch on the edge of the side of the box and prevent it travelling any further.

An alternate design for the hinge can be used to prevent the lid falling back. In this case strips of metal, or bearers, are placed on the outside of the box on either side of the cheniers. When the lid is opened its bearer will eventually touch the bearer on the side of the box and prevent the lid opening further. The bearer can be made small to keep it inconspicuous or can be elaborated on as a design feature.

A Hinge for an Oval Box

In using a hinge for an oval box as an example I can explain the use of bearers more fully, combining it with the making of a hinge for a curved surface. The bearers on a round or oval box will project and must therefore be considered as a design feature. The oval box will have been made in basically the same way as the square one. The metal will have been turned up into a ring and soldered, the top and base soldered on, the lid cut off and its bearing inserted. The curve of the box will govern the number of cheniers to be used but for this exercise the box should be of a size to comfortably hold five cheniers.

The basic arrangement and fitting is the same as before. The bearers are made of two strips of metal of 0·050 gauge. Saw and file out a curve on each to fit the curve of the box.

Solder one bearer at the edge of the lid and the other at the edge of the box where they meet. The bearers must be flush with the rims of both lid and box, and in fact touch each other. The inside of the bearers must now be grooved to accommodate the cheniers. Hinges cannot be made in a curve, so the bearers must hold the cheniers in a straight line that runs the length of the bearer and comes as close as possible to the outside of the box. Cut the line with a back saw to about one-third of the depth of each bearer and open it up to a groove with a gapping file of the same diameter as the chenier, as before. The five cheniers are then soldered in position, with three on the box bearer and two on the lid bearer. The cheniers can be handled as five separate units or one single unit as I have described. Before the box could open the outside edges of each bearer must be bevelled. Then when the lid is opened these bevelled faces will move towards each other until they meet and the lid can go no further.

If the cheniers are set ¾ of the way in, the lid will be prevented from travelling too far

A round or oval box will have bearers to carry the hinges

The bearers can be a decorative feature

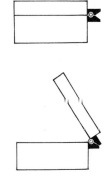

Bevel the edge of the bearers

133

Follow the procedure of broaching and fitting the rivet as described. The bearers can now be refined by shaping the outside edges, and enamelling, chasing, engraving or decorating the top bearer in some other way to make it a feature of the design.

Examples of the decorative use of hinges can be seen in the work of Fabergé and in the design of enamelled Battersea boxes.

Boxes

Green jasper notecase with gold and rose diamonds. Fabergé

Small boxes can often be considered as a part of jewellery, either in the form of lockets or jewel boxes, pill boxes, stamp boxes, the equivalent of sovereign cases, or the principle can be extended to include compacts and cigarette boxes.

Of the possible shapes, square or rectangular boxes are harder to make than round or oval ones, so I will describe the making of a square box.

Having decided on the proportions of the box, cut a strip of metal of 0·035 gauge of the height required and long enough to make the four sides. Anneal it. Measure on it the four equal lengths and mark them. Chamfer, ie bevel, the two ends on one side only. Using a back saw, make a light cut into, but not through, the metal (approximately one-third way) on the three dividing lines. Open these up to a V shape with a three-square needle file, but without going any deeper.

Open up the divisions into a V shape

Begin to bend the strip into a square, using flat pliers. As the sides are brought towards a right-angle the V shapes will close. Work on the three joins at the same time and when the V shapes have closed on them all and the sides cannot be shaped further without distorting them, open up the corners again with the back saw. Don't cut any deeper than before or the outside of the corner will become weak and break, but merely cut into the corner to clear away a little more metal. This clearance is then closed again towards a right-angle and the cutting and

Bend the strip into a square

135

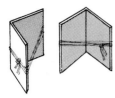

Hold two bevelled sides together with binding wire

Butt join the two rightangles

Inscribe the depth of the lid

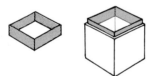

A bearing must be made to locate the lid on the box

clearing continued until the four sides form a square. During the bending process anneal the metal as necessary, and finally pickle before soldering.

There are two other ways of making this square shape. One is to cut the strip into four equal lengths and bevel both ends of each length. The sides are held in position, bevelled edges together, by binding wire or locking tweezers or by pressing them into cuttlefish. Solder two sides together, then the other two, and then solder the remaining joins. The advantage this method has over the previous one is that the outside corners will be absolutely sharp.

Another alternative is to use a strip of metal that is longer than the overall length of the four sides, cut it in half and measure the correct length of one side on each piece. Proceed as in the first instance on one of the pieces, bending and sawing to produce a right-angle. Do the same with the other. There will now be two right-angled pieces that can be aligned quite easily to form a square. Solder them together and saw off the projections from the two long sides. This will give a sharp edge on two corners, while the other two that have been bent into shape will be blunt. To sharpen these, cut through the corners and this cut will usually be sufficient to get rid of the blunt corners, which can then be resoldered.

Despite the simplicity of the shape, it can be surprisingly difficult to achieve an absolutely accurate square if one is inexperienced. I recommend therefore that one makes a former first, on which the shape can be worked. This could be made out of hardwood, laminated wood, lead/tin alloy, or epoxide resins, etc.

The top and base of the box are now to be made using metal of the same gauge. Cut these two shapes slightly larger than the box. Solder them onto the top and the base and trim off the extraneous metal. One now has a hollow squared shape which will be cut through to make a lid. Decide on the depth of the lid and inscribe this depth with a pair of dividers on all four sides. Saw along the inscribed line, thereby making a lid.

A bearing must now be made to locate the lid firmly on the box. Using thinner metal, about 0·025 gauge, and of a greater height than the sides of the box, turn up the box shape in the same way, but fractionally smaller so that this thinner bearing can be inserted inside the box to fit tightly. Solder it in position. The lid should now fit down neatly over the bearing. The bearing may need to be filed down a little if it is too high.

A round or oval box would be made in the same way, by turning up and shaping, its top and base would be soldered on, the lid cut off and the bearing inserted in the same way.

The boxes can be subsequently decorated by a variety of techniques: repoussé, enamelling, niello, engraving, etching, or by setting with stones.

Gold ring with movable bezel,
Thracian 6–5th century BC
Archaeological Museum, Sofia

Byzantine gold ring, Rumania
12th century AD
National Museum of Antiquities,
Bucharest

Rings

Gold ring from Pompeii, 1st
century AD
Museo Archaeologico Nazionale,
Naples

Rings must surely be the most personal form of jewellery. In present-day usage, the giving of them in celebration of birth, engagement and marriage symbolizes the most precious gift.

In ancient usage it is thought that the ring may have been a development of the cylindrical seal, engraved with the owner's personal device. The signet ring was in use in the earliest history of Egypt, and from here the custom of wearing rings passed later to the Greeks, Etruscans and Romans. Prior to the sophistication of making rings from metal, the ancient civilizations provide examples of primitive rings made from reeds or plaited fibres, from hair, bone, shell, horn, ivory, amber and other organic matter, and later faience and stones such as agate, onyx, chalcedony and jade were used.

While rings were given as love tokens and betrothal rings from an early time (examples exist of iron Roman betrothal rings, 2nd century B.C.), the wedding ring, as a separate ring, was not used at that stage, but the betrothal ring would also be used at the wedding. It is impossible to define when it became the common practice to have a separate wedding ring, but it would appear likely to have begun in England in late medieval times.

Gold and emerald ring for an
Egyptian mummy, 4th century
AD

Shanks

A ring can be a plain continuous band, as is a wedding ring, or the band can be interrupted to hold a setting. In the latter case, the band is then referred to as the shank of the ring. If the simple wedding band

Coronation ring for William IV,
1830. Gold set with a sapphire,
over which is a cross formed by
five rubies, with a diamond
surround

137

A knife-edged shank and setting

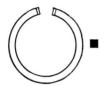

Cut a space out of the square wire for the setting

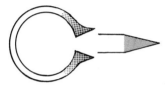

Lay the shank on its side and splay the two ends

File the shoulders to a knife edge

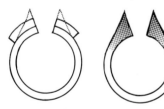

For a very high setting, solder a second length of wire on to the shoulders. When splayed, this will provide twice the height

A horizontal split shank ring

A vertical split shank ring

described earlier had been made and a setting soldered on it, or into it, one would have an example of a shank and a setting constituting a ring. Using the same principle, this type of shank can be designed with a great number of variations.

A thinner shank is used in traditional types of ring. The shank will have been refined by simple, delicate shaping to be visually integrated with the setting.

The two most frequently used basic, traditional types of shank for a setting are (1) a blunt knife-edged shank and (2) a split shank, which can be split vertically or horizontally.

1. A KNIFE-EDGED SHANK

Use a piece of square wire approximately 0·093 gauge, and turn it up, with half-round pliers, to the finger size. Cut sufficient wire off one end to allow the setting to sit between the two ends. (With experience one will learn to judge the correct length of wire needed to meet the setting, and it will not be necessary to cut off and perhaps waste the extra piece, but when inexperienced it is easier to fit the finger first and then shorten the wire to hold the setting.)

Anneal the shank. Allow it to cool. Place the shank on its side on the bench block, and using a shallow dome-faced hammer, spread the two ends so that they splay out in a fan-shaped way. The ends are now filed to fit the taper of the setting. Solder the setting in place between the ends, and check the roundness of the shank on the ring mandrel. The shoulders of the shank are now filed into a blunt knife edge, curving from the shank up towards the top of the setting, but leaving sufficient metal free to set the stone.

If the setting is very high, this gauge of wire would not spread sufficiently far when hammered. To overcome this, with a minimum loss of metal, cut two pieces of the same gauge wire approximately 10 mm ($\frac{3}{8}$″) in length, curve them to the same arc as the shank, and solder them with hard solder along the ends of the shank. Each end is thereby built up to twice its original height, and can be spread in the same way, to accommodate the higher setting. It is then filed and finished as before. Hard solder must be used to avoid any colour differences in the join.

If a half-round shank were required, the square wire can be rounded off. While there may be slight wastage in this, it is preferable to attempting to make the shank from half-round wire, as this will not spread nearly as much as square wire.

2. A SPLIT SHANK

This can be made with either square or half-round wire, and turned up allowing for the setting as before. To make a horizontal split shank, saw down from each end to approximately 8 mm. To make an easier entrance for the saw, bend the two ends out of line, and when the cuts have been made, realign the ends of the shank. Alternatively, the slots could have been made when the wire was in the flat.

This slot is then opened out to a forked shape, using a penknife to force the ends apart. Curve them into a more pleasing shape with half-round pliers, to the point where they will fit the setting. Refine the ends by filing, either into smooth points, or file and carve them into a scroll shape.

For a vertical split shank, the same procedure is followed, with one difference. Whereas for the horizontal split shank the slot was made parallel to the sides of the shank, in this case the slot will be made parallel to the top and bottom of the shank. It is opened up in the same way and finished with the bottom fork following the curve of the shank and the top fork curved, with half-round pliers, in a gentle curve towards the top of the setting. Both ends are filed to fit the taper of the setting and the setting soldered in. The filing to shape of the ends is critical and if correctly done there will be no need to tie the setting in place with binding wire.

In soldering the setting into split shanks, there are four soldering points. Do not attempt to solder all four points at once, because if the setting moves out of alignment it will have to be removed, and the whole soldering process started again. Instead, solder one point, check to see that the alignment is correct, and if so solder the point diagonally opposite. Check again and then the other two can be soldered simultaneously.

However, if despite these precautions the setting had become displaced in the soldering and had to be removed, the simplest way of doing this is as follows. Grip the shank with locking tweezers and place them on the charcoal block. Put a heavy weight on the other end of the tweezers to prevent movement. Tie some binding wire around the setting from top to bottom, leaving the ends free. Reheat the ring and when the solder flows gently pull the setting, by the wires, out of the shank. The soldered areas will then have to be cleaned, and the setting refitted and resoldered into the shank.

Make a saw cut from each end for approximately 8 mm

Bend the ends out of alignment to make it easier to saw

Open up the slot to a forked shape

Curve with half round pliers

The ends could be carved into a scroll shape

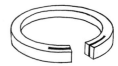

Saw into the shank for approximately 8 mm

Solder the four points of the setting to the shank in this order

Coat of arms of the Medici, three interlinked rings, each set with a natural pointed diamond crystal

Gold, amethyst and sapphire Bishop's ring, English, 13th century

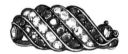

Gold ring with diamonds and rubies, late 18th century

The girdle of a stone is its widest part

The setting must have a ledge, or bezel, for the girdle of the stone to rest on

Types of Setting

A Collet

A collet is the setting that holds the stone in place, and can be a plain band pushed over the stone to secure it or a number of individual prongs to hold it, known as claws. There are numerous ways of making collets, depending upon the cut of the stone. The girdle of the stone, ie the widest part, must rest on a level base, known as a bezel. If it is not firmly seated on a level base, it may fracture when being set, or tilt, and will look, as it is, unprofessional.

As an example, the simplest but incorrect way of holding a stone on the shank of a ring is merely to make a band of metal that fits the stone, but it will be obvious that the stone is not balanced correctly, and when this band is pushed over the girdle of the stone to set it the pressure applied will in all probability unbalance the stone and could result in an uneven setting, or could fracture the stone.

The correct procedure is to make a ledge, or bezel, for the girdle of the stone to rest on. There are several ways of doing this, and the two simplest methods are:

1. To solder two pieces of metal together to make a ledge.
2. To use a thicker piece of metal and to carve part of it out to make a ledge.

Let us assume that in both cases one is going to make a setting for a round stone 6 mm ($\frac{1}{4}$") in diameter (it can be either cabochon or faceted). The first method has the advantage that in the one operation enough material can be made for a number of settings apart from the original one.

To Make a Setting

The procedure is to take a strip of metal 12 mm ($\frac{1}{2}$") wide, 90 mm ($3\frac{1}{2}$") long, of 0·022 gauge. Cut another narrower strip, 10 mm wide and fractionally shorter than 90 mm, of 0·028 gauge. Solder the narrower, thicker strip along the centre of the wider thinner strip. Then saw along the centre of both. You will now have two strips of bezel, adequate for at least eight settings for stones of 6 mm diameter.

Enough bezel for a number of settings can be made simultaneously

The bezel is then shaped with half-round or round-nosed pliers to fit the size of the stone, and the overlap sawn off. Adjust this setting until it fits the stone as closely as possible, and solder the join. Use hard solder for both soldering operations.

The second method is to take a strip of metal 6 mm ($\frac{1}{4}$") wide and 25 mm (1") long, of 0·048 gauge. Turn it up with the pliers to the shape of the stone, and cut off the overlap to make it fractionally smaller, so that the stone rests on the rim of the setting, with half the metal rim showing and half obscured by the stone. Solder the join. You can now see what has to be cut away to allow the stone to sit on a ledge or bezel inside the setting. There is a scorper specifically for this purpose called a Bull Stick. Using this, the inside of the wall of the setting can be carved away until it is thinned sufficiently for the stone to sit on the bezel.

Make the setting fractionally smaller than the stone, then carve away the inner wall to make a bezel

Tapered Settings

If the design calls for a tapered setting, this can be made by either of the previous methods, but if the first method is used it would only be used to make one setting, because of an inevitable amount of waste involved. The diameter of the top of the taper must be slightly larger than the diameter of the stone. (It is always better to err on the generous side, as enlarging or adding is always more difficult.) Measure the diameter of the stone, add a little extra, and draw this length on paper. Design the height and degree of the required taper below this to give you a plan of the setting.

The plan is to be turned into a three-dimensional shape. To do this, extend the sides of the taper down until the lines intersect. This point is the centre of the circle that will produce the correct arc for the tapered setting. Using a compass, start to draw a circle from one end of the top diameter. This will curve around until it passes through the other end of the diameter line. Continue the circle on for some distance. Draw a similar circle through the base line of the plan.

Given the diameter of the stone, one arrives at its circumference by multiplying the diameter by $3\frac{1}{7}$. Use a pair of dividers to measure this diameter $3\frac{1}{7}$ times along the circle, and draw a connecting line from these two points to the centre, which establishes the arc of the tapered

The plan of the setting, multiplied by $3\frac{1}{7}$

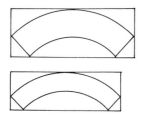

The patterns for tapered settings

The two pieces soldered together

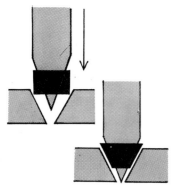

Turn the arc into a tapered collet and cut off any overlap

setting. Bear in mind that while this paper pattern may be a perfect fit for the stone, when it is transferred to metal, an allowance must be made for the thickness of the metal. In metal, $3\frac{1}{7}$ times the diameter would always be just too short, therefore I work on a multiplication of $3\frac{1}{4}$ and even more, as the metal increases in thickness.

This theory is obviously also the basis for making a cone. A cone-shaped setting might be used for capping the top of a pear-shaped stone, or tear-drop shaped stone.

If one is going to make a tapered setting by the first method, ie soldering two pieces of metal together to make a bezel, a second pattern will need to be made for the ledge, but only two-thirds of the height.

Glue the first pattern onto a sheet of 0·022 gauge metal, and the second onto a sheet of 0·028 gauge, and saw out both shapes. Solder the narrower, thicker one onto the wider, thinner one. Turn it up with half-round pliers so the stone will ease gently into the setting. Solder the join.

To make a tapered setting by the second method, the same principle of using a thicker metal and carving out the bezel applies.

COLLET PLATE AND PUNCH

The tool specifically designed to taper settings is the Collet Plate and Punch. It will form a cone of either 30° or 45° from which the bearing or ledge can be carved out. One can make a tapered setting and true it up with the plate and punch, but its most important use is in turning a cylinder into a taper, like a section of a cone. The punch and the plate are made as a matching taper. The cylinder is placed in the hole of the plate and the punch is driven into it by hammering. As the cylinder will be of a softer metal than the hardened, tempered steel of the punch and plate, it will take the shape of the taper as the punch is driven into it.

Select the hole in the collet plate that most nearly approximates the size of setting (or collet) required, and taper the cylinder. If after being hammered in, it is too big, move it into the adjoining smaller hole. Tap the top of the collet with a hammer and force it in to reduce its diameter. There is no need to use the punch in this case. If the collet is too small, it is possible to stretch it by reversing the plate and placing the collet over a hole that is slightly smaller than itself. Insert the punch into the collet and hammer it. This will spread the diameter at the top of the collet. If it does not spread it sufficiently, it can be enlarged a little more by putting it on the tapered end of a bick iron and tapping it gently with a planishing hammer.

If you do not have a collet plate and punch, the reverse side of draw plates can be used as collet plates, although they will not have a matching taper to the punch.

Collet plates and punches are available in other shapes, so that you can get a tapered square, oval and hexagonal collets, or they could be made to order for a required shape.

The collet plate and punch turn a cylinder into a taper

Coronet or Claw Setting

A tapered collet is used as the basis for a coronet or claw setting. The claws will ultimately secure the stone in place. With a pair of dividers, divide the top surface of the collet into six equal parts (or whatever is required in the design). Mark a line down from the top to establish the length of the claws. Saw out a U-shape from the top divisions almost down to the length of the claw, and continue until the six claws have been roughly made. Make their sides parallel, but leave adequate metal for the final filing to a taper. It would be too difficult, unless one is experienced, to pierce out this taper accurately with a saw. Refine the claws to a taper with a double half round file, followed by a round file or gapping file for the base of the U-shape, slanting the file slightly down to soften and facet the base of the U-shape.

A coronet or claw setting

This setting can be used as it is, or a variation made on it, known as an 'organ pipe' claw. There are two ways of doing it. In the first, the base of the setting can be filed away to follow the U-shape but leaving points beneath the centre of the U-shape. The curve must be rounded with fine files, emery papered, and polished. A smaller collet of the same taper must be made, emery papered and polished, and the six points of the setting soldered to it.

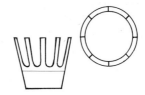

Divide the top of the collet into eight parts

The alternative way of doing this is to allow enough depth in the original collet to cut off the lower collet, and after the organ pipe shapes have been filed out, the lower collet is soldered back on.

As with every type of collet, a ledge or bezel will have to be added or carved out. In this case the bezel is carved out of the top of each claw, and the top of the claw is subsequently pushed over the top of the stone.

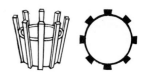

A collet with outside claws

Another type of claw setting is one in which the claws are soldered on the outside of the collet, and in this case the collet itself provides the bezel. The stone sits on top of the collet (if it is not a flat-backed stone, the inside of the top of the collet will have to be bevelled slightly to allow the stone to sit in it), and the claws rise above the collet to hold the stone. The claws can be made of square, round or half-round wire, and are left standing proud of the collet, or they can be tapered away towards the base.

An organ pipe setting

A CUT-DOWN SETTING

An alternative version of the claw setting is called a cut-down setting. In this the gauge of metal of the collet is sufficiently thick for the claws to be carved out of it, by cutting down from the top with a flat scorper or the appropriate needle file, leaving the claws exposed.

Firstly, a bezel must be cut out, and the position of the claws decided upon. The space between the claws is then cut away, almost down to the bearing. The outside of the collet is then channelled out between the claws to leave them in relief. The claws are usually tapered towards the base and the bottom of the setting slightly bevelled.

Charles I's signet ring, and its impression

A KEYED-IN CLAW SETTING

The setting for a large central stone surrounded by smaller stones, known as a 'cluster', can present a problem. While the smaller stones may be pavé set or thread set, if the design calls for the central stone to

A cluster ring with a keyed-in setting

143

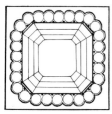
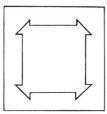

Saw out a square of metal large enough for all the stones

A trapezium shape is cut out of the corners

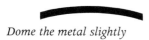

Dome the metal slightly

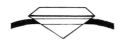

The girdle of the stone will stand above the surface of the metal

The claws are wedge shaped and in cross section trapezium shaped

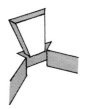

The setting must be high enough to ensure that the culet does not project

A setting for a trap cut stone

stand above the others, keyed-in claws are the best way of setting it. Apart from the design element, the fact that the claws stand proud make setting easier. In the following example, the setting will be made for a square trap cut stone. The setting of the small stones is described in pavé or thread setting, and I will deal only with the claw setting here.

Saw a piece of metal to the shape required to carry all the stones, of 0·050 gauge. Dome it slightly. The shape of the central stone is drawn on the metal fractionally smaller than the stone. This is drilled and saw pierced out at an angle so that the girdle of the stone will stand above the surface of the metal. The claws will be wedge-shaped, with their points removed and their sides bevelled, so that in cross-section their shape is that of a trapezium. (In stone cutting this shape is called a trapeze cut.) The corresponding shape is cut out of the inside corners of the mount, so that the claw can be keyed into it, and soldered in from underneath. Ensure that the claw stands sufficiently proud for a bezel to be cut into it.

A Setting for a Trap Cut Stone

In setting a trap cut stone, the design will probably have to be governed by the depth of the stone – if it is a very deep stone the setting must be designed with sufficient height to ensure that the culet of the stone does not touch the finger. The shank, in this design, does not go beneath the setting, but is soldered onto each side of it, to allow maximum light to penetrate the stone.

The design is based on using thick metal from which to 'carve out' the setting shapes. Two sheets of metal are used, the top one larger than the other, and this becomes the collet, while the smaller one, which is thicker, becomes the strengthening component that is ultimately soldered to the shank. The two are joined by long external claws which determine the height of the design, adequate to encompass the stone. (They can be made of sheet, square or half-round wire, but one flat surface will be essential.)

For the top, use a rectangle of metal considerably larger than the stone and no thinner than 0·050 gauge. Draw the shape of the stone on it, drill a hole within the shape and saw it out, keeping at least 1 mm ($\frac{1}{25}$″) away from the inside edge of the shape.

Using appropriate files, file up to the true edge at an angle. These angles must match the angles of the sides of the stone, from the girdle to the culet. If accurately matched, the stone should fit down securely into this aperture. Saw off the excess metal of the surround and file it parallel to the inner angle. The outside corners are filed flat. Whereas it was vital that the inside angle should match the stone, the outside one need only conform to the required design.

The smaller sheet of metal, of 0·0935 gauge, is worked in the same way as the larger one, with the central shape sawn out. It is made thicker, so that the shape of the shank arc can be carved into it and still leave an adequate wall, as well as allowing for angling the sides. The claws are made of the appropriate length, tapered and a flat is filed onto one face. This fits against the flat corners of both the top and bottom 'frame' of the setting.

18 carat gold ring, with pink
tourmaline Rod Edwards

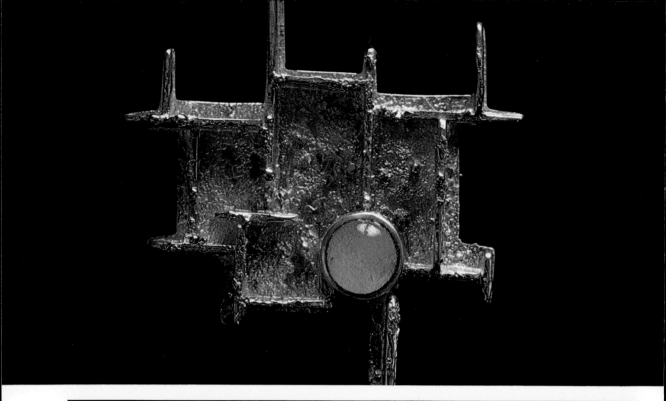

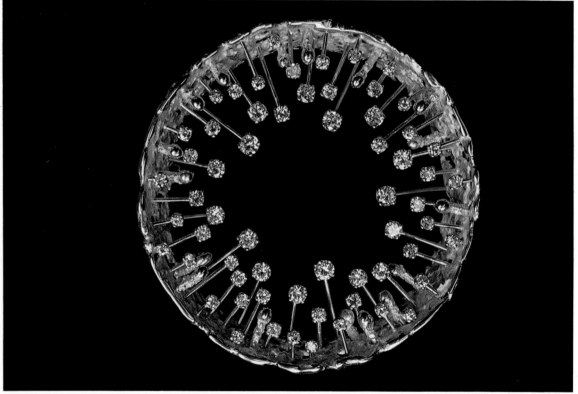

Above: *Silver brooch with 18 carat gold textured surface, and a cabochon emerald* Kathleen Grant

Below: *18 carat gold brooch with diamonds* John Donald

The claws can be soldered onto the corners of the collet one by one, held in place with locking tweezers, or the collet and all four claws could be positioned in cuttlefish to hold them while they are being soldered, the bottom frame then positioned, and soldered to the claws. Cut off extraneous claws, trim, file and solder the setting to the shank.

An alternative approach is to make a frame for the bottom unit, from strip metal 2 mm ($\frac{1}{12}$") wide by 0·050 gauge. Turn it up into a rectangle that harmonizes with the top frame in shape but is only two-thirds of the size, and solder the corner. File a flat on the outside corners.

Place it lengthwise in a swage block in the channel that most nearly approximates the arc of the shank. Lay a cylindrical punch along its long axis and gently hammer it down into the channel to curve it. Doing this will angle its sides and if necessary, they can be refined to match the angles of the top frame. Link top and bottom frames together on their corners, with the long tapered claws. Solder claws to corners of top frame first. Insert the bottom frame inside the four claws at their base and solder them.

Cut off any extraneous claw, file smooth and solder the setting into the shank.

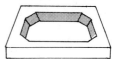

File out the shape of the stone at an angle

Both bars are positioned

A Setting for a Rectangular Stone

To make a setting for a rectangular stone, use a strip of metal with parallel sides, wide enough to accommodate the depth of the stone plus the added depth needed to enclose the arc of the shank.

Measure the sides of the stone and mark across the strip where these corners will come.

With a back saw make a cut across the strip at these marks to one-third of its depth and open this up to a V-shape with a three-square needle file. Bend it to a right angle with two pairs of flat pliers. If it doesn't bend sufficiently to make a right-angle, enlarge the cut with the back saw or a fine saw until enough metal has been removed for it to bend correctly. Bend all three cuts to form right-angled corners and bevel the two ends of the strip to a 45° angle so they will meet to make the fourth corner. Solder this join with hard solder, and at the same time run a little solder in the other three corners. A bezel can be seated inside the collet or carved into the collet, or an inner strip could be soldered in to make a bezel.

The metal must be wide enough to encompass the arc of the shank, as well as the depth of the stone

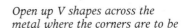

Open up V shapes across the metal where the corners are to be

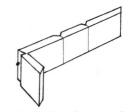

Bend the V shaped cuts to form corners

Saw out the V shapes

TAPERED RECTANGULAR SETTING

To make a tapered rectangular setting, mark where the corners will come across the strip as before. A V-shape is then sawn out, to three-quarters of the width of the metal. Saw out the three V-shapes and saw each end parallel to the adjoining angle. Make a shallow saw incision from the apex of the V to the edge of the metal and bend the metal on this line with a pair of flat pliers, until the angled sides meet. Run a saw through the join to bevel each side so that the angles meet perfectly (or the V-shape could have been bevelled previously with a file).

Bevel the inside of the corners so that the sides will meet when bent

Bend the three corners in this way to make a rectangular tapered box, and solder the join with hard solder, at the same time running a small piece of solder in each corner to strengthen it. If the setting has been made in accurate measurements of the stone, the stone will fit down into the setting and the taper of the setting will prevent the stone from falling through with the angle of the taper itself providing a bezel. Or a bezel can be carved into the collet.

Setting with Very Fine Claws

A setting with very fine claws could be used for delicate stones

If the design calls for a number of very small claws, they can be cut out of the collet itself. The collet can either have a bezel in it, or if the stone is flat-backed, it can rest on a base and the collet can be merely a band of metal soldered to the base to hold it. In either case, the top of the setting can be made into fine claws by using a round needle file to file out a series of tiny U-shapes around the rim, the tops of which can then be used as claws. This is a particularly good type of setting for delicate stones, such as opals or emeralds. When setting a very delicate stone, the softer metals such as 22 carat gold, or pure silver, or platinum, should be used for that part of the collet that actually holds the stone, to minimize the risk of damage to the stone. However, with this type of setting it is not essential to use the softer metals because so little pressure is required to push each of the many tiny claws over the stone.

Setting with Wire Claws

Wire claws

There are instances in which a claw setting is required, but the design may make it difficult or impractical to use the claw settings previously described. A wire claw could provide the solution. In setting a stone in a bowl shape the other types of claw would be difficult both to solder into position and to manipulate in setting. It is almost impossible to solder four or more free-standing claws in place without at least one becoming unsoldered in the process.

Wire claws could be useful for setting a stone in repoussé work as, being very fine, a greater number can be used than with other types of claw (which can be helpful if the work is large), and yet remain unobtrusive. It is perhaps in enamelling that the wire claw is of most value. The heat of the kiln would be sufficient to loosen a soldered claw, but the wire claw would remain secure because of its construction.

Drill a hole for each claw in the appropriate place. Take short pieces of round wire and taper their ends. The wire is then forced through the hole so that the tapered end projects on the back. Solder and cut the projection level with the back, file, emery paper and finish. The claws on the front can then be cut down to the required height for the setting.

Setting from the Back

When the stone is fitted through the setting it is held there by claws pushed over its base

This method is used when setting a very high cabochon stone that would otherwise require very long claws or a very high bezel to gain sufficient purchase on the stone. Setting from the back is used when the design requires the metal to sweep over the edges of the stone in an uninterrupted flow. It is also used when setting delicate stones or enamels, or painted porcelain or the glass of a locket, all of which might be damaged by the normal pressures of setting from the front.

The setting must be shaped to fit the taper of the bottom of the stone. When the stone is fitted into the setting from the back, the fact that the tapers match will prevent it being pushed fully through the setting. In shaping the setting, see that the stone will ultimately fit with its base level with the base of the setting. Drill shallow holes to hold the required number of claws in the base of the setting, and solder the claws in. Cut the claws to the required length, and when the work has been finally polished, the claws can be pushed over the base of the stone to set it.

Settings for Pearls

Pearl cement is used when setting pearls for two reasons:

1. Unlike most other adhesives it is white, and it will not discolour.
2. Its application is easy and if it were ever necessary to remove the pearl, for repair or some other reason, the removal is also easy.

It is not unlike sealing wax to use, in that a small piece is flaked off the rod of cement and melted with a very gentle heat. The pearl can be removed by re-warming the pearl cement over a gentle flame, taking care not to let the flame touch the pearl, and then the pearl can be unscrewed, or withdrawn from the cup and peg. Should the pearl become scorched its outside skin or skins can be removed, with a very sharp knife, exposing an unblemished layer beneath.

If modern adhesives are used instead, for their specific advantages, bear in mind the disadvantage that it will be impossible to remove the pearl. The bond of the adhesive will be so great that the pearl is bound to be damaged if one tries to remove it.

When setting round pearls, a shallow cup is made in the doming die to fit the pearl. The outside of the cup could be fluted to decorate it. A hole is drilled through the centre of the base of the cup, in which a piece of wire must be soldered. Pearls will have to be partially drilled for setting, so make sure that the wire fits the hole in the pearl. The pearl will finally be cemented onto the wire, but the wire must have a thread or a twist on it to carry the cement up into the hole and give it a greater purchase inside the pearl. The wire can be given a thread with the die, or two fine wires can be twisted together, or a round wire can be flattened and twisted.

A method of setting three-quarter pearls (ie a pearl with part of its surface ground flat) is by using a split pin. (This is a piece of round wire sawn down the centre, but not right through). The split pin is soldered onto a base and a minute wedge of metal is inserted point downwards in the slit, but left protruding. The hole is opened up slightly in the centre of the pearl by angling the drill. (When the pearl is pushed onto the split pin and wedge (and pearl cement), the wedge is forced down inside the split pin, widening the pin so that it spreads into the cavity of the pearl. Because of the split pin and wedge technique it would be impossible to remove the pearl if it were ever necessary. In the other

Split pin and wedge

The setting of a half pearl requires a pearl drill bit

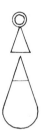

A metal cone is made to fit the point of the stone

A jump ring is pushed down the stone into the slot

Gypsy setting

Saw out the shape of the stone and file to match the angles of the sides of the stone

Roman setting

method of cementing pearls onto a threaded wire, it is possible to remove the pearl by heating the cement gently and unscrewing the pearl.

Great care must be taken when cementing pearls if heat is being used because the pearl could be destroyed by the heat. As with the setting of nearly all stones, pearls must be set when the work has been completely finished (polished).

The setting of a half pearl or any other hemispherical stone requires a special type of drill bit which, while it can be bought, does not cover all diameters of stones. You may therefore have to make one. The construction of this is dealt with in the section on special tools.

A Setting for a Pear Drop Stone

This type of stone is generally used in a hanging or pendant form. A small metal cone or bell shape is made to fit the pointed end of the pear drop, with a jump ring or the necessary fitting for suspending it at the apex. The difficulty is to hold the stone securely, and this is overcome by incising a groove in the stone just within the depth of the cone. If the stone is soft enough, the groove can be made with the sharp edge of a carborundum stone or an emery stone. In some softer stones, an ordinary file will make a groove, and for harder stones a diamond saw or burr would be required. If the stone is very hard and you do not have the necessary equipment, take it to a lapidary.

This groove is then fitted with an open jump ring that has had to be gently pushed down the stone until it springs into the slot, and the projecting curve of the jump ring is filed off to match the taper of the stone. The ring is then carefully soft-soldered inside the metal cone.

Gypsy Setting

In this type of setting the stone will look as if it has emerged through the metal. The setting is made flush to the stone without claws or beads to hold it. (In this it has a similarity to a setting from the back.) A hole is drilled as usual and a bezel cut for the stone. The stone is pushed onto the bezel, which should have been made to be a tight fit. The top surface of the metal surrounding the stone is filed down with a half-round or double half-round file – in some cases a round file could be used. The metal surround is to be filed away to leave a small rim standing, and in setting, this rim is pushed over or hammered over (using a pushing over tool) the edge of the stone. The surface is then smoothed off with a half round or a round file, emery papered and burnished to produce a concave surface that runs smoothly up onto the stone, giving the effect that the stone had grown through the metal without distorting the surface.

Roman Setting

A Roman setting is of a similar nature and is generally used for signet rings in which a seal stone is set (ie a stone that is carved with a crest).

A hole is drilled and saw pierced, smaller than the diameter of the stone and a bezel cut for a very close fit. Should the stone have a sharp girdle, gently blunt the sharp edge if possible on a carborundum stone or a stone grinding machine, or have a lapidary do it. There could be a risk otherwise in this type of setting of chipping the edge of the stone.

When the stone is bedded on its bezel, take a half round scorper and cut a groove on the surface of the metal around the stone and just a little away from its edge. This will produce a metal rim, as did the Gypsy setting, and in the same way this rim is pushed and burnished over the stone, leaving the groove as a decorative border.

Bed the stone into its bezel

Incise a rim

Thread and Grain Setting

Thread and grain setting is the most advanced type of setting and is generally used in expensive jewellery for precious stones, whether they are in line, as in an eternity ring, or clustered together as in a brooch. The technique requires a great deal of skill and patience, and it may be advisable to give this type of setting to a professional setter.

The technique is that the stone is held in position by one or more grains of metal. These are, in fact, incised up from the metal surrounding the stone.

As an example, I will describe the setting of a round diamond in a square piece of metal. The object is fully to display the stone and leave only the minimum of setting visible.

It is easier to start with a square of metal larger than needed, and having drilled a tapered hole to fit the stone, the square can then be filed down to leave only a minimum border. A diagonal cut is made from each corner towards the stone with a spit stick, stopping just before the stone, and leaving the shaving of metal intact and still joined to the metal base. Ensure that the stone is properly seated in the hole by gently pressing down on its table with a pushing-over tool. This will cause the stone to bite into the metal slightly and seat firmly. (Bear in mind that while this can be done with a diamond or another hard stone, it is not advisable with softer or brittle stones.) The shaving of metal is now to be formed into a grain to hold the stone. A graining tool is used for this. At its end it has a hemispherical depression, and this is placed over the shaving of metal and pushed down, using a circular, rocking motion to round the shaving into a grain. As the grain is being rounded, it must also be pushed downwards so that part of it covers the edge of the stone. These minute grains are sufficient to secure the stone in its setting.

For added security three grains can be made in each corner. Two of these can be used to secure the stone by incising the lines parallel with the edge of the square, and the third grain incised diagonally from the corner, but left merely as decoration, away from the stone, as it is unlikely that there will be sufficient room for it at the edge of the stone.

The corners of the metal square now have the incisions across their surfaces with the grains at the end. The incision can mar the appearance of the corner and the area must be worked on to give a better finish. Cut a V-shaped channel in the corner with a highly polished flat scorper

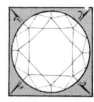

A diagonal cut is made from each corner towards the centre

The shaving of metal is left joined to the base

A beading tool forms the shaving into a grain

The grain is pushed over the edge of the stone

The corner can be decorated with V shaped cutting

The Tiffany diamond. The 'ribbon' holding it is covered with diamonds that would have been set by thread and grain setting.

and carefully shape the underside of the grain with the scorper to make it appear as though it is fully in the round, standing proud of the base. This must be done with the greatest care or the grain could be accidentally cut off. The V-shaped channel is cut to add a design element between the grain and the outside edge of the square, and, still using the spit stick, cut in such a way that the outside edge is left sharp. This can now be cut flat with a highly polished flat scorper to give a bright rim, or alternatively the edge can be serrated with the pattern of a millgrain wheel. Millgrain wheels and graining tools come in a number of different sizes. (The graining tool is polished and sharpened by rotating its depression over its corresponding number on the fion block.)

This final V-shaped cutting can be an important element in the design, and can be used to make star shapes, or scalloped edges around the stone, or if stones are clustered in a complicated design the V cutting can be used to emphasize the design. The principle of making the grains remains the same regardless of how the V cutting decorates the metal surround.

FOR A MASSED EFFECT

The visual effect of a collection of small stones can often be greatly improved by massing them together. By grouping small diamonds closely an impression of greater size can be given, and the colour of small stones can be emphasized by massing them. There are two ways of setting to achieve this effect, peg and cut away setting, or pavé setting.

Peg and Cut Away Setting

This is used for flat-backed stones such as rose cut diamonds or garnets, turquoise and half-pearls, while pavé setting can be used both for flat backed stones and faceted stones.

In peg setting the stones are secured by pegs made of round wires that have been inserted through the backplate and soldered. The stones are massed so closely that only the tips of the pegs are visible when the work is complete.

A lot of Victorian jewellery used this technique and as an example of it I will describe the setting of the Victorian turquoise bracelet shown in the drawing. This used graduated stones.

This is a hollow bracelet, made as a three-sided channel into which the fourth side, the top, which will finally hold the stones, is subsequently fitted. The metal for the sides can be turned into an oval from a flat strip, using flat and half-round pliers, or cut out as an oval from sheet, using 0·060 gauge. The metal for the base plate would be 0·028 gauge and for the top 0·036.

Dome the base plate to curve it across its width, then turn it up into an oval to match the sides. Bevel the sides and the baseplate where they meet and solder them together. This provides the three-sided channel.

The top, which will hold the stones, is made in the same way as the baseplate, but domed in the opposite curve. It is now filed so that it will fit down into the three-sided channel, slightly below the surface

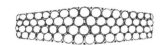

A hollow turquoise bracelet

The sides and the base provide a three-sided channel into which the top will fit

150

but not more than a quarter of the full depth, leaving the centre hollow.

The stones are to be staggered in placement and their position is marked on the top, fitting them as closely together as possible, with edges touching. Probably the easiest way to progress is to scribe around one stone, mark the position of its peg, and move on to scribe around the next stone. The peg's position is to be in the space between the stones and this will subsequently be drilled through to hold the pegs.

It will be necessary to cut the top in half to fit it into the three-sided channel from each end so if it is cut at this stage, it will make the handling of the whole piece easier.

When the positions of all the stones and pegs have been marked, drill holes for the pegs, keeping them slightly less in diameter than the pegs themselves, which are to be made of 0·038 round wire. The peg ends must be slightly tapered. It will be easier to handle if a length of wire is used, tapering at one end, pushed into the hole and then cut to approximately the same height as the sides.

The wire is tapered again and the process repeated.

Solder the pegs from underneath, and file off any projections.

The two top pieces can now be fitted into the channel and soldered in position and the joins between them soldered.

One now has a hollow rigid bangle, but if it were required, it could be made into a hinged bracelet and locked by a tongue and snap. The sides of the bracelet are now to be filed to a scalloped edge that follows the contour of the stones. The gauge of metal is sufficiently thick to allow a considerable degree of form to be shaped into it.

At this stage the meaning of the name 'peg and cut away setting' will be made apparent. The pegs have been made and the outside edges of the setting are now to be cut away to leave outstanding claws. File away the unwanted metal between the claws with a fine needle file and refine the shape of the claws with this file. The metal between the claws is then to be cut down to the level of the bracelet top, that will hold the stones. File both top and bottom edge of the metal between the claws into a gentle curve, so that if viewed from above the sides recede. A particular virtue of this type of setting is that the way in which the stones are held is inconspicuous. Seen from above the outside claws should be minimal and the pegs between the stones become inconspicuous in the play of light and shadow.

The pegs may need to be filed down until they are less than half the height of the stones.

After all finishing and polishing has been done, start the setting by placing two adjoining stones in positions, and use a beading tool in a rotating movement; spread the peg or pegs between the stones down against them so that each peg holds two stones. The outside claws are then pushed over the stones to complete the setting.

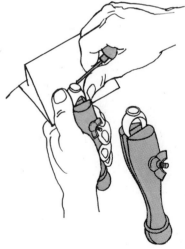

Using a ring clamp for setting

Pavé Setting

Whereas peg setting is generally only used for flat-backed stones, pavé setting can be used for both flat-backed or fully faceted stones. The finished appearance of pavé setting is almost identical to peg setting,

Dome the top of the ring and attach the shank

Place the stones in staggered rows

but the setting method is even less conspicuous as the stones are held by grain settings and these tend visually to disappear in the reflection of light from faceted stones.

To illustrate the setting, a domed ring of faceted garnets could be made. Dome the shape of the ring, attach the shank, finish and polish it.

The dome is now to be completely covered in stones of predominently the same size, but with a range of variation to allow for accurate spacing.

Position the first stone on the centre of the dome and work outwards in staggered rows, placing the stones as close together as possible. Mark their positions by dimpling the metal with a scorper or centre punch where the centre of the stone is to be.

If flat-backed stones are to be set, holes for them are opened up, using a pearl drill of the same diameter as the stone. The pearl drill gives the necessary flat based hole with straight sides.

If fully faceted stones are to be set, their placement is dimpled on the metal, and this is drilled right through the metal, then opened up with a tapered burr slightly smaller in diameter and of the same taper as the stone, so that the girdle of the stone will sit just below the surface of the metal.

The stones are held in place by grain setting. The grains are made as described in Thread and Grain Setting, within the triangle between every three stones. The area is minute but it is possible to incise the shavings for either three grains or one larger one. For the former, the incisions are cut from the centre of the space outwards to where the stones touch, or if the latter, then the opposite way, converging in the centre where all three shavings are rounded into one grain. This is then spread to push down firmly on all three stones.

When the dome is covered with stones the outside edge is finished by filing the metal to follow the shape of the stones, and this edge is burnished over the edge of the stones.

IV GEMSTONES

Rocks, Minerals and Crystals

Rocks, Minerals and Crystals

It may be of help to classify the use of the terms 'rock', 'mineral', 'crystal'. A rock will have been formed by a natural process on the earth's crust and usually consists of a mixture of minerals – granite, for example, is mainly feldspar, quartz and mica.

Unlike rocks, which can be almost random mixtures, minerals have a specific composition that is constant within that mineral. It may be a single chemical element, eg gold or sulphur, or a compound of chemical elements, but what remains constant is that any part of the mineral will have the same composition as any other part. Were it to be powdered, each grain would still have the properties of the whole.

Crystals are composed of minerals, but what segregates them from minerals as a whole is that they are formed in a regular geometric arrangement. This is obvious in their external form, but even were this to be broken up the internal structure would still follow the same crystalline form however much the fragments may be reduced.

The rock mass that surrounds and embeds gemstones is called the matrix, and in fragile stones such as opal, the stone is often cut leaving a base of matrix to strengthen the stone.

Pendant with a jacinth cameo, c. 1580, possibly South German Schatzkammer der Residenz, Munich

Jewelled statue of Knight of
St. George, circa 1590

Gemmology

Garnet

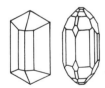

Topaz

Chrysoberyl

Staurolite

The subject of gemmology is a highly specialized, complex and fascinating one and its range is beyond the scope of this book. Gemstones will be dealt with on the basis of their decorative use in jewellery rather than the detail of their crystalline, chemical and optical properties. It is, however, essential that the jeweller should have learnt some of the properties of gemstones before attempting to work with them. The layman has many misconceptions about gemstones, thinking perhaps that within their family they are all alike (that one garnet may differ from another garnet only in size), that stones are virtually indestructible and will stand up to any amount of rough handling and so on. This is, of course, not so. Each stone is unique – a highly individual mineral with its own characteristics. The hardness, softness, brittleness and other aspects of stones must be understood before the jeweller can design and work with the particular advantages and disadvantages of each gemstone.

It used to be common practice to divide gemstones into the two groups of precious stones and semi-precious stones. Precious stones were generally understood to be diamonds, emeralds, rubies and sapphires. Semi-precious stones could range from an extremely fine aquamarine, for example, to an agate. Because of the enormous range it covered, 'semi-precious' is now falling out of use and the name 'gemstones' covers the whole range.

154

As explained gemstones are minerals found in the rocks of the earth's surface. The greater majority of them occur in definite crystalline forms. The various kinds of crystal can be divided into six orders: the cubic, tetragonal, orthorhombic, hexagonal, monoclinic, triclinic, and most of the interesting properties of gemstones can be traced directly to their crystalline structure. It is this structure that gives the stone its natural lines of cleavage and direction of weakness, and thereby governs the lapidary's cutting of the stone. The minerals may be brilliantly coloured or subtle and lustrous, but their quality remains hidden until exposed by the work of the lapidary who cuts and polishes the stone. By the cutting their beauty is revealed, either by its transparency and depth of colour, as in emeralds and rubies, or by colour alone as in lapis lazuli and turquoise, or by exposing the light and brilliance in a diamond. Opal is an exception in that it is a hardened gel.

An important factor is the rarity of the stone. The mineral itself may be quite common but really fine specimens of suitable size and quality for cutting may be quite rare. This is so with emeralds. A flawless emerald of fine colour is much rarer than an equivalent quality of diamond.

Gem minerals are generally hard minerals. This is essential if they are to be cut and set in jewellery, for their durability is vital, as is their resistance to abrasion and their ability to take and retain a high polish. The scale generally adopted to measure hardness is that drawn up by Friedrich Mohs in 1822. This lists ten minerals in ascending order of hardness, the softest being:

1	Talc	6	Orthoclase feldspar
2	Gypsum	7	Quartz
3	Calcite	8	Topaz
4	Fluorspar	9	Corundum
5	Apatite	10	Diamond

The figures denote an *order* of hardness (resistance to scratching) but have no quantitative significance, ie a harder mineral will scratch a softer one, and of the ten minerals selected each will scratch one with a lower number in the scale, but not one higher in the scale. The numbers do not denote equally measured degrees of hardness, for the difference in hardness between (9) Corundum and (10) Diamond is much greater than between (8) Topaz and (9) Corundum.

* I am most grateful to Robert Webster and his publishers and to De Beers Industrial Diamond Division Ltd, for their permission to reprint diagrams and information, and to the Institute of Geological Sciences for their help in supplying gemstone photographs.

Crystalline structure of gemstones showing some of their variations

Beryl (includes emerald)

Turquoise

Zircon

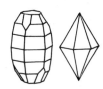

Corundum (includes ruby and sapphire)

Quartz (includes amethyst)

Diamond

Tourmaline

155

Principal Gemstones of the World

German Trophy Jewel, c.1615,
enamelled gold with rubies.
Sir John Soane Museum

KEY: Colour:
B – Blue. Bk – Black.
Br – Brown. G – Green.
Gy – Grey. M – Mauve.
Pk – Pink. R – Red.
W – White. Y – Yellow.

Name of Gem	Mohs's Hard-ness	Specific Gravity	Colour	Remarks
Agate	7·0	2·62	Various stratified colours	Used for industrial and ornamental purposes.
Alexandrite	8·5	3·72	G. Daylight. R Artificial Light	Imitated by synthetic corundum and spinel.
Amazonstone	6·5	2·57	G	Subject to damage through easy cleavage.
Amethyst	7·0	2·65	M	In jewellery the most important violet stone.
Aquamarine	7·5	2·70	B G	The most prized today are the sky blue stones.
Aventurine Quartz	7·0	2·65	G R & Br	A massive quartz with inclusions giving a schiller.
Beryl	7·5	2·70	G Y B W & Pk	Emerald, aquamarine, morganite are beryls.
Bloodstone	7·0	2·62	G splashed R	This stone is used as a seal stone, and is green with red spots.
Bowenite	5·0	2·58	G	A jade simulant. Wrongly called 'new jade'.
Cairngorm	7·0	2·65	Y-Br	Brown quartz often used for Scottish jewellery.
Cornelian	7·0	2·62	Y & R	Brownish-red chalcedony is sometimes called carnelian.
Cat's Eye – Chrysoberyl	8·5	3·72	Y-G with ray	Chrysoberyl cat's-eye is the more valuable and is heavier than quartz cat's-eyes.
Cat's Eye – Quartz	7·0	2·65	Gy W & Br with ray	The ray in quartz cat's eye is less sharp.
Chalcedony	7·0	2·62	G, B & Gy	There are many coloured varieties, including a chrome green.
Chrysoberyl	8·5	3·72	Y G & Br	Yellow chrysoberyls were used in Victorian jewellery.
Chrysoprase	7·0	2·62	G	Some agate is stained so as to resemble chrysoprase.
Citrine	7·0	2·65	Y	Much citrine is amethyst turned yellow by heating.
Corundum	9·0	3·99	W Y R B M Pk Br	The species which provides rubies and sapphires, also star stones.

Name of Gem	Mohs's Hard-ness	Specific Gravity	Colour	Remarks
Corundum (Synthetic)	9·0	3·99	W Y R B M Pk Br	Made in all colours except emerald green. Also as star stones.
Diamond	10·0	3·52	W B G Br Pk Bk Y	The hardest substance known to nature.
Eilat Stone	4·0	2·8–3·2	Variable G, B & Bk	Usually tumbled.
Emerald	7·5	2·69	G	The most highly prized variety of beryl.
Emerald (Synthetic)	7·5	2·65	G	Generally has lower S.G., than natural emerald.
Fluorspar	4·0	3·18	W B M Pk Y G Br	The massive variety is known as 'Blue John'.
Garnet – Almandine	7·5	4·20	M-R	When cut in the cabochon style are called carbuncles.
Garnet – Andradite	6·5	3·85	Bk	Sometimes used for mourning jewellery.
Garnet – Demantoid	6·5	3·84	G	The most valuable of the garnets.
Garnet – Grossularite	7·25	3·63	G	A recent discovery
Garnet – Grossularite	7·0	3·45	G Pk R W	The green material has been miscalled 'Transvaal jade'.
Garnet – Hessonite	7·25	3·65	Br	Has characteristic orange-yellow colour.
Garnet – Pyrope	7·25	3·75	R	Used in much jewellery of the Victorian period.
Garnet – Rhodolite	7·50	3·84	R-M	Rhododendron-red colour.
Garnet – Spessartite	7·25	4·20	Br-Y	Rare and not often found in jewellery.
Hematite	6·0	5·10	Bk	Used for intaglios and as an imitation of black pearl.
Hiddenite	6·5	3·18	G	A rare stone resembling emerald.
Jade (Nephrite)	6·5	3·00	G, W & Br	Used for carvings, beads and other small articles.
Jade (Jadeite)	7·0	3·34	W, G, R, Br, Bk & M	The most prized of the jades. The so-called 'Chinese jade'.
Jasper	7·0	2·65	Br R Y & G	A colourful massive material used for small objects.
Kunzite	6·5	3·18	Pk	This stone is the lilac-pink variety of spodumene.
Labradorite	6·0	2·69	Gy-Iridescent colours	A rock-like mineral with a play of colours, also transparent yellow.
Lapis Lazuli	5·5	2·85	B & W	A deep blue ornamental stone. Often contains pyrites.
Malachite	3·5	3·80	G	A dark green banded ornamental stone.
Marble	3·0	2·71	W & G	Also called 'onyx marble'.
Marcasite (pyrites)	6·0	5·00	Metallic Y	The mineral used for jewellery marcasite is pyrites.
Mocha Stone	7·0	2·62	W with RG markings	May be said to be an alternative name for moss agate.
Moonstone	6·0	2·55	W & B Chatoyancy	Moonstone when cut en-cabochon shows bluish gleams.

Name of Gem	Mohs's Hardness	Specific Gravity	Colour	Remarks
Morganite	7·5	2·7–2·9	Pk	The pink variety of beryl. Named after J. P. Morgan.
Moss Agate	7·0	2·62	W with RG markings	Agate with tree-like markings of red, green or black.
Nephrite	6·5	3·00	G & W	The more common and less valued of the jades.
Onyx	7·0	2·65	Bk & W Banded	Often used for intaglios and cameos.
Opal	6·0	2·10	W Bk & R Iridescent	Opal on a dark ground (Black opal) is the most prized. Some opal is stained.
Peridot	6·5	3·33	Y-G	Characterized by its oil green colour.
Prase	7·0	2·62	G	A dull green stone of the quartz group.
Rhodochrosite	4·0	3·60	Pk	A pink banded material used as an ornamental stone.
Rhodonite	6·0	3·54	Pk Flecked Bk	An ornamental stone pink in colour with black veins.
Rock Crystal	7·0	2·65	W	Has industrial uses as well as for beads and statuettes.
Rose Quartz	7·0	2·65	Pk	Very rarely clear. Used for small carvings.
Ruby	9·0	3·99	R	Some ruby when cut en-cabochon shows a six rayed star.
Rutile (Synthetic)	6·0	4·25	W Y R B	Stones have exceptional fire and double refraction.
Sapphire	9·0	3·99	B Y G W Pk & M	Sapphire, more commonly than ruby, produces starstones.
Sard	7·0	2·62	R	A brownish-red chalcedony used for seal stones.
Sardonyx	7·0	2·62	R & W Banded	Red and white banded chalcedony.
Serpentine	3·0	2·60	G R	A red and green ornamental stone, see also Bowenite.
Soapstone	2·0	2·7	W. Gy. Br & G	Used for carvings.
Sodalite	5·5	2·30	B	Like lapis lazuli but a lighter blue and has pink spots.
Sphene	5·5	3·40	Y Br & G	Sphene has more fire than diamond but is rather soft.
Spinel	8·0	3·60	R B G Y Bk W & Pk	Stones like ruby and sapphire but show no dichroism.
Spinel (Synthetic)	8·0	3·63	W B G P R Y	Made in many colours imitating stones of different species.
Spodumene	6·5	3·18	Y Pk & G	The yellow stones are called spodumene (cf. kunzite)
Strontium Titanate	6·0	5·13	W	A synthetic stone sold under the name 'Fabulite' and 'Diagem'.
Sunstone	6·0	2·66	R-Br Spangled	Coloured schiller due to inclusions of an iron mineral.

Name of Gem	Mohs's Hardness	Specific Gravity	Colour	Remarks
Topaz	8·0	3·53	W Y Pk B & Br	Values given for the brown and pink stones.
Tourmaline	7·5	3·10	All colours	Rubellite and indicolite are red and blue tourmalines.
Turquoise	6·0	2·75	B	American turquoise has lower density.
Yttrium Aluminate	8·0	4·57	W & G	Sold as YAG, 'Diamonair' and 'Cirolite'.
Yttrium Oxide	8·0	4·84	W	Diamond simulant.
Zircon	7·5	4·1–4·8	B W Y Br G R	B and W stones are heat treated from Indo-China rough.
Zoisite	6·0	3·35	B. M & Br	Sold under name 'Tanzanite'.

ORGANIC SUBSTANCES

Name of Gem	Mohs's Hardness	Specific Gravity	Colour	Remarks
Amber	2·5	1·05–1·1	Y & R-Br	Sometimes contains insects and plant spores.
Coral	3·75	2·68	W Pk R & Bk	Best colour is a deep rose red. Black coral has specific gravity 1·33.
Jet	3·5	1·33	Bk	Jet is a type of hard coal.
Pearl	4·0	2·70	W Various Tints Bk	Freshwater pearls have less 'orient' than oriental pearls. Pink conch pearls are non-nacreous.

Mr. Robert Webster F.G.A. has kindly permitted the reproduction and condensation of his chart 'Principal Gems of the World – and their Properties'.

*Pectoral shaped like a falcon,
gold, lapis lazuli, turquoise,
cornelian, obsidian and glass.
Found in Tut-ankh-amun's tomb*

A liturgical comb with a crucifixion scene, ivory, early 10th century, Ottonian.

Organic Gems

Diadem of carved coral and gold, c.1837.

Jet hair ornament, c.1870.

An earring in Pique (tortoiseshell with gold or silver inlay), c.1865.

Unlike gemstones, there are gems that are organic in nature – living entities, as it were. Pearl, coral, amber, jet, ivory and tortoiseshell are all in this category.

Natural Pearls

Natural pearls come from shellfish – the pearl oyster and the pearl mussel. (Very seldom will the edible oyster produce a pearl, and they will be only tiny.) Pearl oysters live in the sea, and pearl mussels in rivers and streams. Some good specimens of pearl mussels are found in the fresh water rivers of Scotland. Pearl oysters grow in the southern oceans of the world on rock banks in the more shallow waters. The Persian Gulf is particularly productive, as are Western Australia, the Gulf of California and the Gulf of Mexico.

Unlike some gemstones, pearls cannot be synthesized (or made up), but they can be cultured. About 500 years ago the Chinese discovered that if a foreign object were introduced between the shell and body of a fresh-water mussel the object would eventually become coated with a layer of nacre. A small stone, or a splinter of wood would be inserted, the mussel would then be returned to the river and live there for a few years until the coating was completed.

Many attempts were made to improve on these ancient methods, but it was not until the early part of this century that the Japanese made enormous improvements in causing shellfish to produce pearls, and so began the cultured pearl industry. Japanese waters have many species of shellfish which produce natural pearls, but only a few of these are suitable for use in 'culturing' a pearl. The most commonly used (partially because of its hardiness) is the Akoya oyster, or Pinctada martensi.

The culturing of a pearl takes from three to six years – on average three and a half years.

Cultured pearls are not as valuable as natural pearls, but in establishing value a lot will depend on the quality of either.

The Loch Buy Brooch, silver with rock crystal and river pearls, Scottish, c.1500. This was made by a tinker; twisted wires are used extensively both for decoration and to delineate the form.

Pearl Shell

Pearl shell, predominantly found in the waters of northern Australia and the Torres Strait, is used for mother-of-pearl buttons, knife handles and inlay, etc.

The shell with brightly coloured blue/green nacre is called Paua shell in New Zealand and Abalone in America. It is found in the Great Barrier Reef of Australia, in New Zealand waters and off the coasts of Florida and California.

The shells for cameo cutting are the Helmet shell (cassis madagascariensis) and the giant conch shell (strombus gigas), both from the West Indies. They are usually sent to Italy to be carved.

Jet

Greatly favoured in Victorian times for its intense blackness and the high polish possible, jet was used in a great amount of 'mourning' jewellery. It is a fossil wood, derived from driftwood that has been subjected to the chemical action of stagnant water and subsequently compressed by great pressure.

Coral

Coral comes from the warmer oceans of the world and grows in branching colonies that may be of enormous size, as in the Great Barrier Reef, off the east coast of Australia. However, there are many species of coral and the one that produces the reds and pinks that are valued in jewellery is not a reef builder. Its scientific name is Corallium Nobile or Corallium Rubrum. Coral is a polyp of jelly, with numerous tentacles. Its life is spent submerged on rocks and it deposits around its soft body a hard skeleton of calcium carbonate. This becomes, in a sense, a scaffolding within which the coral lives and dies, and upon which the new young coral builds.

Two of the medallions of a bracelet of mosaic in semi-precious stones or marble, Florence, c.1870. This type of work is also known as Pietra Dura.

Amber

Amber is a fascinating material because of its extreme age, the true amber having originated in the Oligocene period 40 to 50 million years ago. In those prehistoric times, as sticky resins oozed from the wood of coniferous trees they trapped insects, beetles, butterflies and even small lizards. (It is still possible to see these animals, encased in amber chunks.) Amber comes in a large range of yellows, reds and browns, although green and blue have been found. It can be translucent through to completely opaque and has a warm, slightly greasy, feel.

Ivory

Ivory has been used from the most ancient times, from pre-history as is shown by carvings on the ivory of mammoths found in the caves at Perigord, in France. There is evidence also of it having been used in all the ancient civilizations, from Egyptian, Assyrian and Mycenean onwards.

Ivory is soft enough to be filed, carved with the ordinary chisels used for wood carving or worked on a lathe, band saw, or by a drilling machine – the final polish being given with fine pumice or whiting, using water or methylated spirits.

Tortoiseshell

This does not in fact come from the tortoise, but from the carapace of a sea turtle, the Hawksbill turtle which lives in tropical seas, predominantly off the Malay Archipelago, the West Indies and Brazil. The carapace is formed of plates that overlap each other like tiles on a roof. The tortoiseshell is fashioned very easily and can even be softened in boiling water, or hot linseed oil. It is polished with putty powder and oil and finished with a soft leather. Gold, silver and mother-of-pearl are inlaid into tortoiseshell. (Furniture was inlaid with tortoiseshell from Roman times but brought to a peak by Boule, a cabinet maker to Louis XIV.) Tortoiseshell inlaid with silver, called pique work, was popular in Victorian times.

To repair tortoiseshell, wrap the break in wet tissue and grip this area with a pair of hot tongs. The steam generated will seal the break. The wet tissue prevents the tortoiseshell from overheating and melting.

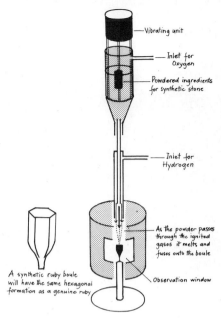

The principle on which a
Verneuil furnace works

Labels on diagram:
- Vibrating unit
- Inlet for Oxygen
- Powdered ingredients for synthetic stone
- Inlet for Hydrogen
- As the powder passes through the ignited gases it melts and fuses onto the boule
- A synthetic ruby boule will have the same hexagonal formation as a genuine ruby
- Observation window

Synthetic and Other Stones

Synthetic and Other Stones

Stones can be synthesized, that is, made by man, and produce most striking and beautiful specimens. They have practically the same physical properties as the natural stone. To be of commercial use they must be large enough to cut and able to be produced more cheaply than mined stones.

A synthetic ruby was made about 1885 by the direct fusion of small fragments of natural ruby under intense heat but this method was superseded by a French chemist, Auguste Verneuil, who pioneered the synthesizing process about 1891.

In the Verneuil method a finely powdered mixture of alumina and colouring oxide (chromium oxide for ruby) is passed through a furnace, subjected to gases, and melts, falling onto a ceramic pedestal called a candle. It solidifies there, but as the powder continues to be passed through the flame the mixture grows upon the candle like a stalagmite. In this method of making synthetic stones the material produced is called a 'boule'. By 1930 Carroll Chatham in California had produced a synthetic emerald and by 1969 Pierre Gilson of France and Zerfass of Germany had produced their own types of synthetic stones. Despite the fact that they are made synthetically, they can be very expensive. Some synthetically produced stones (strontium titanate, rutile, white

Art Nouveau Jewel by René Lalique 1898.

163

Diamond plume

sapphires, white spinel) can have a great similarity to diamond in appearance, as can the newly produced Yttrium Aluminium Garnet (known as YAG). The diamond can be synthetically produced but only in minute sizes for industrial use mainly as an abrasive, although progress is being made to produce diamonds of a size suitable for jewellery.

Composite Stones

These are simulations of gemstones made by joining two pieces of stone together, of which the bulk is usually an inferior material. Composite stones are generally described as doublets (if there are two layers) and triplets (if there are three layers). This will usually be done to give a better colour or appearance to the gemstone, or to provide it with a harder wearing face. For example, the top layer of an opal triplet is made of rock crystal to protect the opal.

True doublets are those wherein both parts are of the same type of genuine stone, eg precious opal cemented to a base of colourless opal. Opal is often used in doublet form as it is frequently found only in thin seams. When cut it would need the strength of its own matrix left on, or a backing stone added. (Turquoise too is sometimes cut with some of its matrix remaining for added strength.)

Faked or Simulated Stones

Stones can be faked to appear better than they are, but with a refracto-meter or by using the specific gravity test and, with experience, most fakes can be detected. The stone most used to simulate diamond, both legitimately and fraudulently, is the white zircon which is rendered colourless by heat treatment.

The diamond doublet can be the most effective of diamond fakes. This stone is constructed with a crown (the top half of the stone) of real diamond cemented onto a pavilion (lower part of stone) of an inferior material. A more unusual fake is the so-called 'piggy-back diamond' where a large flat diamond with a large culet (the facet at the back point of the stone) is set on top of a smaller one. The culet of the top stone rests on the table facet of the lower stone, giving the appearance of a very much larger stone.

Rubies can be simulated by red spinels and some garnets, and imitated by a composite stone with a crown of red garnet and a base of red glass.

Blue sapphires may be simulated by natural blue spinel and imitated similarly to garnets, by a doublet with a blue glass base, and emeralds are most commonly imitated in the same way, although a pale emerald can be painted on the back to enhance the colour. This can be detected, but it is obviously difficult to do so if the stone has been set in a closed setting.

Foiled Stones

Stones that are of a pale or poor colour are often mounted with a closed setting and the back of the stone 'foiled' with a suitable coloured paper. In early times it had been the practice to 'foil' a blue sapphire by backing it with the blue part of a peacock's feather. This is quite a legitimate practice and was used frequently in Victorian times but it must, of course, be made clear to a customer that the stone is foiled to enhance its colour – or the practice could be misunderstood as an intention to deceive the customer as to the quality of the stone.

Sawing, Faceting and Polishing Stones

I cannot describe the work of a lapidary in detail as it is not within the scope of this book and a lapidary is a specialist in his own right. However, there are lapidary machines that are sufficiently uncomplicated for the student to use for simple work. The basic process of reducing a large piece of rough stone to a manageable size is carried out using a cutting and slabbing machine and lapping and polishing is the next stage. Cutting cabochon stones is relatively simple since minor errors can be obliterated with subsequent cuts. Faceting, however, must be done with accuracy and great care. If you are interested in faceting stones, practise with inexpensive materials such as quartz, citrine and rock crystal.

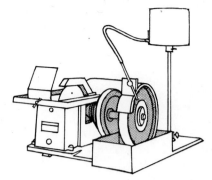

'Robilt' lapidary combination unit

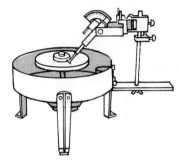

'Robilt' stone faceting machine

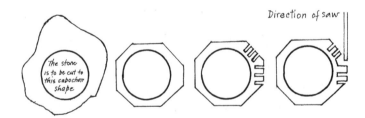

The trim saw shapes a cabochon stone by a series of straight cuts and notches

Cuts of Gemstones

Statue of Sainte Foy. Gold and precious stones (Conques-en-Rouergue Aveyron). 10th/11th century

A cabochon cut stone is one that has been smoothly cut, without facets, into a domed shape. It is the simplest cut and its outline may be circular, oval, elliptical, or any freer variation of a curved shape. Stones that have optical effects such as star-stones or cat's-eye stones must be cut in the cabochon shape. Sometimes, as with garnets, the back of the stone is slightly hollowed out to give more colour to a dark stone.

In the cutting of faceted stones the primary object is to get the best out of the stone as it is cut from the rough, with a minimum of waste. The shape of the stone will dictate the most economical way of cutting. The diagrams show the conventional styles of cutting.

Gemstones can also be carved, either as intaglios (or incised carvings) which are often used as seals, or as cameos where the carving stands in relief.

VARIOUS CUTS

Although the brilliant cut is the most popular for gem diamond purposes, there are other cuts which are equally beautiful. Apart from the single cut which is used on very small stones for fancy settings, these cuts are employed on stones of unusual shape in order to utilize as much of the original stone as possible.

Brilliant Cut: 58 facets. Cut exactly the same whether diamond is large or small, except for omission of tiny facet at point in very small stones.
Single Cut: 17 facets. Employed on very small stones used for decoration, as on the shoulders of a ring etc.
Marquise: 58 facets. Proportion of width to length varies slightly according to shape of rough.
Baguette: 25 facets. Used for decoration and in elaborate designs.
Emerald Cut: 58 facets. Sometimes used to accentuate quality of large, flawless stones.
Square Cut: 30 facets. Most often used in working out designs for jewellery.

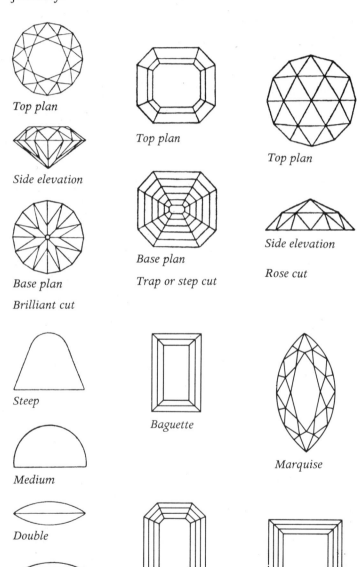

Top plan

Side elevation

Base plan

Brilliant cut

Top plan

Base plan

Trap or step cut

Top plan

Side elevation

Rose cut

Steep

Medium

Double

Hollow

Cabochon cut

Baguette

Emerald cut

Marquise

Square cut

Detail of necklace, North Italian, c.1570.

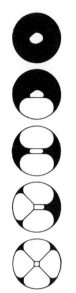

Order in which lower corners of diamond are ground

Order of grinding top corners and bezels

Fashioning Gem Diamonds*

There are a number of properties which set diamonds in a class of their own, but the beauty and value of diamond as a gem are consequences of a unique combination of very high refractive index and optical dispersion, coupled with the durability which results from extreme hardness and chemical inertness.

By taking advantage of its refractive index, the cutter is able to bring out all the hidden fire and brilliance of the gem, but in doing so he has to overcome the problems brought about by its hardness – a hardness which is surpassed by no other substance, manufactured or natural, on this earth. 'Hardness' is a property which has hitherto escaped precise scientific definition; quoted figures usually refer to scratch hardness (abrasion resistance) or indentation hardness, but it must not be confused with 'toughness' or the ability to withstand impact.

It is important to remember that this 'toughness' is very closely related to the cleavage properties of diamond. A thorough knowledge of the cleavage directions in diamonds is therefore the first essential for cutters. To start with, a description will be given of the practical aspects of the diamond cutter's art, after which an attempt will be made to show how the science of the diamond crystal affects these operations.

CLEAVING AND SAWING

When a diamond is received for cutting and polishing, the first active step is the division of the stone into segments suitable for shaping into the final jewel. Large stones need to be subdivided into smaller portions, and it is frequently necessary to remove part of a stone which may contain a flaw.

There are two methods by which this division may be accomplished:
1. Cleaving.
2. Sawing.

In a diamond of recognizable crystal habit the identification of the cleavage plane presents no difficulty, but in a stone of ill-defined shape, prolonged inspection and study is necessary. In order to establish at exactly which point to cleave a stone, a cutter may study it for days, weeks or even months in the case of a very large or exceptional diamond, for unless the line is precisely determined the whole stone can shatter into fragments.

Once the cleavage plane has been determined and the place at which the stone is to be cleaved has been decided, a groove, or 'kerf' as it is known in the trade, is made in the stone with a sharp diamond chip. The diamond is then cemented firmly into the end of a special holder, the handle of which is placed in a tapered hole in a block of lead

* Based upon an article by D. M. Rainier, De Beers Diamond Research Laboratory.

*10 carat gold pendant/necklet
with tourmaline, peridot and
aquamarine. The gold necklet
can be worn separately, and is
then finished with a small
tourmaline setting*
Rod Edwards

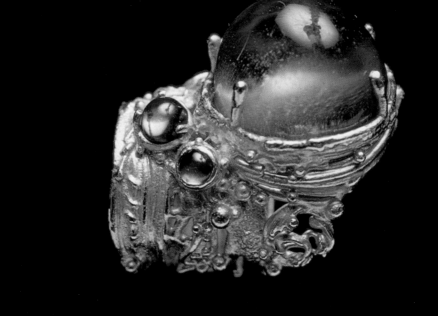

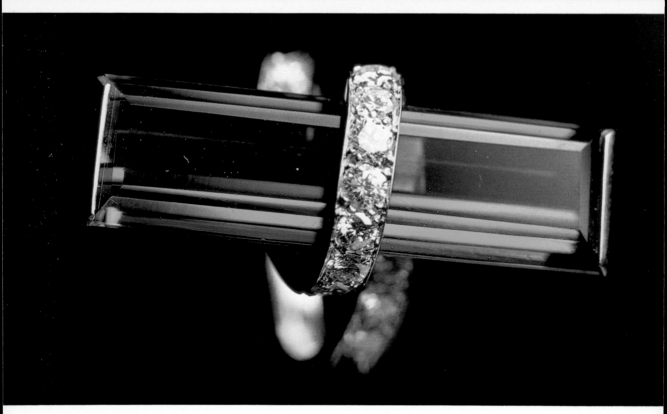

Above: *18 carat gold ring
with cabochon quartz and
tourmalines*
Gerda Flockinger

Below: *18 carat gold ring with
tourmaline and diamonds*
Andrew Grima/Geoffrey Turk

attached to the cleaver's box. A blunted steel knife is placed in the kerf and given a light blow, usually with a mallet, although some cleavers prefer to use a light steel bar.

Sawing

Sometimes it will be necessary to divide a stone in a direction which crosses a cleavage plane. It is then the diamond must be sawn into the desired segments. As in the case of cleavage, sawing can also only be carried out in certain directions which must be identified before starting, and these directions are known as the sawing grain. Today sawing has virtually superseded cleaving with all its attendant risks. Furthermore, when dealing with medium-sized stones and larger, sawing has the added advantage that the stone may be divided in a manner such that two brilliants can be produced from one octahedron, for example, whereas formerly a large part of the diamond used to be removed by bruting. Losses from the entire cutting and polishing process using this method were in excess of 50 per cent of the weight of the original stone. These losses have been considerably reduced by sawing.

It depends on the way in which the stone is sawn whether or not the girdle (which is the periphery at the widest point of the stone) of the bruted diamond coincides with the girdle of the original octahedron. The figure shows the normal method of sawing the octahedron above its girdle in order to arrive at the largest possible final stone. A second, smaller gem will be cut from the upper piece. Occasionally it may be necessary to saw the octahedron through its girdle thus producing two more or less equal gems, but this is not in favour as it is less economical than the other method. In this case a new girdle will be bruted onto the gem.

ORDER OF FACETING

The facets for the Brilliant Cut are put on in two stages. After bruting the stone goes to the 'cross-cutter' who puts on the first eighteen facets. These are the table, which is the large flat facet on the top of the stone; the culet or collette or collet, as it is variously called, and which is a tiny plane facet at the undermost tip of the stone, parallel to and corresponding to the table; four corners and four bezels on the top of the stone; and four corners and four pavilions on the bottom. The actual order in which the facets are ground once the table and culet have been completed varies slightly from one factory to another, or even from one cutter to another, depending on his own preference.

After grinding the table and culet, the first facet to be put on is a corner on the bottom. This is possibly the most critical part of the operation, as the first eight facets must be equal in size and an error here will be repeated on the following facets. The angle of this facet to the horizontal passing through the girdle is also critical, for this angle provides the gem with its fire. The cross-worker has a special gauge for measuring the angle but only his own ability, experience and craftsmanship can tell exactly when the facet has been cut to just the right

Brillianteering the top of the diamond

Brillianteering the bottom of the diamond

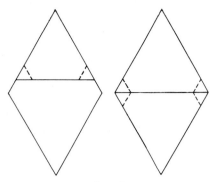

Two ways of sawing an octahedron

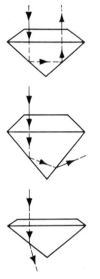

The path of light through a diamond

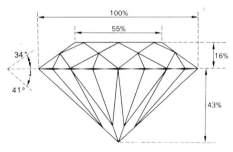

The correct proportions of a brilliant

size. Once he is satisfied, he grinds the second corner directly opposite the first, followed by the third and fourth.

The stone is turned over and the first top corner is ground directly over one of the bottom corners and again to a pre-determined angle. The remaining three corners are then put on, followed by the first bezel at the junction of two of the corners. The size of this must also be judged to a nicety, because when all four bezels have been added the table should be a perfect octagon surrounded by eight equal facets. These facets are sometimes called 'eights'.

The stone is once again turned over and the four pavilion facets are added directly below, and corresponding to, the bezels. There seems to be a little confusion in the use of the term pavilion, as some technical books refer to the entire lower portion of the stone as the pavilion. However, to the diamond cutter the pavilions are the facets which I have just mentioned.

At this stage the diamond is returned to the cutter for further bruting in order to make the girdle perfectly circular. This is called 'rondisting' and once it is complete, the cross-worker puts the final polish on the existing facets and removes the cutting lines left by the grinding operation. This is done in a matter of seconds per facet, by moving the diamond rapidly to and fro across the zoetkring or outer section of the scaife. This completes the cross-worker's share of the operation.

The 'brilliandeur' now takes over and it is his task to add the remaining forty facets, twenty-four on the top and sixteen on the bottom. This part of the process is known as brillianteering and is the final stage.

The first facet to be added is at the junction of the table and two 'eights'. It extends halfway across the junction of each eight with the table, and halfway down the junction of the two eights. This is called a star facet, and there are eight of them. The cutting of these facets is a very delicate operation as very little grinding is required, and the brilliandeur must keep a constant watch, holding the stone on the scaife for only a second or two at a time, and then inspecting it.

The last sixteen facets at the top are called halves or, sometimes girdle facets. This facet connects the bottom of the star facet to a point midway along the junction of the eight and the girdle. There are two halves to each star, and at the completion of this stage the eights will have assumed a kite-shape. Two stars and their four halves are known as a set. Some brilliandeurs prefer to cut all the stars before going on to the halves, others prefer to complete one set at a time.

The stone is turned over and the bottom halves are added directly under the top halves. The point at which these facets intercept the junction between the corners and the pavilions seems to vary, according to different sources of reference, between halfway down and all the way down to the culet. Modern practice seems to favour a point thirteen-sixteenths of the way towards the culet.

This completes the gem and after cleaning in chromic acid it is ready for evaluation and sale.

Identification of Gemstones

Pendant. Crystal hull and enamelled gold rigging. 16th century

A gemmologist will find a microscope essential for distinguishing the origin of stones, separating natural stones from synthetics and for determining the nature of flaws and inclusions in the stone.

A more specialized instrument is the spectroscope. It would be of use probably only to a qualified gemmologist, but it can make positive stone identification possible if, after using the refractometer and microscope, there are still doubts about the stone. It can also be used with rough stones, where the refractometer cannot. It works on the basis of analyzing light in the stone, but would, in general, be outside the scope of the average jeweller.

JEWELLER'S LOUPE

The simple jeweller's loupe (or magnifier) would be quite sufficient for our purpose for inspecting a stone, examining its surface and observing the inclusions within it. The inclusions in a stone will indicate the species to which it may belong, whether it is natural or synthetic, and they are in themselves fascinating to observe.

CHELSEA COLOUR FILTER

This instrument could be useful for a student in that it tests stones in a modified way by transmitting a band of red or green light when a

Chelsea colour filter

stone is viewed through it. It was originally used to distinguish emeralds from their imitations, but has further uses now. It will show red or green of varying hues and tones, depending upon the stone, and will give an indication of the nature of the stone, but is not a definitive test. It is quite useful in that, like a pocket magnifier, it can be carried with you for immediate tests.

LIGHT

The behaviour of light is of considerable importance in gem testing. Stones range from transparent to translucent to opaque, and the action of light upon and within them is invaluable in determining their species.

REFLECTION

Light is reflected from the surface of a transparent gemstone. When this happens, the ray of light hits the surface and bounces off in the opposite direction at an angle which is exactly equal to the angle at which it hit the stone.

REFRACTION

As well as being reflected off the stone, the light enters into the stone. When a ray of light enters in an oblique direction the ray, instead of being able to travel through the stone in a straight line, is caused to alter its course. This is because the light ray has entered a medium denser than the air through which it travelled. This bending of the light ray is refraction. The measurement of this angle is the refractive index of a given stone.

Refractometer

A refractometer is the instrument used for measuring the refractive index of stones.

To use the instrument, place the clean stone with its flat surface, or table facet, facing downwards on the small rectangular glass strip of the refractometer. Although the stone and the glass strip would appear to be face-to-face, a film of air remains between them and prevents optical contact. To get rid of this, a liquid that acts as a wetting agent is used between them. (Among those used are Selenium Bromide No 4 or Methylene Iodide.) The stone is now genuinely in contact with the glass and will therefore transmit a reading to the calibrated scale of the refractometer. The scale is viewed through the eye piece and the reading will be of the shadow edge of the stone, which is in direct relation to the refractive index of the stone. Each species of gemstone has its own characteristic index of refraction which will most usually serve as positive identification. These can then be checked against the Table of Refractive Indices.

Specific Gravity

Another method of identifying a gemstone is by measuring its specific gravity. In brief, the specific gravity is the 'heaviness' of a stone. The difference in 'heaviness' between one substance and another can be worked out numerically by taking water as a standard, and comparing the weight of each substance with the weight of an equal volume of pure water. The specific gravity of a substance, then, is simply the ratio of its weight to that of an equal volume of water. (Water at 4°C is the standard.) Detailed descriptions of how to use the method are in the books I have recommended and, more simply, in the section on casting.

HEAVY LIQUID METHOD

If only an approximate value of the density of a stone is required, a simpler test called 'the heavy liquid method' can be applied. Briefly, three types of liquid of different known densities are used. As a stone will (a) sink in a liquid less dense than itself, (b) float in one that is denser, and (c) remain suspended in a liquid of equal density, an approximation of the stone's density can be obtained by testing it in these liquids.

Identification of Gemstones

An experienced jeweller will usually be able to identify a stone by its colour and natural appearance. (Under even a small degree of magnification, inclusions in the stone and striations or bubbles can be seen. These demonstrate the provenance of a stone – for example, swirls of colour called 'treacle' can be seen in hessonite garnet, 'horse-tail' asbestos fibres in demantoid garnet, 'feathers' in Siamese corundum, 'silk' in rubies from Burma, etc.)

However there are rare and unusual stones within the natural order, as well as modern synthetic and simulated stones. It is therefore less easy to be sure of the exact provenance of a stone, judging by eye alone, but accurate identification can be made by scientific methods. As mentioned, these are a microscope, a refractometer, a spectroscope and a specific gravity test. The most positive method is the use of X-ray crystallography, but this is also outside the scope of the ordinary jeweller.

'Feather' in red spinel

'Needles' in rutile quartz

Liquid 'feather' in Ceylon sapphire

Tiger stripe in amethyst

Inclusions in stones

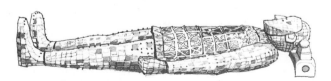

2160 tablets of jade stitched with gold wire make the funeral suit for Princess Tou Wan. Hopei, late 2nd century BC

V FORMING AND DECORATING

Casting

The Cellini Salt. 16th century

General Techniques

Casting is the process of reproducing one original piece into many multiples. An accurate reproduction or facsimile of an article can be obtained, either singly or in numbers, depending on the casting method. It is an ancient technique and there is evidence of prehistoric man having carved impressions of tools and axe-heads into stone to receive molten bronze or copper. These were open casts, and in time covering stones were added to make an enclosed mould. Ancient castings were made in clay and sand, and bronze was cast by the lost-wax method as early as 2230 B.C.

Basically the technique is that a hollow form or mould of the article is made and into this the metal is cast. This cast when removed is a replica of the original article. There are various ways of making the mould – the simplest is to make a cuttlefish bone mould and the most sophisticated and accurate is to make a mould in investment plaster by using the lost wax process. The investment plaster mould can then be used for centrifugal casting, Solbrig casting, gravity casting and pressure casting.

There are other types of casting machines, such as vacuum casting and electrically activated automatic casting, but these are usually too expensive for a craftsman and better suited to manufacturing jewellers with bigger production. Sand casting is still in common use for larger

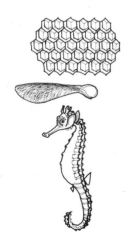

Natural objects can be cast

work like sculpture, but rarely for jewellery as it does not give the necessary reproduction of detail.

The value of casting as a technique for the jeweller is the capacity to give repeats of the design in the cheapest, quickest and most efficient way. It is essential to be able to establish the amount of metal needed to cast a given model. Insufficient metal will fail to fill the mould, or give a poor cast, and too much may result in an overflow of molten metal.

The most accurate way of finding out the weight of metal required is by using the Specific Gravity table. (This is included in the list of tables.) This table shows a comparison between the weights and specific gravity of various substances. By referring to the table one can deduce the weight of metal required to reproduce a model that has been made in another material, eg wax, which of course weighs much less than metal.

Let us assume a model is in wax and is to be cast into silver. The table will show that wax has a Specific Gravity of just under 1·00 and silver's Specific Gravity is 10·50 so the weight of the silver is $10\frac{1}{2}$ times greater than the weight of the wax. Let us also assume that the wax model weighs 3 dwts. (troy weight). It then follows that $10\frac{1}{2}$ times that weight will be needed to reproduce this model in silver, ie $31\frac{1}{2}$ dwts.

Should the model be made of a substance that is not included in the Specific Gravity table, its weight can be ascertained by using the Specific Gravity Test.

There is an additional important factor to be taken into consideration when assessing the weight of the metal required for casting. In all the casting processes the molten metal enters the mould through a passage or sprue, (there may be more than one sprue) and these sprues must be weighed in conjunction with the model to calculate the correct total weight of metal required for casting. A small additional amount of metal must also be added for the 'button'. This is the excess of metal left in the sprue base after the model and sprues are filled, like a reservoir. Its weight adds more impetus to the casting. As sprue bases differ in size, only experience will show you how much extra metal is needed for the button.

Another point in casting is that shrinkage is involved. As the metal cools in the mould it will shrink, although it may only be to a minute degree (approximately 2 per cent). This will probably not affect the design but there is one instance where it could be a disadvantage, and this is in casting a ring. The possibility is that the finger size may be altered. As the metal cools in the shank of the ring mould it shrinks away from the surfaces of the mould. This means that the inside diameter is slightly increased and the outside diameter slightly decreased, and the result could be that the finger size is larger than was intended. A safeguard against this is to make the finger size of the model one size smaller.

If in finishing the cast any bending or hammering is required the cast must be annealed as its molecular structure will have been altered.

□
Wax – unit weight = 1

Standard silver – unit weight = 10.5

18 carat gold – unit weight = 15.5

Platinum – unit weight = 21.5

A simple ring, such as a signet ring, will be cast

Select fine-grained cuttlefish bone

Cut the ends off leaving thick middle section

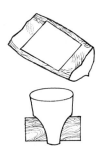

Put a rod of cedar through the shank

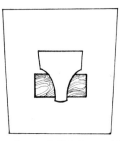

Shape the cuttlefish into a block that will hold the ring leaving substantial space all around

Cuttlefish Bone Casting

Cuttlefish bone casting is the simplest traditional method of casting, and the cheapest, but has inherent disadvantages that are avoided when more sophisticated methods are used. Firstly, it is not suitable for very fine work as the coarseness of the cuttlefish will not give fine enough reproduction, but plain simple forms, eg signet rings will reproduce well. Secondly, it can only be used for a single casting, as the mould will have lost its definition. Additionally, the texture of the cuttlefish will be reproduced on the cast and will have to be filed off, unless it can be utilized for purely decorative purposes.

When making moulds from cuttlefish bone, only articles or models of a hard nature can be used as they must be forced into the cuttlefish bone which is quite dense in texture. Wax, plasticine, rubber or soft wood like balsa, or other soft materials, are unsuitable. To show the different casting techniques clearly the same object will be used in each case: a simple ring, like a signet ring.

We will assume that you have the model you wish to cast, either in the form of an existing ring or the shape made in hard wood, metal or investment plaster. To make the mould, select two pieces of cuttlefish bone with the finest grain, ensure that they are dry, and cut their ends off, leaving the thick middle section. The shell of the cuttlefish is extremely hard and a very coarse saw such as a hack saw will be needed to cut it.

Shape the pieces with a coarse file into two equal-sized blocks into which the ring can be fitted leaving about 20 mm ($\frac{4}{5}$″) clear all round. Smooth off the soft faces of the cuttlefish with coarse sandpaper or emery paper, or rub the two cuttlefish faces together which will have the same effect. If the hard back of the cuttlefish is left intact it adds strength.

Through the inside of the shank of the ring put a piece of round cedar wood of the same diameter as the shank, and long enough to project slightly on either side. This is to block the metal from entering the inside of the shank in casting. Most woods are suitable, but cedar will withstand the temperature of the metal better.

Begin by pressing the model into the smoothed surface of one block, and force it in until the model is halfway in. It may be difficult to press it in to this depth if the model is large, so gently scrape away the depressed areas of the cuttlefish and continue pressing and scraping, but do not destroy the profile of the model in the cuttlefish. Remember always to press the same side of the model down, as there may be slight variations in the two sides. When the model is firmly embedded to its halfway mark, place the second block of cuttlefish on top of it and press this onto the model. Assist its entry by gently scraping out the shape as with the first side, until the model is fully forced into the second block and the blocks meet sufficiently closely so that no light shows between them. Now score the opposite sides of the blocks across to provide location marks for realigning after the blocks have been separated. Another way of aligning the blocks accurately is to embed four pins, or even matchsticks, in the four corners of the bottom block, but leave them projecting and as the top block is forced onto the model, it will also be forced onto these, providing automatic location.

Remove the model and take the wood insert from the shank and put it back in place in the mould, where it now constitutes an integral part of the mould.

In casting, the heaviest part of the model must be at the base. In this case this will be the bulky top of the ring. At the opposite end of the mould make a V cut from the edge of the block to the edge of the model impression and hollow this out to the shape of a half cone. This is called a Gate and is the passage through which the metal will enter the mould. Incise fine lines from the edges of the block to the impression to act as air vents. These need not be matching on each block.

Coat the inside of the impression lightly with a fine oil. Place the two blocks together, correctly located, and bind them with wire.

If casting is to be in silver, place a small piece of zinc, perhaps 3 mm ($\frac{1}{8}$") square, down in the apex of the gate. When the molten silver is poured down the gate, it will melt the zinc which acts as a de-oxidizing agent, thus helping to expel the gases and air in the mould and preventing porosity in the cast.

Melt the metal in a Fletcher crucible held in tongs or heavy pliers and when molten, pour it into the slightly warmed mould. Allow it to cool for 10 or 15 minutes. Separate the blocks. Take out the cast, remove the insert of wood, pickle, wash and dry.

There will be a projection of metal where the gate entered the mould. This is the button. Remove it and the ring is then ready for finishing. The cuttlefish mould cannot be used again as it will have been burnt out. Salvage any unburnt cuttlefish as it can be used as a base when delicate soldering operations require firm location.

Another way of making the mould is to press the ring model into the cuttlefish on its sides as opposed to the first method in which it was pressed in on its shoulders. This obviates the need for the cedar peg to plug the centre of the shank.

If the design calls for a stone to be set in it, make a hole for this through the top of the model and plug it with a cedar peg to stop metal from filling this area, in the same way as described in the first method. The advantage of this is that the hole for the stone does not have to be drilled out subsequently.

Lost Wax Casting

The lost wax process is so named because it actually means the loss of the wax model, which will be melted away. Whereas in cuttlefish casting a solid, permanent model was necessary, in this method of casting the model is impermanent. It is made in wax, enveloped in plaster, the wax is then melted out and the cavity filled with molten metal that provides the cast. The plaster mould is destroyed to retrieve the cast.

This technique has the advantage that the wax prototype can be modelled, carved and shaped very easily, using warmed knives, scalpels, spatulas, and textured equally easily, either using a tool or impressing a textured form, or engraving minute detail. Electrically

Score the opposite sides of the model

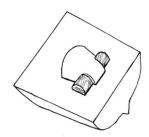

Embed the model to its half-way mark

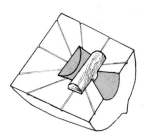

Replace the wood insert, cut out the gate and inscribe air vents

Locate the blocks correctly and bind them

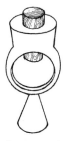

A ring can be cast to incorporate a hole for a stone

heated spatulas and pens provide a consistent heat which is more efficient than having to continually warm knives and spatulas over a spirit lamp. The malleability of the wax allows for a fluidity of design that is not easily achieved in harder materials.

As the many factors involved in this technique are liable to variation, depending upon the manufacturers of the materials and the circumstances in which they are used, I have not indicated specific ratios or temperatures as they would not be viable in all instances.

The varying grades of wax, the proportion of water to plaster, the drying out and heating times for various processes will differ depending upon the manufacturers, and the best results will only be obtained by following their instructions.

WAX

A specific type of dental wax must be used, which is available in sheet, rod or wire form of varying hardnesses. It is essential to use this because of its purity as it will leave no residue on being melted out of the mould. Other types of wax may leave residual matter in the mould, giving a poor cast.

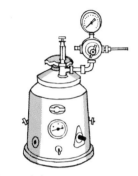

A wax injector

Although a wax model offers great potential for design and detail, the same simple ring used for cuttlefish casting will be used in demonstrating this technique, for the sake of clarity.

One of the great advantages of the lost wax method is its capacity to reproduce exactly every detail of the model, so it is highly suitable for the most intricate and detailed work. The other unique advantage is that reproducing undercuts and crevices presents no problem.

Make the model in dental wax, working on a very lightly greased surface to prevent the work sticking. A sheet of glass lightly smeared with Vaseline could be used, or if the ring is to be made on a mandrel, wrap tissue paper or lightly greased silver foil around the mandrel first. There is a liquid called *Microfilm* that acts as a separating medium and can be used to prevent the wax sticking.

When the model of the ring has been made, prepare it for casting in the following way: invert it and attach the base of the shank to a solid cone of the same wax. This will serve as the passage or sprue through which the metal will enter the mould.

INVESTMENT PLASTER

When casting in cuttlefish, the cuttlefish itself provided the mould, but in lost wax casting the model will be enclosed in investment plaster to provide the mould. This is a particularly finely ground plaster that is able to withstand very high temperatures without cracking. As will become apparent, it is necessary to withstand these temperatures as platinum, for instance, can be cast into it and this only becomes molten at 1775°C (3227°F).

Plaster of Paris, or any other plaster, would be quite unable to sustain the temperature of molten precious metals.

FLASKS

A stainless steel cylinder called a flask will hold the investment plaster to enclose the wax model and sprue. There is a tight fitting rubber lid for this, in the centre of which is a small cone or dome and this is called the sprue base. Attach the model to the sprue base by its own wax sprue, using a warm spatula. Then press the flask down into its lid.

Flasks come in varying sizes. Select a flask that allows adequate coverage of plaster around the model. This should never be less than 12 mm ($\frac{1}{2}$") from the model to the wall of the flask.

When the plaster is to be poured into the flask it must fill it to the brim. As one of the subsequent processes could cause it to overflow, stick a strip of paper around the flask to extend above the rim. This will contain the overflow and allow it to subside down level with the rim again. (It is the equivalent of putting a paper collar around a soufflé dish.)

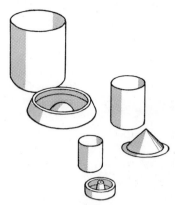

Stainless steel flasks with rubber sprue bases. The middle size has a steel sprue base

INVESTING

Air bubbles in the plaster can prevent a good casting. One way of minimizing them and assisting the plaster in flowing smoothly over all the surfaces and into the undercuts is by the use of a wetting agent. This is a form of mild detergent and it can be brushed over the model with a soft brush, or gently poured into the flask, swilled around, poured out and the process repeated several times, and then allowed to drain off thoroughly.

The flask is now ready for investing, ie filling with investment plaster. Mix the plaster, using water that is colder than room temperature, following the manufacturer's directions, and mix it to roughly the consistency of cream. Some manufacturers recommend adding one or two drops of defoaming agent to the water prior to mixing to diminish the possibility of air bubbles. It is better to mix the plaster in a rubber bowl so that any residue can be allowed to set and removed merely by squeezing the sides of the bowl to dislodge it. Plaster would stick to a china or plastic bowl.

There are several procedures to be completed before the plaster is to be poured into the flask, but in general there will be 10 or 12 minutes for working, but after this the plaster begins to set quite rapidly, so the work needs to be done swiftly. Never pour wet or dry plaster down the sink as it will block the drain – let unwanted plaster dry and put it in the rubbish bin.

It helps to give a perfect cast if the wax model can be lightly filmed with wet plaster before the whole flask is filled. Either paint it with a light coat of plaster, using a soft brush, or pour the plaster gently into the flask to cover the model, then empty it out and repeat this once or twice until the unit is coated. In all these operations work carefully and gently to avoid dislodging the model from its sprue base. Never dust the model with dry plaster prior to filling the flask as it will prevent a perfect casting.

Now tilt the flask and pour the plaster gently down the side to fill

An alternative version of casting flask with a metal lid to which the wax model is attached

A casting flask with its lid, sprue base and sprued model

179

the flask and the paper collar will prevent its overflowing.

As mentioned earlier, air bubbles in the plaster are a hazard in casting. If they should lodge against the wax model, the plaster hardens around them and they become, as it were, part of the model and are filled by the molten metal in casting, forming nodules. This results in a poor cast and if the nodules have formed in undercuts they can be very difficult to remove.

VIBRATING TABLE

Vibrating table

There are two methods of getting rid of air bubbles – one is a vibrating table and the other is a vacuum chamber. The vibrator is efficient and quite adequate for a small workshop. The vacuum chamber is a much more expensive and sophisticated piece of equipment but would justify its cost if one intended to do a great deal of casting. The bowl of investment and then the invested flask should both be vibrated or vacuumed if possible.

In use, the vibrating table, with the flask upon it, shakes the bubbles to the surface of the wet plaster where they burst and disappear. If the sprueing has not been correctly done, the vibration can dislodge the sprue, and one would have to start all over again.

It is possible to improvize a simple vibrating table. As the principle is to vibrate the flask very gently, this can be done even by putting the flask on a bench where a piece of machinery is in motion. Other improvizations can be devised, but as it is essential to get rid of the air bubbles, if one lacks equipment this can be done just by tapping the sides of the flask gently and repeatedly with a piece of wood or a mallet. Painting on the investment will also help to give a good cast if you do not have a vibrator.

VACUUM CHAMBER

The vacuum chamber unit works on the principle of drawing the air out of the vacuum chamber containing the flask and consequently drawing the air bubbles from the plaster in the flask. Each manufacturer's unit will be differently designed, with its own instructions on air evacuation that must be followed meticulously. The chamber may be made of glass, like a bell jar – or if made of steel, it will have a sealing glass lid, as it is vital to be able to observe the process. As the air is evacuated from the chamber and drawn from the plaster, the plaster will rise within the flask and would overflow if the flask had not been taped with its paper collar. Each vacuum unit will have a specific time for this evacuation of air (it can be as brief as 30 seconds) and a gauge will indicate when the vacuum should be turned off.

After the flask has been vibrated or vacuumed, put it aside and allow it to set. This setting or drying out time varies with the make of plaster – some manufacturers suggest 24 hours should elapse before burning out the wax and casting – with others the drying out can be as brief as two hours. It is in the nature of the plaster to still feel slightly damp, although it can be ready for casting.

After the required time has elapsed the flask is ready for the burn out of wax. This can be done either by burning out on a gas ring or putting the flask directly into a hot kiln. I prefer to burn out over a gas ring which is slower but there is less chance of the wax expanding due to the sudden heat and thereby possibly cracking the plaster.

Before starting to burn out, remove the rubber or metal sprue base from the flask. The flask can be put directly on the gas ring or a wire mesh support could be made to hold it slightly above the gas.

The dome in the rubber sprue base will have left an impression of itself in the plaster at the apex of which the end of the wax sprue will be visible.

Place the flask on the gas ring, or on the support, tilted slightly so that the wax can run out freely. As the flask heats the wax will start to run but on contact with the gas flame the wax completely burns away, leaving no residue whatsoever, either on the gas ring or within the flask.

If the flask is to be burnt out in the kiln, tilt it as before, by supporting it on a piece of fire brick and switch on the kiln to a low temperature and gradually bring it up to a heat sufficient to complete the burn out. Again the wax will completely disappear.

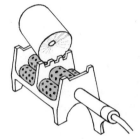

Burn out of wax over gas unit

CASTING

The flask must now be made extremely hot to receive the molten metal so that the metal will retain its heat as it fills and penetrates every part of the mould. If one endeavoured to cast molten metal into a cold flask the metal would probably solidify at once at the entrance, or if it entered would solidify before it made an adequate cast. (Never allow the flask to get cold as it must not be reheated.)

Heat the flask to approximately 900°C (1650°F) in the kiln (only a kiln will give such intense heat). Stand the flask upright in the kiln with the sprue hole at the top.

I have found it better to heat a kiln slowly by degrees rather than starting it at a high temperature, as abrupt heat can ultimately shorten the life of a kiln and repairs can be costly. The temperature gauge will indicate when the kiln has reached 900°C, but if your kiln does not have a gauge you can judge by the appearance of the flask. At 900°C this will look white hot. The flask can now be removed from the kiln with tongs and asbestos gloves and although it will cool very slowly, it is now ready for casting into, and remains so as long as a red/pink colour shows within the sprue hole. The flask can be allowed to cool down to 700°C (1290°F). Both of these temperatures are subject to the manufacturer's instructions.

The three methods of casting into the flask will be described subsequently but whichever method is to be used requires molten metal. This can be prepared while the flask is heating in the kiln. I have stressed the need to be accurate about the weight of metal for casting earlier. It can be dangerous to attempt to cast with too much molten metal as it will splash, and too little will give an inadequate cast.

Tongs

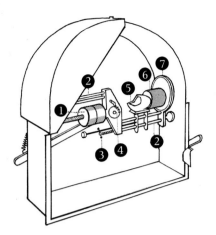

Vertical centrifugal casting machine

1   Counter weights
2   Supporting rods
3   Spring loaded rod
4   Ratchet
5   Crucible
6   Flask
7   Back plate

Silver, gold and platinum can be bought in granulated form specifically for casting. If scrap metal is to be used make sure that it is perfectly clean and that there is no solder on it. Pass a magnet through it to collect any iron or steel particles that may be present. (These could be minute particles of files, broken saw blades, etc.) Should these or any other foreign body be in the melt, they could block the outlet of the crucible or the inlet of the flask in pouring. This is dangerous as the metal is poured at such speed that if its passage is blocked it can only splash backwards. You could be showered with red hot metal, so it is advisable to wear protective glasses and asbestos gloves.

Centrifugal Casting

Centrifugal casting machines can be either horizontal or vertical, but both work on the same principle. I will describe the use of a vertical machine. It has an arm called a casting arm on a central axis. This has on one side the flask with the crucible held against it and on the other side, counter-weights that can be adjusted to balance the arm. The casting arm is driven by a spring activated device which, when released, rotates the arm at a very high speed, causing the molten metal in the crucible to be shot into the flask.

The metal will have been melted in the crucible while it is in position on the casting arm, and subsequently shot through the outlet hole of the crucible, which will be directly in line with the inlet hole (ie sprue hole) of the flask. Therefore the crucible must be held pressing against the flask. This is effected by a spring loaded rod. To load, the crucible is placed in its cradle on the arm and the crucible carrier can then be drawn away towards the centre axis by the spring loaded rod. It is held there by a finger grip so that the flask can be inserted, resting against the back plate, until the spring loaded rod is released gently, forcing the crucible hard up against the flask. They are now in position for casting. As the holes in both crucible and flask must line up, the crucible size would have been previously matched to the flask size.

The total weight of the flask and the crucible containing the metal will vary with each casting. The counterweights on the other side are necessary therefore to balance the arm. They can be screwed along the arm which is threaded, until the correct balance is obtained and then locked in position by turning them one against the other.

The casting machine can now be set for action. The springs which drive the arm must be put in tension. This is done by winding the arm in a full circle, thereby tensing the springs, and then fastening it in this tightened position by using its ratchet and ratchet pawl. (The ratchet is a steel disc with teeth into which a corresponding pawl fits.) This is then locked in position with a safety catch. When one is ready to cast, the safety catch is released and the arm rotates at a great speed.

The metal must be partially melted in the crucible prior to putting the arm in tension; if the metal pieces were to be put in the crucible loose and the arm then tensioned, some metal may fall out in this action. However, if it is partially melted it will solidify in the crucible and the

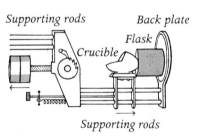

Supporting rods   Back plate

Flask

Crucible

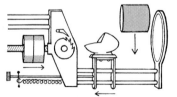

Supporting rods

Casting crucible

movements of balancing and tensioning will not dislodge it. There are at least four ways of melting:

1. Using a gas and compressed air torch.
2. An oxygen and gas torch.
3. An oxygen and acetylene torch.
4. Bottled gas.

(The metal could not be melted using a mouth blown torch as sufficient heat could not be generated.) Oxygen/gas and oxygen/acetylene give greater heat than other methods and consequently greater care must be taken.

A reducing flame, as opposed to an oxidizing flame, should be used. When the metal is fully melted it will resemble the yolk of a fried egg and at this point it spins.

The sequence of events is as follows. The machine is set for action, the crucible is in its cradle with the metal partially melted. The flask which has been heating in the kiln is removed, using tongs specifically designed to hold it safely, and placed on its side in its cradle, with the crucible hard up against it. Before putting the flask in its cradle, place a damp disc of asbestos between the base of flask and the back plate as it helps to cushion the flask when the centrifugal arm is set in motion.

There is no need to hurry in the preceding sequence as the flask can cool to 700°C (1290°F) as mentioned earlier. Melt the metal and when it is in its fluid egg-yolk state it must be cast. Make absolutely sure that the torch has been moved out of range and that nothing stands in the way of the arc of the arm. Release the safety catch and the arm will rotate with great velocity, shooting the metal into the flask. The spin will run down and the arm will come to rest. Apply the safety catch to keep the arm steady.

Remove the flask. It is then to be cooled by immersing in water, but to do this gradually, rest it on another empty flask standing in a sink and run the water in slowly to cover both flasks. This allows a slow cooling of the flask and casting. When the flask is cool it is taken from the water and the investment plaster is dug out and put in a waste bin. Obviously one must be careful not to damage the delicate parts of the cast in doing this. It does not come cleanly away from the cast and may need to be brushed out in water with a stiff brush or picked out with a fine point like a darning needle.

The cast is then put into a hot pickle for final cleaning, washed and dried. The sprue or sprues are sawn off and the cast is filed, emery-papered and polished to complete it.

SPRUEING

If an object larger and more complicated than this simple ring were to be cast, it would need a number of sprues, both to support it in the flask and permit easy access of metal to all parts.

The sprues need to be as straight and as short and as cylindrical as possible to allow the metal to flow smoothly. Arrange the sprues so they are evenly spread around the model, converging on the sprue base.

A piece of jewellery comprised of identical units, as for instance a

Gravity casting can be done in a hand-held crucible

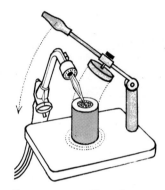

Solbrig casting utilizes damp asbestos and steam to force the metal into the flask

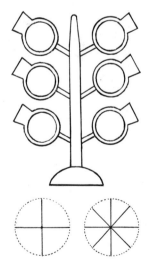

Wax models can be set up in a 'tree' which will be inverted for the molten metal to travel down the trunk into the models. The models can radiate at a number of angles depending on their size

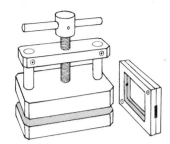

A hand-operated Vulcanizing Press, used with an aluminium mould frame

necklace, could be produced in one casting. If the units are small enough they can be sprued to give a multiple casting. This would be governed by the size of the flask – if there were too many units for a particular size of flask two castings might be necessary. Let us assume the wax models are leaves – each model must have its own sprue which joins the central sprue. The small sprues are positioned so that they radiate up and out, rather like the branches of a tree, and the metal when flung follows this natural course.

Each wax model of the leaf would, in fact, have slight variations in it as it was made by hand, but it is possible however to obtain identical replicas by making a rubber mould.

Rubber Mould Making to Produce Wax Models for Casting

This is the one technique used in casting that is essentially for mass production. All the previous methods have been concerned with producing a single unit, but this is the technique for producing multiples. In this case the mould is permanent. It is flexible, can produce an almost unlimited number of models and is capable of reproducing work of the finest detail. Also undercuts present no problem. As in cuttlefish casting, an existing prototype is required and it is this that will be duplicated. The prototype must be made of metal (excluding lead) and rhodium plated to give a very smooth surface which facilitates removal of the prototype from the rubber mould.

Metal prototype ring and metal sprue

There are at least four types of rubber that can be used for the mould. The processes are basically the same but the equipment varies and can be very expensive. The vulcanizing rubber process is perhaps the most efficient and the equipment needed for it is the most expensive. This tends to put it out of the range of the craftsman/jeweller, but it is used extensively in manufacturing. The major expenses are incurred by a vulcanizing press and a wax injector. The vulcanizer cures the natural rubber which is used, by pressure and heat, which gives the mould a longer life than any of the other types of rubber. The wax injector ensures the minimum risk of faulty wax patterns.

The other rubbers used are synthetic, and while they do not have the long life of natural rubber, are perfectly adequate for use by the craftsman/jeweller. These are silicone rubber, polysulphide rubber and 'hot-pour' compounds.

I prefer silicone and this is the process I will describe. Silicone comes in the form of a thick fluid and must be mixed with its chemical reactor (also a liquid) which acts as a catalyst. Together they form a compound that will set to a rubbery consistency. It is most essential to mix them in the correct ratio as described in the directions.

The same signet ring that has been used before is to be the prototype. The first step is to sprue the ring, but in this case the sprue must be of metal and soldered to the shank. The model and sprue are then rhodium plated.

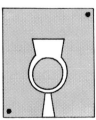

The ring is sunk into a block of plasticine

Make a block of plasticine. The ring is to be sunk into this so it must be sufficiently large to allow 12 mm ($\frac{1}{2}''$) clearance. Lightly coat the ring and sprue with Vaseline thinned with a drop of alcohol or Microfilm to prevent the plasticine sticking to it. Press the ring and sprue in until they are set halfway into the plasticine block, with the sprue reaching the end of the block. Make locating holes about 1·5 mm ($\frac{1}{16}''$) diameter at diagonal corners. Now build a plasticine wall around the block as high again as the block itself. Coat the inside area and the partially exposed model with a separating agent (*Microfilm* or *Vaseline*).

It is essential that the proportions of silicone and catalyst are measured according to the manufacturer's instructions. This is most easily done by using cheap plastic cups for weighing, particularly as the ingredients are messy and the cups can be discarded afterwards. Weigh two empty cups, then put the silicone in one and the catalyst in the other. Now weigh them again and deduct the weight of the cup from the total of each. You will now know the weights of the ingredients. The silicone must have been very thoroughly stirred before pouring into the cup. Pour the catalyst into the silicone and mix with a plastic spoon.

At this time you need only enough to fill the plasticine box to its brim. Let it set. Setting time is governed by the ratios used and the brand of silicone used, and the times vary from 15 minutes to 48 hours. Silicones and their catalysts can be an irritant to both skin and eyes, so care must be taken when handling them.

When this top half of the mould is set, remove the plasticine wall and take the silicone piece with the model out of the plasticine block. Invert it. You then have half a mould in silicone. To get the other half build another plasticine wall all around the silicone block as high as before. Paint with the parting agent. Now mix a second lot of silicone and pour it into the box to fill it to its brim. Let it set. When set, remove the plasticine wall, separate the two halves, take out the model and check that the sprue hole entrance is clear. Wipe off the parting agent. The silicone will have filled the locating hole in the first half of the mould, automatically supplying a peg in the second half of the mould. These locating pegs will hold the two halves of the mould together.

The mould is now ready to be filled with hot wax. It can be quite difficult to get the wax to flow right to the base of the mould before it starts to cool and solidify. One solution to this is to use a metal icing syringe. Its cap is taken off, it is filled with molten wax, recapped, and should it cool, as it is metal it can be reheated. The nozzle is put into the sprue hole, the plunger pushed in, and the hot wax is forced down into the mould. There is a fair chance of getting a good wax model just by pouring hot wax down the sprue hole from a heatproof dish. The difficulty is to pour the hot wax through the narrow opening quickly enough to prevent the wax solidifying on contact with the sprue hole.

When the wax has been poured and allowed to cool, the mould can be opened. If the wax pattern is faulty it can often be corrected by hand, adding and smoothing the wax.

The rubber mould can now be used to produce a number of identical wax patterns which can be invested singly or in a group by attaching their sprues to one central sprue. When invested and burnt out, they can be cast by the methods described previously.

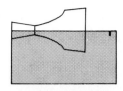

Press the ring and sprue halfway into the block

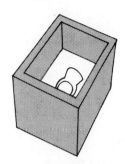

Build a plasticine wall around the block

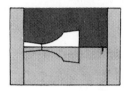

Pour the silicone into the plasticine box

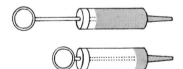

A metal syringe for icing cakes could be used to inject wax

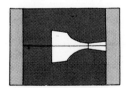

Invert the model and pour in the second lot of silicone

Specific Gravity

The specific gravity of a substance is its weight compared with that of an equal volume of water at its greatest density which is at a temperature of 4°C. Specific gravity is used to establish the denseness of a substance, and consequently its weight. (One cubic centimeter of water at 4°C is the weight of a gramme, and so the specific gravity of any substance is also the weight in grammes of a cubic centimeter of it.)

SPECIFIC GRAVITY IN RELATION TO CASTING

Although specific gravity can be used for other purposes, such as establishing the weight of a gemstone, my concern with it here is solely to determine the weight of metal required for a specific casting from a wax model. There are a number of detailed and complicated tests for arriving at specific gravity, but the following test is the simplest and adequate for this purpose.

It is based on water displacement. One needs a glass measuring flask that is marked on the side in centimetres. Pour water in, to the halfway mark or more. Attach a thin strong wire to the sprue of the wax model, with wax. Push the model down into the water. The water will rise to a level which we will call point X. Note this level. Take the model out. Now put into the flask the metal to be used in casting, in small pieces, adding as necessary until the water rises again to point X. This is then the metal equivalent of the wax model and sprue – and the amount required to cast them. What has not been taken into account is the additional metal that will form the 'button' by partially filling the sprue base former. I would generally add another 15 to 20 per cent of metal for this, but it would be governed by the design of your sprue base former.

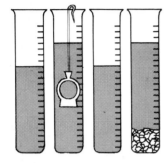

Specific gravity test, for use in casting. Put water in calibrated flask and note the level. Add wax model and sprue which will raise water level. Note this, and remove model. Add casting metal to flask until water reaches higher level. This establishes amount of metal required for casting that model

Enamelling

The Townley brooch, 10th or 11th century. Gold and Enamel. French or German

The Technique of Enamelling

Enamelling is the technique of fusing coloured glass to metal.

It is used as decoration on jewellery and other objects because of its particular property of giving a coloured glazed surface that can be transparent, translucent or opaque, to a metal surface.

The enamels are made by amalgamating silicon, feldspar, soda, borax, flint, sand or combinations of these and several other components, and the colours are obtained by adding metallic oxides. Of the various techniques used in jewellery, enamelling requires the least equipment, as the principle is to place the powdered enamel on a metal base and melt it until it fuses onto this.

From this basic principle the technique extends to include Cloisonné, Plique-à-jour, Limoges, Champlevé and Baisse-taille.

It will be apparent that in enamelling there is a certain amount of overlapping of tools and equipment used in jewellery, so it is not necessary to buy other than specific tools for this technique. Existing tools can often be altered or adjusted, and the innovator can save time and money and achieve excellent results by applying his skill to improvization on existing equipment.

The earliest example of cloisonné enamelling. Mycenaean 1200 BC. A sceptre with a pair of gold hawks, the whole set with cells of white, green and mauve enamels

Pyrometric cones

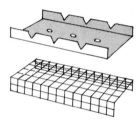

Enamelling support and rack

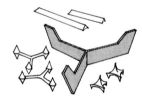

Enamelling supports and spurs

Asbestos gloves

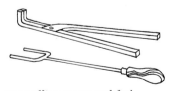

Enamelling tongs and fork

THE KILN

The kiln should be capable of a controlled temperature up to 1030°C (1886°F) and have a temperature control gauge and a pyrometer as well as an aperture for observing the processes taking place inside. Enamel fuses at approximately 850°C (1560°F), but the kiln could also be used for other techniques requiring higher temperatures.

If the kiln does not have a temperature gauge, pyrometric cones can be used. They are used in pottery making to determine the satisfactory completion of a firing. Their composition and structure are such that they bend when subjected to heat for a period of time. They are placed inside the kiln in alignment with the spy hole. Three consecutive grades are used, which give adequate indication of how the firing is progressing. Cones can be used to check evenness of heat distribution in kilns by being placed throughout the firing chamber, and it is advisable to do this before first firing any new kiln.

Although one may have turned the switch for the kiln to 'On', the kiln will not function until the door is closed.

A useful feature which could be incorporated into a kiln is a steel box to act as a lining to the kiln. It would need to be open at the front for loading, and on four short legs to allow easy removal from the kiln. You would have to make this to fit your own kiln.

Its purpose is to keep the inside walls of the kiln clean, protecting them from fumes and their residue, and protecting the kiln floor from fallen enamel.

This type of kiln could also be used by a craftsman concerned with centrifugal casting or niello work. Ideally one would have a lining box for each process as there are chemicals in each technique that could be detrimental to the one that follows it. The lead used in niello work, for instance, can be particularly detrimental to gold or silver.

EQUIPMENT

In addition to jeweller's tools, one will need a pair of long-handled tongs, an enamelling fork, cradle supports, and spurs made of stainless steel for supporting work, asbestos gloves, heat-resistant michrome wire mesh (for racks), nitric and sulphuric acids, a range of copper sieves, a timer (similar to a kitchen timer), several spatulas or palette knives and a set of small china bowls. Also gold and silver foil, gum tragacanth, pure alcohol, several assorted sable hair brushes, a spray or atomizer, and, of course, enamelling, gold, silver, copper and/or gilding metals. Hydrofluoric acid is necessary for removing enamel in case of repairs. Great care must be taken in the use of this acid as it burns and can be harmful if breathed in. Ideally it should be used in the open air.

METALS

Gold is without doubt the best metal for enamelling, as there is no oxidization. Silver will oxidize but to a certain extent the enamel will minimize oxidization.

Silver for enamelling should ideally be a special alloy that includes a higher degree of pure silver, and consequently has a higher melting point than sterling silver. Sterling silver will melt at 925°C (1742°F). As enamel fuses at approximately 850°C (1560°F) there is very little margin before the metal's melting point. Copper is also a fine metal for enamelling and is probably the most commonly used. Brass, ie, commercial brass, is not suitable for enamelling. Gilding metal is also used frequently, mainly commercially, for the production of lapel badges, name-plates, etc. It is a metal which has the colour of gold and polishes extremely well. Bronze and nickel can also be used.

Mortar and pestle

THE ENAMELS

Enamels can be bought in rough chunks, for grinding, or ready ground. If you choose the former, the enamel chunk must be ground in a porcelain mortar with a pestle, to a powder. Large pieces can be coped with more easily by heating them and then plunging them into cold water, which will crack them into smaller pieces.

When they are sufficiently broken up, just cover with water (this prevents the enamel chips from being thrown out of the mortar) and start to grind, using the pestle with a rotary action.

Keep changing the water when grinding until it becomes clear, which will mean that any impurities will have run off on the surface of the water. (When enamel has been bought already ground, even more care must be taken to ensure that it is washed absolutely clean.)

To dry the ground enamel, place it in small trays, which can be made from aluminium foil, and put them into the kiln at a very low heat. Or they can be placed near the mouth of the kiln and covered with a saucer. Remember that ground enamels must always be kept covered unless actually being used, preferably in an airtight jar, as some enamels can deteriorate if left uncovered and could collect dust. Label the jars with the relevant notes for easy reference in future use.

The enamel must then be sieved through a diminishing range of sieves, which will finally result in a regular sized grain.

It is advisable to use a face mask when sifting to ensure that the fine particles of enamel and enamel dust are not inhaled.

When grinding, always sieve into a clean dish or tray. As when soldering or melting, always make sure that the tools are cleaned after use, so as not to contaminate future work.

Preparation for Enamelling

Prepare the metal prior to laying on the enamel by ensuring that the metal is absolutely clean by pickling, rinsing, and drying; then, with either fine emery paper or fine steel wool, clean the surface, wash thoroughly and dry. Try not to handle with your fingers, but use tongs. As an alternative, brushing pure alcohol or carbon tetra-chloride over the surface achieves the same result of complete cleanliness.

Vulture headdress from figure of goddess. Egypt 380–343 BC. One of the earliest and extremely rare examples of enamelling. The blue and white scale-like sections in front and back of the headdress are fused glass, ie enamel. The gold cloisons are exceptionally fine – bearing in mind the whole headdress is only $1\frac{1}{4}$" high and $1\frac{1}{8}$" wide.

Electric sprayer

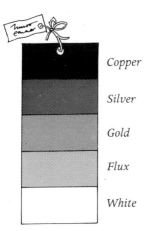

Copper

Silver

Gold

Flux

White

Colour sample

APPLICATION OF ENAMEL

Manufacturers generally give the melting temperatures of their enamels, but enquire about these if they are not available. There are soft, medium and hard enamels, and the soft enamel fuses at the lowest temperature and the hard enamel fuses at the highest temperature.

The enamel can be applied in one of two ways: dusted on as a dry powder, or applied in the form of a wet paste. In this case it would be mixed with water and gum tragacanth added to it to help keep it in position. It can be put on with a spatula, and excess moisture can be mopped up by gently pressing blotting paper against the edges of the piece.

If the enamel is to be dusted on, the dry powder is sifted onto a coat of gum tragacanth that covers the metal. When it has settled it is re-sprayed with gum and a second layer of enamel, and built up in this way to cover the surface evenly.

Whichever method is used, the enamel must be dry before firing.

The kiln is gradually brought up to the required heat, the enamel piece is supported on a rack or stainless steel supports and very gently moved into the kiln. The fusing time can be very brief, a few seconds would be sufficient for a small piece, but firing depends on many factors such as the size of the kiln, the hardness of the enamel, the size of the piece, etc. The enamel will have fused when it becomes smooth and shiny. Remove it carefully and allow it to cool slowly away from draughts.

To finish the piece, any unevenness must be levelled off. Start by grinding with a carborundum stone, keeping the work wet all the time, and then grind with wet pumice on a felt bob. After washing and drying the piece can then be given a final firing which will leave the surface smooth and bright.

When making celled enamels, such as Cloisonné, the walls can be glued on, or soldered on. In the latter, gum tragacanth is mixed with borax in soldering the cells to the base. Great care must be taken so that no solder is left visible as it would show through transparent or translucent enamels. Use hard solder, bearing in mind that enamel fuses at approximately 850°C (1560°F) and a hard solder would be able to withstand this degree of heat. The recommended solder is alloyed of one ounce of fine silver and five pennyweights of pure copper.

When the cells have been fixed to the base and have been thoroughly cleaned, fill them with the enamel paste and fire in the kiln. After firing, allow the work to cool slowly. The enamel may have shrunk within the cell and if so must be replenished with enamel and refired. Any holes or flaws that may have appeared can be cleaned out and refilled at the same time.

The application and firing of enamels is a specialized technique and, as in all cases of specialization, I recommend books dealing specifically with the subject in the Bibliography.

COUNTER ENAMELLING

When the metal is ready for use, the back as well as the front must be coated with enamel. Failure to coat both sides of the metal will allow distortion to take place. The reason for this is that the metal will expand in the heat, and the enamel will melt and fuse onto it in its expanded state. As the metal and enamel cool, they contract but at different rates. If the metal had been coated on one side only the brittle enamel would not be able to cope with the more rapid contraction of the metal, which would curve or bend due to the unequal pressure, and the enamel would crack or chip.

By coating both sides with enamel, on fusing and cooling the metal is sealed within the enamel and held in its expanded state, and as the pull on both sides is equal and the contraction is equal, the metal will not distort nor will the enamel crack. This is called counter enamelling.

The enamel on both sides should be as equal as possible, and less than the thickness of the metal itself. The underside enamel can be used as decoration or may merely be a way of using up waste enamel.

COLOUR

As the beauty of enamelling lies in its colour, it is extremely useful to have a series of samples that show how both transparent and opaque colours alter when fired, and also how these colours will vary depending upon what underlies them. This is self-evident with transparent colours, but even opaque ones alter in relation to the number of coats they are given. Therefore make a sample of all the colours in use, both transparent and opaque.

With transparent colours, it is vital to know how they will appear over various bases, and the most efficient way of demonstrating this is to take a rectangular piece of copper a few inches long and divide it into five equal bands. If a hole is bored at one end a tag with all the relevant information, such as gauge and type of metal used, suppliers and their code number for the colour, time and temperature of firing, can be recorded, and the sample available for easy reference.

Prepare the copper sample for enamelling and counter enamel it. Leaving one of the end bands as plain copper, coat the band next to it with white enamel, and the remaining three with clear flux, and fire it. Leaving the middle band as clear flux, cover the remaining two bands with a strip of gold and a strip of silver foil. Then coat the whole piece with the coloured enamel, and fire it again. When this is completed the sample will clearly show the effect of that particular colour over copper, over white enamel, over flux and over foil, and in each case the colour will be different, being most brilliant over the foil, and then the white and flux, and finally deepest on the copper.

The same principle is applied when making samples of opaque colour to show how one, two or three coats will alter the colour of the enamel. Coat the whole copper sample and fire it, then coat half of it and fire, and again coat half of the two-coated area and fire.

Some knowledge of colour theory is important in enamelling, as the unique quality of this aspect of jewellery is the intense brilliance of colour that the medium gives. Because of the vitreous nature of enamel, when fired the transparent enamels do have depth and intensity of colour quite unlike flat paint.

Vulture pectoral of Tut-ankh-amun, gold, lapis lazuli, blue, green and red glass. This is considered to be one of the earliest examples of enamelling, 1362–1353 BC

Gold and enamel earring. Byzantine

Eagle brooch, pierced enamelled gold from treasure of Empress Gisela, c.1043.

191

Gold miniature case with champlevé enamel in black and white, c. 1620.
Private collection

Small Diptych of translucent enamel on gold. Obverse: Pierre II, duc de Bourbon, with St Peter. Anne de Beaujeu with St Anne
Reverse: Charlemagne and St Louis, King of France.
French circa 1490.
The Wallace Collection, London

Types of Enamel

CLOISONNÉ

The first enclosed enamels, and probably the oldest method of enamelling is Cloisonné (from the French word meaning partition or cell). The appearance of Cloisonné work can be compared to a bee's honeycomb, with each of the little cells filled with enamel. The partitions or walls of the cells are built up with very small rectangular wire (ie thin and very shallow). The wire is shaped into the pattern to contain the enamel and held in position on the pre-prepared base with gum tragacanth, or the walls can be soldered on.

CHAMPLEVÉ

Champlevé is also a compartmentalized enamelling of ancient origin, but in this case the enamel is introduced into a sunken cell, instead of a built-up one. The sunken shapes can be cut, carved, engraved, etched or stamped into the metal, or the design can be pierced out of a metal sheet, which is then soldered to a base, thereby giving the containers for the enamel.

BAISSE-TAILLE

Baisse-taille enamelling follows the same principle as Champlevé, but with the difference that the base and the cells have been decorated with a design. This can have been made by carving, stamping or chasing a design into the metal and the whole area is then overlaid with transparent enamel so that the design shows through.

This work was greatly used in the 14th century, and the grounds were generally chased. If relief moulding is introduced into the base, it gives an extremely rich effect as the chasing of the bright metal shines up through the transparent enamel, which alters its colour according to whether it lies thickly in a depression or skims over a raised surface.

PLIQUE-À-JOUR

Enamelling may be 'à jour', that is transparent, or 'à nuit', ie applied on a thin plaque; the latter, including Cloisonné, Champlevé and the other better known methods, has always been more widespread.

Plique-à-jour enamelling is similar to Cloisonné, except that the celled design is free-standing without a backing. The cells are filled with transparent enamel, and the result resembles a stained glass window.

The walls to hold the enamel in Plique-à-jour must be slightly curved or keyed to support it. A suitable shape can be made by drawing rectangular wire through a round drawplate, using a hole that is slightly smaller in diameter than the depth of the rectangular wire. This will give you the required U-shaped curve to hold the enamel. A special drawplate could be made if sufficient of this shape of wire was needed.

When the design has been made from this wire, place the cellular structure on a sheet of mica, which will act as a base during firing, and the enamel will not stick to it. The enamel is mixed with gum tragacanth to help to hold it in the cells. To prevent the design moving on the mica while it is being filled, anchor it with steel split pins or adjustable tweezers – even clamping it with paper clips or tying it down so that you can work on it freely.

The enamel and gum tragacanth mixture must be allowed to dry before firing. If it should be necessary to keep an area free from enamel, a thin coat of paste made from powdered rouge and methylated spirits can be painted on, and will not interfere with firing. Instead of using wires, the cellular structure can be made by piercing the design out of a sheet of metal of suitable thickness. This can then stand vertically for filling and firing.

Because of the delicate nature of its construction, Plique-à-jour is unsuitable for very hard wear, but is particularly beautiful when used so that the light can shine through it, for its full stained-glass effect (eg as in earrings).

Ram shaped box and cover.
Chinese cloisonné. Enamel.
AD 1736–96.
Victoria and Albert Museum

RESIN ENAMELS

There are now available synthetic enamels, made of resin, that can provide a very cheap way of putting colour on metals. There are a number of types available, some of which require a hardener.

ÉMAIL EN RÉSILLE SUR VERRE

An extremely difficult technique in enamelling was practised in France in the early 17th century, but only for a decade or two by a few highly skilled craftsmen. It is called émail en résille sur verre. The technique consists of engraving a design into coloured glass, usually dark blue or viridian, in a low intaglio. These intaglio hollows were lined with exceptionally thin gold foil and then filled with powdered enamel, which was to fuse at a temperature low enough not to affect the glass base. The result was delicate and subtle in the extreme.

Limoges school of enamelling
(1151–1160), plaque from the
tomb of Geoffrey Plantagenet.
Le Mans Museum

LIMOGES ENAMEL

Of the surface enamels, Limoges or Painter's Enamel is the best known. As its name implies, one is painting in enamel and a high degree of draughtsmanship and creative skill is required.

In the 15th century French craftsmen at Limoges established that the metal divisions to contain enamels were not essential; and began to work without them, painting directly in enamel. It is a delicate and complicated procedure, particularly if rendering realistic forms as those craftsmen did. The modelling of these forms requires accuracy and a sure knowledge of the relative hardness of the colours being used. As many firings may be required the harder colours should have been painted first so that the heat from subsequent firings of softer colours does not destroy the first layers.

Grisaille is another method of surface enamelling, but in this case the

Rhenish school of enamelling,
Samson carrying off the gates of
Gaza, 12th century.
Victoria and Albert Museum

Grisaille enamel. An ornament of 17th century

painting is in monochrome, not colour. It was very popular in 16th and 17th centuries. A dark-coloured ground (often blue or black) was laid on copper and the design overlaid in layers of white enamel, building up a strong three-dimensional effect, as the dark ground showed through the white. For this, of course, a considerable knowledge of form and draughtsmanship was needed.

ADDITIONAL WAYS OF DECORATING ENAMELLED SURFACES

There are additional ways still of decorating enamelled surfaces – by encrustation, by gold leaf, by gold and silver foil, in paillon form, as well as by sgraffito or stencilling.

In sgraffito the surface of the work is scored with a sharpened tool such as a lining scriber, through a fine coat of enamel that has been previously dusted onto the metal. Spray lightly with tragacanth to secure the design.

Stencils can be used in enamelling to block off part of the design while powdered enamel is dusted over the rest, and patterns can be built up by using the same stencil for subsequent coats, but in different positions.

The Alfred Jewel. Gold and Cloisonné enamel. Found at Athelney, Somerset. Around its edge it bears the inscription in Anglo Saxon: 'Alfred had me made'. English 9th century. Ashmolean Museum, Oxford

Niello

The Fuller Brooch. A Fibula Silver inlaid with niello. 9th century Anglo Saxon. British Museum

The word 'niello' derives from the Latin 'nigellum', the diminutive of 'niger' meaning black, and this was taken into Italian as 'niello'. Niello work is so-called because the process uses the black niello alloy for decorative purposes on metal. There are many ways of putting the niello design on the metal base, but the principal is to recess an area to hold the niello – for instance, by engraving. If used over a larger area, the recession can be made in a similar way to the recessed space used in champlevé enamelling, or by chasing, or punching, or repoussé work.

The earliest examples appear to have been found in Egypt, later in Cyprus and Greece, and it is thought that ancient niello was an alloy of copper and silver sulphides. After a period of decline it was practiced again in Roman times when its composition was silver sulphide only – as far as we know the technique was widely employed by artist/goldsmiths up to, and during the 15th century particularly in Florence. In the 11th century A.D., Theophilus made various alloys for niello work, the principal one being:

Silver	2 parts
Copper	1 part
Lead	$\frac{1}{2}$ part

and an unspecified amount of sulphur.

(My experience proved satisfactory when I used sulphur that was twice the quantity of the other three components, ie 7 parts of sulphur to $3\frac{1}{2}$ parts of silver, copper and lead. It is possible that one could use up to 10 parts of sulphur successfully.)

Gold and niello ring of King Ethelwulf of Wessex, Anglo-Saxon AD 839–58 British Museum

*Mycenaean 1550 to 1500 BC.
Ornamental daggers with inlaid
blades. Late Bronze Age – made
by Cretans for the mainland
market. Gold hilted dagger of
bronze inlaid with gold, silver
and niello. Decorated with a lion
hunt*

*The only dagger with the hilt
surviving intact comes from
Pylos – decorated with hunting
leopards*

From the works I have studied and my own practical experience, I agree with Herbert Maryon that Theophilus gives the safest and probably the best alloy, as it contains the least lead, which is not a very satisfactory metal to work in conjunction with gold or silver, because if it is carelessly used it may seriously damage the metals.

Cellini, Wilson, Bolas, Rosenberg and others have their own alloys for this technique, and an interesting one is found in Ernest Spon's *Workshop Receipts*, a book in four volumes which also includes chapters dealing with almost everything from plumbing to embalming, and makes entertaining reading.

The ingredients used are basically the same, altered slightly either by adding to or subtracting from the different metals or chemicals, but generally they are composed of sulphur, silver, copper, lead, antimony, bismuth, in various combinations of quantity, some using borax, sal-ammoniac and quick-silver.

This technique has to some extent died out in the West, and most of the present-day work is done in the East, in Thailand and Malaya particularly. There does however appear to be a slight revival of interest now, shown particularly by students in the West eager to become more knowledgeable about the various techniques that can be used by craftsmen. Niello work was used frequently by medieval armourers, and the engraving that was done to receive the niello could be inked in to 'print' the design, to check on its progress. This became part of the technique of artists using an inked engraved line, as in etching, and from it the process of intaglio printing was developed.

The principle of niello is very similar to that of enamelling, insofar as both processes fuse a decoration onto a metal base under heat – in niello, 'black' metal is fused onto metal, in enamelling, coloured glass is fused onto metal. Niello can be used on the same metals as those used in enamelling, and in a similar manner to champlevé or cloisonné. It can, as with enamelling, be heated either in a kiln, or with a blow torch or Bunsen burner from underneath, to fuse the decoration into position.

When working with niello it is advisable to have an extractor fan on, as the fumes (predominantly of lead and sulphur) can be harmful if much work is to be carried out over a period of time. Lacking an extractor fan, a face mask is an adequate substitute.

To make the blackened or dark smoky-blue colour that is characteristic of niello, melt the silver and copper together and when molten, stir well with a carbon or graphite rod, or a ceramic rod, all of which will withstand the temperature of the molten metal and yet can still be handled.

Now add the lead, which, having a much lower melting point, will melt almost instantly. Stir it again and remove any dross that will have risen to the surface. (Dross being the impurities, given out when metal is melted. It is generally not found in gold or silver, but is usually found in the baser metals, particularly lead.) In another crucible have the sulphur which has already been melted or heated, and into this crucible pour the niello alloy and mix all thoroughly together. There are some schools of thought which suggest that the sulphur is not melted or heated but just thrown in. It is really a matter of experimentation to find out what gives the best result, but the aim is that all the ingredients must be mixed into a homogeneous mass. Then pour onto an oiled sheet of steel or into an ingot mould. On cooling the lump of niello can be broken up and ground to a powder, then sieved through an 80 gauge mesh. (Note the similarity to the enamelling technique.) Another way to break the big lumps into smaller pieces, as in enamelling, is to pour the molten metal into a fairly deep vessel containing cold water. As it hits the water the niello breaks up, which facilitates the later grinding processes.

When the niello has been ground and washed in distilled water, pour off the impurities that may float to the surface (as in cleansing enamels) and then, as an additional precaution, run a magnet through the niello to pick up any iron or steel dust that may be present. Store the cleaned niello in a stoppered bottle with distilled water covering it. This will ensure that it remains free of impurities.

To use the niello powder, dry it in front of the kiln or in the kiln at a very low temperature, as in drying enamels. When ready for use, the niello powder can be laid into the recessed areas with a spatula. If the walls of the recesses are undercut, it is a decided advantage, but if they cannot be undercut it is advisable to coat the recesses with a weak borax solution to ensure a firm cohesion when the niello fuses. Try not to overspread the niello as if the niello is made too hot it will burn into the surface of the metal, and would then have to be filed away, making the metal appreciably thinner.

Sprinkle a little powdered borax or sal-ammoniac over the work as a fusing agent, and place the piece in the slow kiln at a low temperature. Watch carefully until the niello has fused and take it out of the kiln immediately as it should not be overheated or its lead component will corrode the gold or silver.

Should the niello begin to spread or wander, push it back into position with a hot spatula, and also use this to firm the niello down if necessary. Allow it to cool off and do not quench. File away any excess niello but not quite down to the metal. Re-heat the piece – or pass a hot iron over, not on, the work (as in making Crème Brûlée) then with a lightly oiled burnisher, quickly burnish down the remaining niello until it is level with the metal surface, which will remove any air bubbles that may have arisen.

Using a leather buff and pumice powder, begin to polish, following this by rubbing with Water-of-Ayr stone and then with a mop charged with either crocus or tripoli. Finally finish with the soft rouge mop. Care must be taken when polishing to see that the work is not pressed down too hard on the mops, as the niello could be dragged or scoured out. If that happens, wash thoroughly, and pass the hot iron over the work to re-fuse it, then finish again. If scoured out too deeply, the piece would have to be re-filled with niello and re-fired.

When files are used for niello work, keep them exclusively for that technique and don't use them for other work, because minute particles of lead remaining in the file teeth may get mixed with other lemel.

Gold belt buckle with niello, from Sutton Hoo ship burial, 7th century AD.

VI SPECIALIZED TECHNIQUES

Electroplating

Electroplating and electroforming are highly specialized techniques involving the use of complicated, critical equipment which can be very expensive and could be potentially dangerous. The solutions used in plating contain cyanide and apart from the obvious dangers of accident, even the inhalation of the fumes presents a definite danger.

I will give a simple description of the techniques, but I would strongly recommend that the work in which you wish to utilize their advantages should be given to the specialist firms that deal with electroplating and forming.

Electroplating or electro deposition is the technique of depositing a metal coating onto a chemically clean, electrically conductive surface, in an aqueous solution, by applying a low voltage DC current.

The plating solution is based on a salt of the metal to be plated (ie the salt of silver is silver cyanide) with other chemicals added to increase conductivity, assist anode dissolution and brighten deposits, etc.

The solution is electrolyzed by applying a low voltage DC current, with the negative lead connected to the work piece and the positive lead connected to the anode. This is the basis of electroplating, and the description can now be broken down into a more practical details.

The article to be plated should be suspended by 22 gauge or 24 gauge soft copper wire by utilizing any holes or projections in the contours.

The first operation is cleaning, and for successful plating the article must be 100 per cent chemically clean. Any scale or oxide must be removed by pickling. Heavy grease should be removed by immersing in carbon tetrachloride, and normal cleaning or degreasing is carried out in alkaline hot cleaners.

Commercial cleaners are sophisticated solutions and are most likely to be sold only in large quantities. However, a strong, hot household detergent can be used instead as a cleaner for soaking the article in, and subsequently brushing over the surface with a soft brush should remove any remaining dirt.

After rinsing in clear cold water, one can tell if the article is genuinely clean by allowing running water to flow across its surface. If any dirt or grease remains, the water will 'break' around it instead of flowing smoothly without interruption. If the flow is interrupted, it means that the cleaning is insufficient and the cycle should be repeated.

A typical commercial cleaner would have the following formula:

Tribasic Sodium Phosphate	4 oz to a gallon of water
Sodium Metasilicate	4 oz to a gallon of water
Wetting Agent	$\frac{1}{8}$ oz to a gallon of water
Temperature	80°–90°C

As all electroplating is dependent on a controlled electric supply, it is important that this should be fitted up with care. The current necessary is low voltage DC, but of a comparatively high amperage. In commercial operation a rectifier is used, but they are expensive and even the smallest type marketed has an output of 8 volts 50 amps which is more than would be usually needed. The commercial rectifier would be worthwhile if it was going to be utilized sufficiently to warrant its cost.

However, for the craftsman/jeweller a small car battery charger of 4 amp rating or a car accumulator could be used after adaptation. Both these units emit 12 volts, and as plating is usually operated at 0·75 to 4 volts approximately, a variable resistance must be included in the circuit to reduce and control the voltage. A commercial slide resistance unit will do this or a unit could be cheaply and simply constructed.

To do this, obtain a spiral electric fire, element 350 watts, a voltmeter 0–10 volts, and an ammeter 0–5 amps from a radio or electrical shop. The spiral element (or resistance wire) is supported on a couple of metal brackets, one end being connected to the positive source of the battery or charger. The connection to the anode in the plating bath is made by a flexible lead with a crocodile clip, which will vary the current according to the position in which it is clipped onto the spiral element.

In commercial plating it is quite common to copper-plate an article first, prior to the subsequent plating of gold or silver. This is done because a copper 'flash' provides a good key and could be utilized to cover solder. It is also a necessity on alloys of tin, lead or zinc because of their porosity.

The copper solution for this purpose is based on cyanide, which is highly toxic, and a typical formula would be:

Copper Cyanide	$3\frac{1}{2}$ ozs to a gallon of water
Sodium Cyanide	5 ozs to a gallon of water
Temperature	45°–60°C
Current Density	5–10 amps per square foot
Voltage	3
Anodes	Pure copper
Tank	Steel, plastic, glass, ceramic

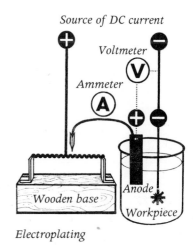

Electroplating

The free cyanide content will gradually decompose, and if any trace of green sludge appear on the anode surface, a little more sodium cyanide should be added. For normal undercoats, 5–10 seconds in the solution should be sufficient.

This solution, like nearly all other plating preparations, is available from plating supply houses and I recommend its use as proprietory salts are far more convenient for the jeweller. They come fully prepared either in mixed salt or solution form together with explicit working instructions.

Having carefully copper-plated the article, this is then swilled in clear running water to remove every vestige of chemicals ready for the next process.

Silver plating, like copper plating, is again a cyanide-based solution and although this can be made up from the following formula, I would advise that proprietory salts are used instead.

Silver Potassium Cyanide 30 per cent	6 ozs to a gallon of water
Potassium Cyanide	$\frac{1}{2}$ oz to a gallon of water
Potassium Carbonate	2 ozs to a gallon of water
Temperature	Room (18°C)
Current Density	2 amps per square foot
Voltage	0·75 volt
Anodes	Pure silver 99·99
Tank	Plastic, glass, ceramic

If the article has been copper plated, it is essential that it is connected electrically before immersion in the solution. Failure to do this can result in a simple immersion deposit of silver which has virtually no bond strength. The plating time will depend on the thickness of deposit required. A generally accepted first-class standard is 0·025 mm (0·001″) to 0·037 mm (0·0015″) thick. If real weight of silver is required, then

$$\frac{463}{\text{Amperage} \times \text{time (minutes)}} = \text{Weight in ozs Troy}$$

After a certain amount of use the anodes will become dark brown in colour denoting a lack of free cyanide. Add potassium cyanide sparingly until the anodes regain their matt white colour. A shiny crystallized appearance of the anodes denotes either lack of metal in the solution (in which case add silver potassium cyanide) or too low a temperature.

The deposit from this simple silver solution should be milky white and this can be brightened either by burnishing or scratchbrushing. In this instance the article is scratchbrushed using a fine brass wire wheel revolving at approximately 1400 rev/min. Water containing either a wetting agent or size is dripped onto the wheel as it revolves to soften the abrasive power.

Gold plating over the last decade has seen enormous technical advances, primarily due to the electronics and aerospace industries, and the 'hard bright' gold solutions that have been developed are now extensively used in the watch and jewellery industry. However these solutions require professional operation and sophisticated equipment.

For the individual jeweller who merely requires a colour or a thin deposit of metal, the time-proven cyanide-based solution is perfectly satisfactory. This can be made up as follows:

Potassium Gold Cyanide (40 per cent Fine Gold) $\frac{1}{2}$ oz/gallon
Potassium Cyanide   2 oz/gallon
Temperature   60°C
Anodes   Fine gold sheet or stainless steel
Tank   Enamelled iron or steel

The article being gold plated must be agitated or kept moving in the tank. Temperature variation of up to plus or minus 5°C and voltage variation combine with the degree to which the article is agitated in the solution to produce a complete range of colours from a cyanide gold solution.

If a stainless steel anode is used, the metal deposited will denude the solution and regular additions of gold potassium cyanide will be necessary. After some degree of use, a pinch of potassium cyanide should be added to the solution.

In all these foregoing solutions cyanide has been used. This is a highly toxic material and fatal if absorbed orally. Rubber gloves should always be used when handling any of these chemicals, and obviously great care must always be taken.

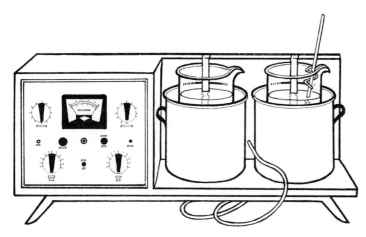

An Electroplating and Electroforming Unit

Silver gilt bracelet
F. E. McWilliam 1961

201

Gold and diamond coronet for the investiture of HRH the Prince of Wales in 1969. This was designed by Louis Osman and it was made by electroforming

Electroforming

Electroforming, by definition, is the production of articles by electroplating metal onto a reusable or expendable mandrel or mould.

As a process it has its origins in the 1830s at the birth of electrodeposition, when people like Spencer, Jacobi and Jordan were experimenting with silver and copper plating on gutta percha moulds. Among the patents subsequently filed at that time were those of the famous Elkington cousins who started the electroplated domestic tableware industry. There are still many splendid electroformed wall plaques in existence, for which the original master was beautifully chased and engraved.

However, during this period there was no shortage of skilled craftsmen, such as silversmiths, chasers, engravers, etc, and despite its capacity for mass production, electroforming was not competitive enough in price to allow for development. It become dormant as a process until the late 1930s and the Second World War. The post-war boom in microwave technology, spark erosion technique and plastic moulding produced a great interest in copper and nickel forming for tools, wave guides, etc.

In the silver and jewellery trades, it gradually became apparent that there was now a shortage of skilled craftsmen, and therefore of handmade work, and this encouraged investigation into methods of mass production. A research and development programme was instigated by B.J.S. Electro Plating Company Ltd in order to produce a commercial precious metal electroforming process.

By utilizing and modifying modern plating solutions and employing modern plastics technology, a practical 'forming' process was evolved, culminating in the manufacture of the coronet for H.R.H. The Prince of Wales. Today, many thousands of grams of silver and gold are electroformed as complete items and as piece parts in the silver and jewellery trades.

Electroforms

There are two ways of producing an electroform. The first is by taking a re-useable negative impression of the master and plating from the final outside surface inwards. The second method is by moulding the article in wax or a low melting point alloy (ie tin/bismuth), plating it, and when the plating is sufficiently thick, melting out the original pattern and leaving the electroplated shell.

The first method is the more commercial process. The master pattern should preferably be made of metal, but wax and plaster can be used. If plaster is used, it must be thoroughly sealed first. Three basic moulding materials can be used – epoxy resin, poly vinyl chloride and silicone rubber. The choice of which of these to use will be governed by the master pattern. The rubber cures at room temperature, the resin is exothermic and generates some heat, and the PVC has to be oven cured.

The master pattern is placed in a suitable moulding box and the mould material poured in. It is advisable to paint the master pattern with wax or a release agent and if possible to put the box under vacuum to remove any air bubbles. When thoroughly set the mould is removed from the box, warmed, and the master pattern extracted, leaving a perfect negative impression. A copper wire should then be pinned to the edge of the mould prior to metallizing and plating.

The second method of electroforming using a wax or a low melting point alloy casting uses the sculptor's lost wax casting technique, and this has been explained in the section on casting. The next operation is to make the surface of the mould electrically conductive for the plating process. Attach a copper wire to the mould by which it can be suspended.

The simplest, cheapest and oldest method of making a surface electrically conductive is by dusting it with graphite or plumbago. This black powder is brushed into the surface of the mould area to be plated, using a very soft brush and applying the powder liberally. If the surface is large, it will be necessary to have a number of connecting wires, as graphite is not a very good conductor, particularly in the initial plating stage.

There is also a fine silver flake which is applied in much the same manner as graphite. This has a greater capacity for conducting electricity. A silver dispersion (ie a silver powder in lacquer) is the most efficient of this type of material and is applied by brushing. The commercial process of metallizing is wet silvering. This necessitates not only initial cleaning of the mould but sensitizing in a stannous chloride solution and then precipitating silver onto the surface by spraying with a solution of silver nitrate and a reducing agent such as formaldehyde.

Electricity is lazy. It will plate or form heavily where accessible and lightly where difficult. The more that is plated on, the more it will build up badly

In plating over a large surface, the plating will get thin in the centre

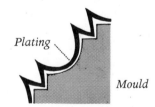

Plating

Mould

Plating will build up badly around a sharp cornered mould

A round edged box will plate more evenly than a square edged one

This involves the use of a twin-nozzle spray gun and sophisticated equipment, and I do not advise attempting to use it when one of the simpler methods can be used instead.

SILVER FORMING

The commercial silver plating process has to be sophisticated to achieve the desired metallurgical properties. As the forms have been made from pure silver, they will become soft when soldering has to be done. One solution to this problem has been patented by B.J.S. Electro Plating Company Ltd, who have produced a silver deposit which age-hardens after annealing. However, providing highly complex electro-forms are not attempted the simple silver plating solution described in electroplating can be used.

It is important that the area is measured reasonably accurately and the current applied at 3–4 amps per square foot. Agitation of the solution is helpful – an aquarium aerator will be sufficient for most purposes.

The addition of 5 gm per litre of potassium hydroxide and 3 gm of sodium thiosulphate per litre should aid the conductivity and grain refinement. When the mould is put into the solution, start with a small current (30 per cent of final) and increase as the surface coating builds up. If the electroform has to be soldered, care should be taken not to break the current as this causes exfoilation of the silver when heated.

To calculate the thickness of deposit, the following formulae can be used:
1 square foot 0·001" thick weighs approx. 0·008 ozs Troy.
463 amp/min (Time of deposition in mins × amperage) = 1 oz Troy.

The foregoing has been based on a set-up of 2 to 3 gallons tank capacity. If a larger set-up is envisaged, then constant filtration, agitation and accurate electrical control will be necessary.

GOLD FORMING

Gold forming has only recently become commercially viable. The forms are of 24 carat and easily solderable. However there are many proprietary solutions available which do not meet these requirements and would, in addition, result in electroforms that are highly stressed and subject to distortion. Care should be taken, therefore, when selecting a solution, to ensure that the deposit will meet all the necessary requirements. These solutions are expensive and build slowly.

Design Criteria

The moulding materials used in electroforming, if effectively employed, will reproduce very fine surface detail accurately and many times. It is important therefore that the master pattern be as near perfect as possible. This characteristic of 'honest copy' allows for the reproduction of natural materials and items such as leaves, rock faces, leather, wood grain, etc. Moulds will only reproduce in one plane, therefore

204

items in further dimensions (ie back or top, etc) will need to have multiple moulds and the forms fabricated.

It should always be remembered that plastics have a $1\frac{1}{2}$–2 per cent shrinkage on curing. Shallow undercuts in the master pattern are acceptable, but obviously deep undercuts impose a great tear strain on the mould during parting, particularly if a number of forms are to be made from the mould. Sharp edges and corners will also tend to cut the mould and these should be softened or radiused if possible. Boxes, for a long time an electroformer's production dream, suffer from corner weakness.

This means that due to the way the plating 'grows' in the corners, they are weak and should be avoided as a project. Electro deposition does not cover evenly over an area. Because electricity is lazy and the attraction is for the highlights, peaks and edges which build up quicker. Therefore the centres and valleys are weaker.

Electroforming is a process that can be complementary to the silversmith and goldsmith, by the utilization of skills from a totally different source. It also offers one major advantage: the craftsman need produce only one master pattern, from which can come absolutely accurate reproduction in unlimited quantity.

The Gold Helmet of Ur, circa 2700 BC. The original is in the Iraq Museum and this electroformed copy is in the British Museum

Romania. Gold helmet from Coţofeneşti, 4th century BC. Cap of helmet decorated with rosettes, and lower section with apotropaic eyes and rectangular cheek and neck guards.

Silver Rhyton in the form of a deer's head, before 4th century BC, from Rozovetz, region of Plovdiv.

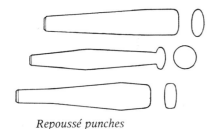

Repoussé punch should be held upright

Repoussé punches

Repoussé and Chasing

Repoussé is the technique of raising-up design and ornament three dimensionally from one flat sheet of metal. Chasing is the more detailed work of defining and completing the three-dimensional shapes. In repoussé the metal is hammered up from the back to make the bigger forms of the design, and chasing is done from the front to refine the detail and add the final precision to the design. However, these two techniques overlap and interchange very much.

The metal will be repeatedly worked from both back and front, as work on the reverse is taken as far as needed and the metal then turned over to continue raising, forming and detailing it from the front, and reversed again to continue raising from the back, so that both repoussé and chasing are used on both faces of the metal.

Embossing is also involved, as the actual process of raising the metal is often called 'bossing' it up, and engraving too may be used on the design to incise particularly fine sharp detail. Repoussé work therefore can be seen to include four techniques, but for simplicity I intend to include embossing and engraving within the meaning of repoussé and chasing.

The real quality of good repoussé lies in the visual effect of the one sheet of metal having been hand worked, to give the heights and recesses on which the fall of light and shade will enhance the design. There should not be the impression that the work was made by joining several pieces of metal.

As the metal is being stretched and enlarged, too thin a gauge could be distorted. In general 0·028 gauge would be suitable for small work and 0·036 used for larger work.

As the metal will be raised by hammering it with punches, it must be laid over a base that is resilient enough to accept the forming of the metal. Pitch is the traditional material for this, but as it is brittle it needs to be rendered more plastic by combining it with other materials.

The recipe for the pitch composition is made by melting together six parts of pitch, eight parts of plaster of Paris (or brickdust), one part of resin and one part of linseed oil. (Linseed oil or tallow is used to soften the mixture and in cold weather slightly more may be needed to give the right consistency.) Handle the pitch carefully as it is inflammable.

The metal is to be stuck on to the pitch base and must be supported by it at all times to avoid distortion. Small work can be handled easily in a pitch bowl. For this a cast iron bowl is filled with the pitch mixture and the metal will stick when placed on the hot pitch. The bowl can be rested in a ring of coiled rope to keep it steady, and angled into any position. Small work can also be raised without pitch by handling it on an engraver's sand bag, or a base of lead or wax, but the definition will not be as clear as if worked on pitch.

For larger work, a pitch board is used. This is a block of hard wood, larger than the design, onto which a base of pitch is poured. It may need a second coat for thickness. The metal front is greased and pressed face down onto the hot pitch. Press its sides into the pitch gently so that the pitch will overflow slightly onto the edges and so secure them.

When the design has been decided on, it is transferred to the back of the annealled, pickled metal either by drawing directly on to the metal, transferring the drawn design by using carbon paper, or gluing the paper design on and pricking its shape through onto the metal. In either case, the design will need to be lightly but clearly pricked into the metal so that it doesn't disappear as the work progresses.

Because the work will mainly be done in reverse relief and therefore may be confusing, it could be helpful to make a three-dimensional plasticine model of the design to refer to. It also may be easier to start by practising on simple symmetrical shapes, maintaining centre lines and other reference points that could be useful. Leave a margin of at least 25 mm (1″) of metal all around the design which can be subsequently saw pierced out.

Repoussé and chasing tools are basically the same and predominantly interchangeable except that those used for repoussé will usually have blunter, rounder heads, and chasing tools will be flatter, finer edged. They are small punches, about 10 cm (4″) long, sometimes misnamed 'chisels'. Both will have the corners rounded off so that they cannot dig sharply into the metal. They will be made of hardened and tempered steel, but could be lignum vitae, boxwood or hard brass if these serve the purpose better. They come in four main groups – bossing tools, with curved blunted ends for raising the main bulk of the design, tracers for delineating and detailing, shaping tools, such as burnishers, and texturing tools, with ends that may have a pattern of repeating units, hatched textures, matted or grained surfaces etc.

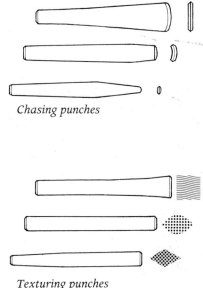

Chasing punches

Texturing punches

Repoussé. Inscribe the design on the metal. The repoussé is started by beating up from the back, and completed by chasing from the front

207

Repoussé hammer

A sandbag and rope ring for resting work on

The Agighiol Treasure. Silver helmet worked in repoussé and poinçonné (perforated stamped) partially gilded, c. 400 BC National Museum of Antiquities, Bucharest

Repoussé Acanthus Leaf by William Stace, c. 1890

Repoussé work is a good example of an instance where it may be very helpful to make your own tools for specific purposes.

Boxwood punches and mallets with rounded ends can be used for hammering up large work. There is a repoussé hammer designed with a special handle to give it the springy action needed in this work. It also has a broad face, making it easier to strike the repoussé punches.

In use the repoussé punch is held upright and most easily managed by holding it with thumb and first finger of the left hand, using the second finger to keep it in position, and the third and fourth fingers pressing down on the work to guide the punch along. The hammer is used with a light, easy regular motion, and should be handled so that you are looking at the work as you move along, and not at the hammer.

The chasing punch is angled in use, however, so that the design is more clearly visible as you are working on it.

The large areas of metal must be hammered when the pitch is warm, partially for resiliency, and partially to maintain contact with the pitch all the time. The detail can, however, be put in when the pitch is cool.

Start by raising the largest areas of ornament first as they will most probably be the highest, and work down with the differently shaped punches, as the design requires, through increasingly smaller sections until the detail is reached. If the pitch cools, warm it via the metal with the torch.

The aim is to keep the punch on the move all the time, with light tapping rather than hammering, and circling steadily over the whole area to indent lightly and then circling again to indent further, as if one were stroking the metal with a series of gentle punch marks, gradually forming by a continuous fluid forward movement.

As the metal gives and stretches it becomes work hardened and will need annealling.

To release the metal so that you can work on the other side or for annealling, heat the metal to melt the pitch, and hold it in the heat for a few seconds so that the grease and pitch coating will be easier to remove. Do this by rubbing initially with cotton waste and clean oil or paraffin, and then brush hard with turps and dry out in boxwood sawdust. Pitch that may have been burnt on is hard to remove, and the simplest way may be to anneal the work fully and plunge it into cold water.

When the other side of the metal is ready for working, it must be greased and stuck down again into the pitch and the repoussé process continued. When the forming is complete the work will need to be finished in the usual way, but being careful to preserve the textures.

The acanthus leaf design illustrated was made by William Stace, designer, modeller and repoussé worker in about 1890. After raising, it was outlined with a blunt tracer, restuck on the pitch and modelled with a planisher that had been allowed to rust, to give it the texture of a very worn mixed mat punch. The design was then matted with a soft-grain mat punch throughout the leaf. The vase shape from which the leaf springs was partly formed from the front, for delineation, and then put in from the back and the stem finished with smooth planishers to contrast with the soft grain of the foliage.

Mycenaean gold pendant in shape of a pomegranate with granulated detail. Total height 36 mm, diameter 25 mm. From Enkomi, Cyprus, 1400 BC

Granulation

Granulation is a form of surface decoration practised by the Ancient Greeks and Etruscans, and evidence suggests that the technique originated in Mesopotamia, Syria and Asia Minor. A primitive example was found in the treasure of Ur, 2500 B.C., and in the Treasure of Troy II (2200 B.C.) and Byblos (2000 B.C.) fully developed granulation appeared. Granulated work was found in Crete from 1800 to 1100 B.C. and in Greece from 1550 to 1100 B.C. The Dark Ages followed until 800 B.C. and shortly after this, granulation was again practised in Greece and finally brought to its peak of technical perfection by the Etruscans from 700 to 600 B.C.

The technique was of astounding delicacy and precision, and consisted of attaching the most minute spheres of pure gold to a pure gold base without the use of solder as we know it. These infinitesimal spheres are massed to make a decorative area or linear design. There is a bowl in the Victoria and Albert Museum called the Praeneste Bowl which has an estimated 137,000 grains on it, and yet it is only about 75 mm high × 120 mm in diameter. These grains are about the diameter of a fine needle. In the late Bronze Age grains measured as little as 0·4 mm, and in the finest Etruscan work grains as small as 0·25 mm and even 0·14 mm were used. The Enkomi ball pendant illustrated will give some idea of the quality – it has about 4,200 grains on the ball, and the ball measures only 25 mm in diameter and 36 mm in total height.

The knowledge of the technique seems to have died about 1000 A.D.

and remained a mystery until early 1800 when a jeweller in Rome called Fortunato Pio Castellani researched the subject and found that crafts-men in a small village in Umbria were practising a similar technique, but although he used their knowledge to make granulated work the actual technique was never divulged by him.

A jeweller and a scholar, H. A. P. Littledale, working in London, having researched the subject very thoroughly, gave a lecture on it at the Goldsmiths Hall in 1936. In this he described his discovery of what he thought was the most likely solution as to how granulation work was made. He practised the technique by copying a number of pieces of granulated work and in my opinion they are of an even superior standard to the originals. His explanation of the method he used follows.

In 1961, W. Haendel published an article on the subject: 'Eutectic Soldering', and in 1974 Michael Jackson wrote on the same subject – 'Granulation' – based on research carried out at Sir John Cass College, for the Worshipful Company of Goldsmiths.

Mr Littledale's lecture was printed as a paper: 'Lecture IV, February 24th 1936. A new process of Hard-Soldering and its possible connection with the methods used by the Ancient Greeks and Etruscans', and a brief précis of it is as follows:

A very distinctive type of gold work, called granulation, was made in Greece and Etruria from approximately 1400 B.C. to 400 B.C. The art of making it seems to have been lost round about the beginning of the Christian era, and ever since there has been a mystery surrounding it; no one can explain how it came into existence.

(The technique of granulation consists of attaching minute spheres of metal to a metal background as decoration.)

Two methods have been used in attempts to reproduce the grain work of the Ancients – the first is metallic hard soldering and the second autogenous soldering, more commonly known as sweating. The people who started the art of granulation lived in the Bronze Age, that is to say, their tools and domestic utensils were made of copper or bronze. Lacking iron or steel tools it is doubtful if they could have filed their solder up into a fine powder, which is one of the theories that has been put forward. So the explanation of hard-soldering must be ruled out. The other process of joining metals, known as sweating, requires raising the work to such a high temperature that it is on the verge of melting. This, when cleverly done, does make an almost invisible join, but the delicacy of granulation work would never withstand such heat, so the explanation of sweating being used is equally non-viable.

In searching for a third alternative the difficulties of the technique become apparent: although hard soldering was not used, some form of metal to metal joining is essential, therefore some form of 'solder' has to be used. The principal difficulty is to divide the 'solder' – or whatever is to be used – into fine enough pieces, and then to cause it to flow without the flux displacing the tiny grains being used.

The third difficulty is to ensure that the grains do not fall off the work by gravity, as a lot of the work was done in the round. There would have to have been a very reliable adhesive securing the grains underneath the object at the time of heating.

Etruscan Gold Votive Bracelet. 7th century BC.

A solution to the solder dividing was to divide it by chemical means rather than mechanically, and a solution to the flux displacement was not to use any flux. The problem of the grains falling off was left in abeyance, in the hope that it might solve itself.

The joining process was to be based on the use of copper, in some form, as a joining agent. Everyone who has done any practical silver work knows that it is dangerous to use copper binding-wire to hold the work together while firing, because this may cause a melt-up when the work is heated. In fact, it is possible to use that principle actually to make a joint, but not worth doing because of the difficulty of dividing up the copper, a difficulty just as great as that of dividing up solder. And yet it is just that principle which underlies the process to be used. Only, instead of trying to divide the copper mechanically it will be divided chemically.

The principle concerned is that gold and copper, or silver and copper, when in contact, mutually melt each other at a temperature far below the melting-point of either of the metals concerned. The melting temperature is, curiously enough, always the same. Gold and copper flush each other at 890°C, although their own melting points are 1062°C and 1084°C respectively. Silver and copper flush each other at 890°C although their melting points are 962°C and 1084°C. Copper, therefore, is able to cause gold and silver to melt at 890°C.

The diagram of melting points of gold and silver alloys with copper shows at its base the proportion of copper in each alloy: the silver–copper curve shows the alloy to be $7\frac{1}{2}$ per cent copper and $92\frac{1}{2}$ per cent silver, and the gold–copper curve shows the alloy to be 20 per cent copper and 80 per cent gold. That is to say, for each part of copper introduced at first the result will be a melt of four parts of gold – total, five parts of molten metal.

That will not produce strong jointing and so on gold the temperature can be allowed to run up to 940°C with the result that more gold joins the melt. The higher the temperature, the greater the amount of molten metal and the better the fineness. On gold, it is quite safe to raise the temperature to 1000°C, and much of the ancient work was probably fired at least as high as that. The alloy has now 3 per cent copper, 97 per cent gold. In fact, the copper content could be reduced further, for, when fired at 1000°C fine gold can be soldered with an alloy as fine as 23·28 carats. This fineness of the metal in the joints would account for the lack of discolouration in the joints of ancient work which has caused so much interest among researchers.

As stated, copper can cause gold to melt at 890°C, and the intention was to endeavour to use copper in some form as the joining agent. For this it would have to be very substantially reduced in content. This is done by obtaining copper oxide (when copper is heated the oxygen in the air combines with it to form a black scale which is oxide of copper) and adding carbon to it. When these are heated sufficiently the carbon removes the oxygen, leaving behind pure copper in a very finely divided state.

Having explained the general principles they were put into practice in the following way: A copper salt is required – these are many besides

Large gold fibula with granulation and stamping. Etruscan 7th century BC.

Gold earring with pierced and relief figures decorated with granulation from the Aliseda Treasure. 6th century BC.

the simple oxide that has been described, and it was found that the most efficient is copper hydrate $Cu(OH)_2$. This is a greenish-blue salt, scarcely soluble in water but easily ground to a fine powder. This is moistened and its own bulk of ordinary Seccotine glue added to it. It is mixed until very smooth, and can then be diluted with water until very thin indeed. This mixture is a strong adhesive and the grains are simply stuck on the work, using fine brushes to handle them. Used thinly it dries quickly and can be recoated until all the joins are filled up, but without a surplus spreading over the work. It is cleaned up with a brush dipped in ammonia and water and is thus ready for the fire, preferably a muffle furnace.

The adhesive compound will be visible as a green streak filling up every join. The furnace should be at least as high as 900°C. Place the work in the furnace and after some minutes it will attain the same temperature as the furnace. By the time the work has reached a temperature of 100°C the copper hydrate will have changed into oxide, and the green salt turned black. At 100°C plain glue would certainly bubble but the salt seems to take up all the water from this glue and prevents bubbling and displacement. The temperature of the work rises and at 600°C the glue carbonizes, ie burns. One now has copper oxide packed with carbon within the joins of the work. The heat continues to rise. At about 850°C the copper oxide can no longer retain the oxygen it holds. It parts with it to the carbon. All that is left within the joins is a streak of copper. The temperature continues to rise. By the time the copper has got itself reduced (that is the correct term for what has happened) from the oxide to the metallic state the temperature is at 890°C. It has been established that copper and gold when in contact and heated to 890°C will melt each other that is what happens now. The streak of metallic copper in the joint flushes with the gold and the parts are joined. As soon as the flush has taken place the work is removed from the fire. It really is all very simple.

One may wonder 'How could the Ancients ever have come across such a process?' But their tools and vessels were bronze and copper, and as copper when heated, for instance in cooking, produces copper oxide, and as these same copper vessels would have been used in making glue, it is possible that at some time, by accident, the combination of copper salts, glue and fine pieces of precious metal came together, and this fascinating technique evolved from there.

Metal Techniques

Filigree

Filigree is made of the most delicate wires, threads and beads, either as ornament on jewellery, or the whole piece can be made of filigree. The wires can be turned into shape with very delicate round nose and half round nose pliers, and will be so fine that they could even be shaped with the fingers. A very experienced jeweller is capable of saw-piercing filigree work, but the use of wire is easier for most people.

The design can be arranged on a charcoal block, after each individual unit, however small, has been warmed, boraxed and annealed. The borax will hold the units together as they are being soldered. For larger decoration, a pattern block can be made by putting pins or wooden rods into a wood block to establish the pattern, and the wire can be wound around these. This has the advantage that the pattern can be duplicated accurately.

In the same way, a repeating curve is obtained by winding wire around nails driven into a block at staggered intervals. If they are staggered and positioned just on either side of a central line, they can also be used to straighten bent wire. When wire is drawn through the drawplate it tends to come out in a curve, and this is difficult to straighten by hammering because of the risk of damage, but clamping it at one end and pulling it through the wires will straighten it without damage.

To make a very tight scroll out of filigree wire, one can wind it around a needle. Hold the needle upright in a vice, having wound a

Gold Hercules knot, classical
Greek filigree work. From
Ginosa, 4th century BC.

little of the wire around the needle beforehand. Thread the unsecured wire end through a washer and put this over the top of the needle. The washer provides a base on which the wire can be held flat while it is being wound around the needle into a coil. If it has been annealed properly the wire can be spiralled flat, and one wire won't ride up over the other.

Engraving

Examples of engraving

Jewellery engraving may take the form of decorating a surface, or using lettering upon it, as inscriptions on brooches, medallions, trophies and other articles. It is work for a specialist craftsman. Were it for decoration alone, the designer's intention and his ability to engrave may mean that he is able to carry out the work himself, but if lettering is to be engraved on jewellery an additional ability is required, and that is a distinguished craft in itself – lettering and calligraphy.

The qualities of lettering are understood less and less as the printing used in mass media increases, but the craft is one in which aesthetic judgment and sympathy are as essential as in any other. Until the student has some knowledge of the essentials of lettering it is pointless to attempt it – for it oddly enough betrays ignorance more readily than many media.

Die Stamping

An example of die stamping

This is the mechanical process of stamping out metal in relief. Two steel dies are made of the design, the top with the design in relief and the bottom with the design recessed in intaglio. They are placed in the die stamping press, the metal sheet is laid over the bottom die, and the top die brought down with force, pushing the sheet down into the concavities of the bottom die.

The cutting of the dies is an extremely skilled technique, and they are consequently expensive to make, but this is offset by the fact that, once made, their production capacity is unlimited, and they provide one of the cheaper ways of mass-producing jewellery in quantity. The steel die can be carved with a very fine degree of detail and modelling, and is usually reserved for work where this precision is a necessity, as in making medallions, badges or any other work with fine, precise detail such as lettering on it. The craftsmen who make the dies are known as die-sinkers, and are exceptionally skilled in their work, especially as much of it is done in reverse.

Diamond Milling

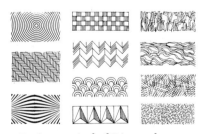

Designs typical of Diamond Milling

Diamond milling is a modern process of applying bright, sharp, cut textures to metal. It is done by machine, using a diamond-tipped tool that will cut an incalculable number of different textures, ranging from those that are precise and regular to freer and seemingly random designs. The tool gives such a bright finish that final buffing and polishing are unnecessary.

214

Its most extensive uses are on wedding rings, bracelets, watch straps, etc, on which its complexity of texture can be utilized in mass production for relatively little expenditure. The machine has not supplanted texturing by hand with gravers, scorpers and other tools, and the two processes can be combined, as for example, in watches, where the dial may be machine-textured and the band of an expensive watch hand-textured, or hand engraving may be overlaid on machined work to add subtlety to the texture.

Engine turning is also a mechanical method of texturing metal, and is done on a complex lathe. It makes a shallow surface texture unlike the deeper cuts of diamond milling, and does require finishing by polishing. It is predominantly used for cigarette cases, cigarette lighters, compacts and similar, simple shapes.

Gilding

Gilding has been used from ancient times. Its earliest application was to use an adhesive to attach gold leaf to an object, and when necessary burnish it into shape. Another procedure known as 'amalgamation' was to pulverize powdered gold in a mortar, and then mix it with mercury until they amalgamated. The resulting 'paste' was spread over the metal, and the mercury was subsequently vaporized, leaving the gold deposit. This dangerous technique has been superseded by electroplating.

Seal Engraving

Seals have been used from ancient times as a form of signature. Literacy has tended to make them redundant, but they retain a decorative use. In the original form the seal would have had the owner's symbol cut into it in intaglio, and this was impressed, originally into clay and subsequently into wax, to make his mark. The earliest seals date from Western Asia, 6500–6000 B.C., and were made of clay, geometrically decorated. From 4000 B.C. onwards cylindrical stone seals were used, originating in Mesopotamia, and subsequently in Egypt and Greece. Amulet seals with apotropaic significance were also used.

By 400 B.C. in Greece the seal had been incorporated into a signet ring, and this version of it has continued until the present. Seal cutting reached its peak in the Renaissance in both aesthetic and practical terms. By the 18th century they were often worn decoratively as fobs on chains. Only soft stone could be used in the earliest times (eg steatite) but harder stones such as hematite and cornelian were later engraved, and as stone cutting techniques developed, amethyst, garnet, agate and rock crystal could be used.

The technique of seal cutting is still practised in both metal and stone, but is becoming more rare and skilled craftsmen fewer. It is an extremely difficult technique, both for the precision and delicacy required on such a small scale, and the difficulty of carving the symbol in reverse.

The Petrossa Eagle, gold and garnets, 4th century Barbarian. Open work piercing of metal of this type was popular in late Roman jewellery, called Opus Interassile

The seal and its impression of Andrea della Valle, Cardinal (1517–1534) Ashmolean Museum, Oxford

Medallion of Emperor Charles V, gold and enamel bloodstone, lapis lazuli, Italian, c.1540

'Fused' or 'Melted' Metal

This is a technique used for surface decoration in which the metal is heated just sufficiently to begin to flow, forming its own free shapes as it does so, and producing a molten, almost 'volcanic' surface texture.

The texturing must be done prior to making up the work, or the heat used may destroy structural solderings. If it is possible, use a metal sheet considerably larger than the final requirement, so that you can select the area where the random flowing of the metal has worked most successfully. The metal may need a number of workings to produce a satisfactory result because one has little control over the shapes it will form.

Start by heating the surface with a torch until the metal is just at melting point. The instant the metal begins to flow, remove the flame. The abrupt removal of heat causes the metal to solidify at once. One then has to persist in the heatings until a satisfactory texture is obtained. Overheating, of course, will ultimately melt the sheet.

Further textures or roughened surfaces are obtainable by scattering small pieces of metal, or metal filings, over the boraxed surface and heating carefully until they fuse.

Gold cigarette case using fused metal as decoration (Samorodok) Fabergé

216

VII IMPROVIZED TOOLS AND TECHNIQUES

Improvized tools and techniques

There will often be instances when you may not be able to buy, find or afford a tool for a specific purpose. You could, of course, order a tool to be made but this would be expensive. It is possible to struggle through, using incorrect tools, but inevitably the result will be less than perfect and additional time will be needed to correct the faults.

This time could be much better spent by making the specific tool for the job. It is not a formidable task and the time it involves will repay you in quality of craftsmanship. I have devised and learnt a number of ways of improvizing, and you will be able to do the same as your knowledge of the craft increases.

JOINTING TOOL OR CHENIER SPACER

A jointing tool or chenier spacer is designed to allow you to cut pieces of chenier or wire accurately into equal lengths (as, for instance, when making the joints for a box or locket). In the first tool shown the chenier is inserted into the aperture in the tool, secured there with a thumb screw and the end filed flush with the face of the jointing tool. The other end is then sawn through and filed flush, the chenier therefore is exactly the width of the jointing tool. (Because the tool is hardened and tempered steel it will not be damaged by the file passing over its surface.) The screws are then released to free the piece of chenier and the process repeated until you have the required number of joints.

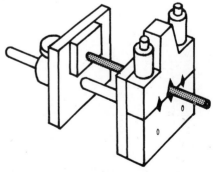

Jointing tool made by Fred Swift

217

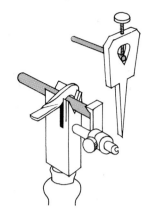

Jointing tool

The tool is available in a range of thicknesses to suit most jointing requirements up to 3 mm ($\frac{1}{8}''$) in diameter and 8 mm ($\frac{1}{4}''$) in length. For the larger sizes of wire or chenier from 3 mm ($\frac{1}{8}''$) to 12·5 mm ($\frac{1}{2}''$) diameter and up to 7·5 cm (3") in length the second tool shown is used. This tool has an adjustable spacing device. The chenier is laid in the V slot, the thumbscrew piece moved to the required length, the chenier is secured in position by the lever and sawn through in the guiding slot made for this purpose.

I use a hand-made jointing tool which was designed specifically for me. It is an improvement upon those that are commercially available, insofar as it will accommodate bigger and longer pieces of wire and chenier even more accurately. It is also more convenient in use as it can be clamped to the bench, leaving both hands free, whereas the other two are hand-held.

Its face is made of two plates on which are three apertures of varying sizes. These can be enlarged to hold wire up to 12·5 mm ($\frac{1}{2}''$) diameter and approximately 7·5 cm (3") in length, by unscrewing the locking screws and separating the two plates. The chenier is inserted and stopped at the required length by the distance spacer. This is locked. The two plates are tightened on the chenier by the screws.

In this case the guiding slot for the saw is immediately behind the face of the plates. When the chenier is sawn through here, it will be flush with the end and at an accurate right angle to the long axis of the chenier, requiring no further filing. Using a back saw that will just fit the slot, it is evident that it would be impossible to make a crooked cut.

A STONE-SETTING TOOL

I describe this tool as a 'pushing over' tool as it is used to push the metal over the edge of a stone as you are setting it. Make it from a rod of Stubbs steel about 3 mm ($\frac{1}{8}''$) diameter and about 7·5 cm (3") to 9 cm ($3\frac{1}{2}''$) long. One end is then tapered and this is forced into a scorper handle. The rest of the rod is polished and its end is left unpolished and flat. When you are holding the tool, the rod should not project much more than 12 mm ($\frac{1}{2}''$) beyond your thumb. If it were too long it would be unwieldy, and because of the extreme pressure to be used there would be a tendency for it to break or bend. Near the end an angle of 90° is filed into it, starting one arm of the angle just before the flat end. This angle is filed halfway into the rod.

The tool can then be used to set a stone that is positioned very close to another stone as the notch will clear the other setting while the first stone and setting are being worked on. The flat end of the tool is held against the setting and when pressure is exerted, the tool pushes the metal over the stone.

An important point to remember about pushing over tools, scorpers and gravers is that you must make certain that the tool is firmly embedded in the handle and that the shaft of the tool is not too fine. Because of the pressure needed, the shafts are likely to break if they are too long or too thin, and this could cause injury.

Leave the end of the pushing over tool unpolished, and should it

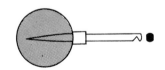

Stone-setting tool

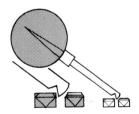

The cut out angle allows it to fit between two stones to push the metal over

become polished by use, roughen it slightly with emery paper, as, if it is too smooth it may slip on to the stone in the course of setting and damage it.

DOMING DIES

There will be occasions when you may want to make domed shapes. Semispheres can be made in the doming die up to about 5 cm (2″) in diameter. If a larger size is needed or a domed shape other than a semisphere or hemisphere, such as an oval, this will have to be improvised by making your own doming die. These can be made of lead, lead/tin alloy, epoxide cream putties, or a close grained hardwood such as boxwood or beech. The tool plumbers use for beating lead is a boxwood mallet and domed shapes could be carved into the thicker end of this, or similar ready-made shapes.

A plumber's boxwood lead beater

LEAD, TIN, ALLOY OR EPOXIDE PUTTY DIES

Dies of lead, tin, alloy or epoxide putties can be made by, in effect, casting around a model of the desired shape. An ideal shape for a hemispherical die larger than those available can be produced by allowing plaster to set in a hemispherical rubber bowl. Mix enough investment plaster to give the size you require in the rubber bowl. When set, merely squeezing the sides of the bowl will dislodge the hemisphere of plaster. This is the model around which the lead/tin alloy or the epoxide putty will be poured.

To facilitate removal of the plaster model make a handle for it from a bolt 5 cm (2″) or 7·5 cm (3″) long, or from strands of heavy twisted wire. Before the plaster sets in the bowl put the handle part way into the plaster and hold it in position until setting is complete. When set, remove the plaster dome and dry it out thoroughly in an oven or kiln.

Make a handle for the plaster model

The lead or epoxide is now to be poured around this shape. This can be done in a tin large enough to accommodate the dome, leaving roughly 25 mm (1″) on either side and 12 mm ($\frac{1}{2}$″) at the bottom. If there is a rim on the tin cut it off or it will interfere with the removal of the contents. If necessary, cut down its height so that the dome can be handled conveniently within the tin. Slightly grease the inside of the tin to facilitate removal. Melt the lead and pour it into the tin or, if using epoxide, mix it and pour it into the tin.

While the lead is still molten or the epoxide still soft, lower the plaster dome down into the tin. Hold its handle with tongs if using lead as the handle will become hot. The plaster dome should be pushed down until sufficient lead or epoxide is displaced to rise to the level of the plaster surface, but do not allow it to overflow onto the surface of the plaster or it will be difficult to remove. Make sure that the lead or epoxide is at least $\frac{1}{2}$″ thick below the plaster dome. Hold the dome in position until the material in the tin is set. When using lead make sure that the tin has no water at all in it or the hot lead will splash.

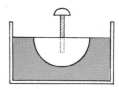

The model is pushed down into the mixture

Neither material will stick to the plaster so it can be removed quite easily by its handle. The lead or epoxide must be taken out of the tin,

The concave die

and if there is difficulty in getting it out, cut the tin away with shears. You will now have your concave die shape. One of the advantages of using a lead die is that metal, when hammered into it is unlikely to be marked in shaping because of the lead's softness.

The model for an oval die can be filed out of the hemispherical plaster dome

OVAL DIE

An oval die can be made by following out the same procedure, but the plaster dome can be filed into the required oval, using a Surform, wood rasps, coarse files, and emery paper. It helps to have made an oval template of copper or brass. Cast this shape as before.

Any domed shape can be made in this way, or another alternative is to simply pour lead into a tin to get a lead block or lead cake, and carve the dome into this, using burrs, fraisers, rotary files, chisels, dome-faced hammers, etc. It may be difficult to make it a regular shape, so use a template for checking.

IDEAS FOR OTHER SHAPES

Explore the field of objets trouvées for shapes on which metal can be formed. There are interesting possibilities in much that is discarded: scrap yards, engineering works, wood workers, plastics and laminate factories, demolition sites, dental and hospital discards, worn out car parts, all have wasted material that an inventive jeweller can use for either form or ideas. The possibilities are unlimited if you can teach yourself to be aware of shape.

TO DOME AN OVAL OR RECTANGLE

As far as I know, dies to dome oval or rectangular shapes cannot be bought. However, the following technique makes it possible to dome these shapes: the doming die is used in conjunction with the swage block to form the metal.

For an oval dome, place the flat metal shape in the largest doming hollow of the die and start to form it with the mating punch for the hole. Keep forming it in the die until you have achieved the depth of dome you want. This may necessitate moving down to smaller holes.

When the depth is reached you will see that the long axis of the oval is higher at the ends than the rest. To counteract this, place it in the closest fitting channel of the swage block with its long axis running along the channel of the block. Lay in it a wooden punch that corresponds as much as possible in size. Start to lightly tap along the length of the punch with a hammer, and this will begin to flatten the raised ends of the oval. As the ends are tapped down, the sides will rise to be almost level. Then invert it and place it on a flat steel block and with a wooden hammer tap the sides, close to the edges, down onto the steel block until it sits level.

A rectangle is domed in exactly the same way.

Using the doming die

ARROW HEAD DRILL

A particularly useful drill for the drill stock is the arrow head drill. It is used either to drill a hole straight through metal or to make a tapered hole.

The arrow head drill is shaped as its name suggests. They can be bought, but it is common practice for each craftsman to make his own for his particular needs.

If you decide to make your own arrow head drill, there are two ways of doing so.

1. Use steel rod which is not hardened and tempered. The rod should be approximately the diameter of the hole to be drilled. One end is ground with a flat on either side, to the required taper of the hole, using carborundum stone, so that a flattened arrowhead shape results. Behind the head the shaft is narrowed. This is done so that when the arrowhead has made the hole the shaft will not touch the sides. The narrowing is continued approximately half-way up the length of the shaft and the other half remains at its original diameter, which fits one of the chucks. It then requires sharpening on an Arkansas oil stone.

The edges of the arrowhead are to be sharpened, but only one edge on one side and the opposite edge on the other side. Sharpen them to roughly a 45° angle. The drill then has two cutting edges. As the drill stock works by revolving in a full circle in one direction, clockwise, and then reversing its direction in a full circle, anti-clockwise, in both movements the two sharpened edges of the arrowhead will be cutting.

When the edges have been sharpened, the drill is then hardened and tempered.

2. The alternative method of making an arrowhead drill is basically similar to the first. Steel rod not hardened or tempered is used, and of the same diameter. The difference is that in this case the steel rod will be spread by hammering at one end to produce the arrowhead, whereas in the first example the arrowhead shape was filed out of the rod. This will obviously produce a bigger arrowhead. If a smaller arrowhead was required, it could be filed to shape or a narrower diameter of rod used.

Spread the end by placing it on a steel block and beating and spreading it with a planishing hammer. This will produce a spade-shaped end which is then filed to the arrowhead shape and sharpened as described. In this case the shaft will not be narrowed because the arrowhead has been made wider than the shaft. The arrowhead drill is then hardened and tempered.

STRAIGHT SHAFTED DRILL

This drill is used for drilling simple straight-sided holes that can be of a very fine diameter, even finer than the finest needle.

In this case, as no filing is required, hardened and tempered steel can be used. Use a fine steel rod and grind a 'flat' on either side near the end. This puts an edge on the rod. Be careful to grind very gently in case you accidentally take the 'temper' out of the rod.

Grind both sides of this edge back at an angle of roughly 45° to

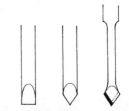

Arrow head drill
Rod flattened
Rod tapered
Sharpened arrow head

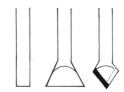

Alternative version of arrow head drill
Rod
Spread rod
Sharpened arrow head

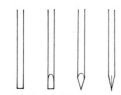

Straight shafted drill
Rod
Rod flattened
Tapered (front view)
Tapered and sharpened
(profile)

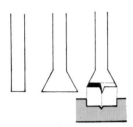

Pearl drill
Rod
Spread rod
Metal

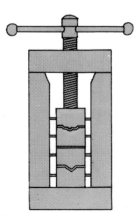

A drawswage

produce a point. These angles are sharpened on an Arkansas oil stone. As this drill is particularly fine, handle it carefully or it will break, and when it requires re-sharpening, hold it in a pin chuck and sharpen it very gently.

PEARL DRILL

A pearl drill is used to cut a hole for flat-backed stones such as half-pearls, etc. Because it must be the same diameter as the stone you are going to set, and these could vary so much in size, you may have to make your own pearl drill. It is generally used in a drill stock, as it cuts in the same way as the arrow head and straight shafted drills, revolving backwards and forwards.

To make it, use unhardened steel rod as before. Spread one end by beating with a planishing hammer to slightly exceed the diameter of the stone. Now straighten this end by filing at right-angles to the shaft, but leaving a central projecting V-shape. The drill is then sharpened in the same way as the arrow head, giving two cutting faces, and leaving the V-shape intact. Harden and temper the drill.

Prior to drilling, a dimple will be made in the metal and the V-point located in this, and then when drilling the two cutting faces will accurately drill out a straight-sided flat-based hole.

A DRAWSWAGE

This is a tool, difficult to buy but not to make, which will easily repay the time spent making it. The tool makes mouldings, like the moulded section of a picture frame, which are extremely arduous and time-consuming to make by hand, particularly if any considerable length of moulding is required.

The drawswage is a rectangular frame made from square steel rod. Within the frame are held two steel forming dies that will, between them, make the shape of the moulding which will be a strip of metal, angled or curved into the decorative form required. This type of moulding cannot include undercuts.

The two steel forming dies are the obverse and reverse of the decorative form. The metal, in plain strip form, is placed between the dies with one end projecting slightly. The top die is pressed down onto the metal strip by a central screw, which is tightened until the strip is held securely. The strip will then be pulled through these dies, in exactly the same way as drawing a piece of wire through a draw plate. The result, however, will be a curved or angled shape according to the design and the dies for it.

The drawswage is put on the drawbench for drawing down the strip of metal as it would be very difficult to draw down by hand. It is placed at the end of the drawbench, between the supports and the pillars as a drawplate would be. As it is so small it may need to be gripped there with a G-clamp or vise. The projecting end is gripped in the draw tongs and the strip drawn almost through, but leaving enough projecting at the other end for the draw tongs to grip there. (This means that each end will be misshapen by the gripping by the draw tongs.) Do not re-move the strip from the drawswage as it is unlikely that it could be accurately repositioned, and therefore the clarity of its edges would be destroyed.

Now reverse the position of the drawswage and grip the other end of the strip, preparatory to drawing down. Turn the screw down slightly to tighten it on the metal and pull the strip through. This process is repeated, tightening the screw gently each time, until the strip gradually takes shape. The metal may work harder and require annealing during the process. If this happens, re-insert the strip as accurately as possible.

When drawing the strip down, add a little beeswax to lubricate it, and make the drawing down a little easier.

If you decide to make this tool, its size will depend on your own requirements but for general purposes I think a drawswage that will take a strip of metal of 12/13 mm ($\frac{1}{2}$") is ample. This would be adequate for frames, decorative edges for boxes, lockets, pendants, or chalices and maces. For this, the drawswage frame should be made from Stubbs steel 10 mm ($\frac{3}{8}$") square rod. The sides can be 5 cm (2") high and the top and bottom 3·75 cm (1$\frac{1}{2}$") long. These four pieces of rod are screwed together. The forming dies can be made out of a length of 10 mm ($\frac{3}{8}$") square rod.

When the design has been decided on you file its shape into the face of one forming die. Carry the shape through to a very high finish – the more highly finished the shapes are the easier it will be to draw the strip through and the better the final result.

With calipers and dividers transfer the design of the first die but in reverse, onto the face of the second die and file this into shape so that the two faces marry and provide the obverse and reverse of the design. At the top a hole is drilled and threaded for the $\frac{1}{4}$" diameter central screw, and its head is drilled to take a crossbar to turn the screw.

The screw will be stronger if it is short – the longer it is, the more work it will have to do and the briefer its life. It is therefore quite a good idea to make a second pair of forming dies and put them in the bottom of the frame. They thereby reduce the traverse of the screw, add a little extra weight and if they are of a design that you may use frequently, are conveniently at hand. The top dies would be taken out and trans-ferred to the bottom so the second pair can be put in place.

In making the tool one would have had to consider at the very beginning how to locate the dies within the frame. They need to be able to move easily up or down within the frame, but without any side-ways movement which would distort the metal strip. This is made possible by filing a channel lengthwise on the inside face of the sides. The dies would have had to be shaped with projecting locating pegs that fit firmly into the channels. At the top of the frame the upright bars have been filed away just sufficiently to allow the die with its projecting pegs to be inserted so that it will drop down into the channel.

The drawswage can also be used to make unusual shaped cheniers, for instance, hexagonal cheniers and triangular cheniers, etc, that cannot be bought.

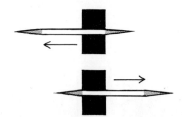

As the strip is drawn through the drawswage each end will be misshapen by the tongs

The forming dies will have locating pegs

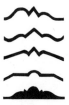

Examples of the mouldings that could be made in a drawswage

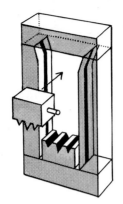

The dies are located by their pegs in channels in the sides

The frame and the dies must be hardened and tempered, and the dies highly polished. This will give clarity and precision to the shape of the moulding.

LINDSTRÖM MICRO PLIERS

As has been mentioned before, tools from other crafts and industries can be used in jewellery and they may make one particular task just that much easier to do. Small tools from engineering and industry can be most useful, and a very good example are the pliers and nippers designed for electronic and computer work by Lindström, a Swedish company, for whom the British agents are Wm. A. Meyer Ltd, 9 Gleneldon Road, London S.W.16. These pliers have a precision machined box joint (whereas not all jeweller's pliers do) in which the frictional resistance and play are adjusted by means of a screw and nut. In addition, the joint surfaces are long, to provide better guidance and support for the jaws than has hitherto been possible. The jaws are precision ground in a machine and this provides closer limits and more even quality.

End cutting nippers

Oblique-cutting nippers

Gripping pliers will grip a very fine wire even against a flat surface

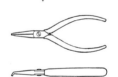

Snipe nose pliers

VIII APPENDIXES

Tables, Standards and Conversions

PENNYWEIGHTS AND GRAINS WITH DECIMALS OF OZ. TROY
TROY WEIGHT WITH MILLIGRAMS

Dwts	Decimals	Grains	Decimals	Oz.	Milligrams
20	1·000	24	·050	·001	31·1035
19	·950	23	·047916	·002	62·2070
18	·900	22	·045833	·003	93·3105
17	·850	21	·04375	·004	124·4140
16	·800	20	·041083	·005	155·5175
15	·750	19	·039	·010	311·0350
14	·700	18	·0375	·020	622·070
13	·650	17	·035416	·030	933·1050
12	·600	16	·033	·040	1244·140
11	·550	15	·03125	·050	1555·1750
10	·500	14	·02966	·10	3110·350
9	·450	13	·027083	·20	6220·700
8	·400	12	·025	·30	9331·050
7	·350	11	·022916	·40	12441·40
6	·300	10	·020833	·50	15551·750
5	·250	9	·01875	·75	23327·625
4	·200	8	·01666	1·0	31103·50
3	·150	7	·014583		
2	·100	6	·0125	1·0 oz = 31·1035 grams.	
1	·050	5	·010416		
		4	·00833		
		3	·00625		
		2	·004166		
		1	·002083		

APPROXIMATE WEIGHT OF 1 SQUARE INCH OF SILVER TO THE VARIOUS SIZES ON THE BIRMINGHAM METAL GAUGE

Gauge size	Approximate weight per square inch			Gauge size	Approximate weight per square inch		
	Decimals of oz.	dwt.	gr.		Decimals of oz.	dwt.	gr.
1	·049 or	–	23½	13	·220 or	4	9½
2	·055 ,,	1	1½	14	·246 ,,	4	22
3	·061 ,,	1	5	15	·268 ,,	5	8½
4	·070 ,,	1	10	16	·286 ,,	5	17½
5	·081 ,,	1	14½	17	·307 ,,	6	3½
6	·093 ,,	1	20½	18	·330 ,,	6	14½
7	·110 ,,	2	5	19	·342 ,,	6	20
8	·126 ,,	2	12½	20	·362 ,,	7	6
9	·143 ,,	2	20½	21	·384 ,,	7	16½
10	·163 ,,	3	6½	22	·406 ,,	8	3
11	·183 ,,	3	16	23	·428 ,,	8	13½
12	·203 ,,	4	1½	24	·456 ,,	9	3

Measures of Length

The metre is the length, at 0° Centigrade, of a platinum bar preserved in Paris, and known as the Mètre des Archives.

1 inch (in.) = 25·39977 millimetres (mm.).
12 inches = 1 foot (ft.) = 30·479 cm.
63,360 inches = 5280 feet = 1760 yards = 1 statute mile = 1·6094 kilometres.
1 millimetre = 0·039370113 inch = about $\frac{1}{25}$ inch.
10 mm. = 1 centimetre (cm.) = 0·3937 inch.
100 mm. = 10 cm. = 1 decimetre (dm.)
To convert
Inches into millimetres multiply by 25·39977
Millimetres into inches multiply by 0·03937

Measures of Weight

Troy weight is used in Great Britain for precious metals: platinum, gold, silver, etc. But the decimal system is now generally employed when dealing with fractions of an ounce. Thus 17½ ounces of silver are written 17·5 oz., rather than 17 oz. 10 dwt. There is no Troy pound.

Avoirdupois weight is in general use for other materials.
1 grain troy = 0·00208 oz. troy = 0·0648 gram = 1 grain av.
24 grains troy = 1 pennyweight (dwt.) = 0·05 oz. troy = 1·5552 grams.
1 ounce troy = 31·1035 grams = 480 grains = 1·0971 oz. av.
16 drams avoirdupois (dr.) = 1 oz. av.
1 ounce avoirdupois = 437·5 grains = 28·3495 gram = 0·9114 oz. troy.
1 pound avoirdupois = 7000 grains = 16 oz. av. = 14 oz. 11 dwt. 16 gr. troy = 453·5924 gram.
1 hundredweight (cwt.) = 50·8 kilograms = 112 pounds (lb.).
1 ton, British = 1016 kilograms = 2240 lb. = 20 cwt.
1 ton, American = 908 kilograms = 2000 lb.
1 milligram (mgm.) = 0·015 grains.
1 gram (grm.) = 15·43235 grains = 0·032151 oz. troy = 0·352736 oz. av. = 0·0022046 lb. av.
1 kilogram (kg.) = 2·2046223 lb. av. = 35·2734 oz. av. = 32·1507 oz. troy = 1000 gram.

CONVERSION TABLES

Grams	into grains	multiply by	15·43235
Grams	,, ounces av.	,,	0·03527
Grams	,, ounces troy	,,	0·03215
Centigrams	,, grains	,,	0·15432
Kilograms	,, ounces av.	,,	35·2739
Kilograms	,, pounds av.	,,	2·2046
Kilograms	,, ounces troy	,,	32·1507
Ounces av.	,, grams	,,	28·3495
Ounces av.	,, kilograms	,,	0·2835
Pounds av.	,, kilograms	,,	0·4536
Ounces troy	,, grams	,,	31·1035
Ounces troy	,, kilograms	,,	0·0311
Gallons	,, litres	,,	4·54102
Litres	,, gallons	,,	0·220215

Weight of Precious Stones

The British legal standard for the weighing of precious stones and pearls, from the year 1913 onwards, has been the Metric Carat of 200 milligrams. This standard corresponds with that in use in the Continental diamond markets, in South Africa, and in the United States. Before 1913 a carat of 205 milligrams was most generally employed.

The weight of a diamond is reckoned in carats and in one-hundredths of a carat (in decimals), though very often the fractions of a carat such as $\frac{1}{2}$ or $\frac{1}{4}$ are used in conversation. But for pearls the carat may be reckoned as being composed of 4 grains. So a pearl may be spoken of as a 2-grainer or 3-grainer. Small diamonds are referred to by the number that would go to a carat: 40, 50, 100, 300 and so on.

Approximately $141\frac{3}{4}$ metric carats = 1 ounce avoirdupois.

CONVERSION TABLES

Fahrenheit to Centigrade
From the number of degrees Fahrenheit subtract 32. Multiply the result by 5, and divide by 9.
Centigrade to Fahrenheit
Multiply the number of degrees Centigrade by 9, divide by 5 and add 32.

Centigrade to Réaumur. The formula is: $\frac{4C}{5} = R$.

Réaumur to Centigrade. It is: $\frac{5R}{4} = C$.

A ROUGH METHOD OF ESTIMATING HIGH TEMPERATURES

Degrees Centigrade	
232	Tin melts.
419	Zinc melts.
500–600	Faint red glow.
650–700	Dull red.
800	Cherry red.
893	Standard silver melts.
900	Bright red.
961	Fine silver melts.
1000	Very bright red, verging into yellow.
1063	Fine gold melts.
1083	Fine copper melts.
1280	White heat.
1350	Steel melts? varies.
1480	Nickel melts. Blinding white.
1500	Iron melts? varies.
1668	Titanium melts.
1773	Platinum melts.

Temperatures obtainable in:

	Degrees Centigrade
Bunsen burner flame	1100–1350
Oxy-hydrogen flame	about 2000
Oxy-acetylene flame	,, 2400
Electric arc	,, 3500
Electric arc (under pressure)	,, 3600
Sun	,, 5500

THE MELTING POINTS AND ATOMIC WEIGHTS OF VARIOUS MATERIALS

Name	Cent.	Fahr.	Atomic weight
Aluminium	659·7°	1219·6°	26·97
Antimony	630·5°	1166·9°	121·76
Bismuth	271·3°	520·3°	209
Brass	1015° varies	1859°?	
Cadmium	320·9°	609·62°	112·41
Copper	1083°	1981·4°	63·57
Gold	1063°	1945·4°	197·2
Ice	0°	32°	
Iridium	2350°	4262°	193·1
Cast-iron	1100°	2012°	
Iron (pure)	1535°	2795°	55·85
Lead	327·4°	621·32°	207·21
Magnesium	651°	1203·8°	24·32
Mercury (solid)	−38·87°	−37·966°	200·61
Nickel	1455°	2619°	58·69
Platinum	1773·5°	3192·3°	195·23
Silver	960·5°	1728·9°	107·88
Steel	1350° varies	2430°?	
Tin	231·89°	417·5°	118·7
Titanium	1668°	3035°	47·90
Water (boils)	100°	212°	
Zinc	419·47°	755·04°	65·38
Common salt	801°	1441·8°	

The figures given above are for fine gold, fine silver, fine copper, etc. Those for alloys would differ.

	Troy oz.	Specific gravity
If platinum of given dimensions weighs	1·0	21·50
Fine gold of same dimensions will weigh	·900	19·33
22 carat	·820	17·60
20 ,,	·765	16·50
18 ,,	·725	15·55
15 ,,	·645	13·50
12 ,,	·590	12·75
9 ,,	·535	11·50
6 ,,	·505	10·90
Silver, fine	·495	10·70
Silver, standard	·490	10·50
Lead	·530	11·40
Bismuth	·455	9·80
Copper	·415	8·95
Nickel	·414	8·90
Brass	·375	8·10
Iron	·365	7·85
Tin	·340	7·30
Zinc	·335	7·15
Aluminium	·120	2·60

The Brown and Sharpe (B. & S.) wire gauge is the standard gauge for sheet metal in the United States.

Number of gauge	Thickness	
	Inches	Millimetres
6/0	·580	14·73
5/0	·5165	13·119
4/0	·46	11·68
3/0	·409	10·388
2/0	·364	9·24
1/0	·324	8·23
1	·289	7·338
2	·257	6·527
3	·229	5·808
4	·204	5·18
5	·181	4·59
6	·162	4·11
7	·144	3·66
8	·128	3·24
9	·114	2·89
10	·101	2·565
11	·090	2·28
12	·080	2·03
13	·071	1·79
14	·064	1·625
15	·057	1·447
16	·050	1·27
17	·045	1·14
18	·040	1·016
19	·035	·889
20	·031	·787
21	·028	·711
22	·025	·635
23	·022	·558
24	·020	·508
25	·017	·431
26	·015	·381
27	·0148	·376
28	·012	·304
29	·0116	·29
30	·01	·254
31	·008	·203
32	·0079	·199
33	·007	·177
34	·006	·152
35	·0055	·142
36	·005	·127

Bibliography

English Girdle book. 1540 AD

Abbey, S., *The Goldsmiths and Silversmiths Handbook*, The Technical Press Ltd, England, 1952.

Adair, J., *The Navajo and Pueblo Silversmiths*, University of Oklahoma Press, USA, 1966.

Aldred, C., *Jewels of the Pharaohs*, Thames & Hudson, London, 1971.

Alexander, C., *Jewellery: Art of the Goldsmith in Classical Times*, The Metropolitan Museum, New York, USA, 1928.

Armstrong, N., *Jewellery*, Lutterworth Press, London, 1973.

Bainbridge, H. C., *Peter Carl Fabergé*, B.T. Batsford, London, 1949.

Bank, Dr H., *Precious Stones and Minerals*, Fredk. Warne & Co. Ltd, London, 1970.

Barsali, Isa Belli, *European Enamels*, Paul Hamlyn, London, 1969.

Baxter, William T. L., *Jewellery – Gem Cutting and Metalcraft*, McGraw-Hill, USA, 1950.

Beard and Rogers, *5000 Years of Gems and Jewellery*, Lippincot, New York, USA, 1947.

Blakemore, K., *The Book of Gold*, November Books, London, 1971.

Blakemore, K., *The Retail Jewellers' Guide*, Iliffe Books Ltd, London, 1969.

Bowman, John J., and R. Allen Hardy, *The Jewellery Repair Manual*, Van Nostrand, USA, 1956.

Bradford, E. D. S., *English Victorian Jewellery*, Country Life Ltd, 1959.

Bradford, E. D. S., *Four Centuries of European Jewellery*, Spring Books 1967.

Brynner, Irena, *Modern Jewellery*, Reinhold Book Corp., New York, USA, 1968.

Buchester, K. J., *The Australian Gemhunters Guide*, Ure-Smith, Sydney, Australia, 1967.

Butts, A., and Cox, C. D. (Editors), *Silver: Economics,* *Metallurgy and Use*, D. Van Nostrand, New York, USA, 1967.

Carli, Enso, *Pre-Conquest Goldsmiths Work of Colombia*, William Heinemann, London, 1964/5.

Cellini, Benvenuto, *Treatises on the Arts of Goldsmithing and Sculpture*, translated by C. H. Ashbee, Edward Arnold, London, 1898 and Dover Publications Inc., New York, USA, 1967.

Cennini, d'Andrea, *Il Libro Dell' Arte (The Craftsman's Handbook)*, translated by Daniel V. Thompson, Jr, Dover Publications Inc., New York, USA, 1954/1960 and Yale University Press, USA, 1933.

Choate, Sharr G., and Bonnie Cecil de May, *Creative Gold and Silversmithing*, Crown Publishers, New York, USA, 1970.

Clark, Geoffrey, Francis and Ida Feher, *The Technique of Enamelling*, B.T. Batsford, London, 1967.

Cunynghame, H. H., *The Theory and Practice of Art Enamelling on Metals*, Constable and Co., London, 1899, 2nd edition 1901. 3rd edition 1906.

Cuznor, Bernard, *Silversmiths' Manual*, N.A.G. Press, London, 1935, 1949, 1958, 1961, 1971.

Dana, E. S., Prof., *A Textbook of Mineralogy*, J. Wiley and Sons Inc., New York, London, Sydney, 1898, 1922, 1932, 1949, 1966. Revised by Ford, W. E.

Desautels, P., *The Mineral Kingdom*, Paul Hamlyn, London, 1970.

Dickinson, J. Y., *The Book of Diamonds*, Crown Publishers Inc., New York, USA, 1965. (Distributed by Frederick Muller Ltd, London.)

Emerson, A. R., *Handmade Jewellery*, Dryad Press, Leicester, England, 1953, 1955, 1973.

Evans, Joan, *A History of Jewellery 1100 to 1870*, Faber & Faber, London, 1973.

Evans, Joan, *English Jewellery from 5th Century AD*

to 1800 AD, Methuen, 1922.

Falkiner, R., *Investing in Antique Jewellery*, Cresset Press, London, 1968.

Fisher, P. J., F.G.A., *Jewels*, B.T. Batsford, London, 1965.

Frank, Joan, *Birthstones of the Month*, published by Colourmaster International, England, 1973, in collaboration with the Jewellery Information Centre.

Garrison, W. E., and Dowd, M. E., *Handcrafting Jewellery*, Robert Hale and Co., London, 1974/5.

Gee, George E., *The Practical Gold Worker*, Crosby, Lockwood and Son, London, 1877.

Gee, George E., *The Silversmith's Handbook*, Crosby, Lockwood and Son, London, 1885.

Gee, George E., *The Goldsmith's Handbook*, Crosby, Lockwood and Son, London, 1897.

Goodden, R., C.B.E., R.D.I., and Popham, P., A.R.C.A., *Silversmithing*, Oxford University Press, London, 1971.

Higgins, R., *Greek and Roman Jewellery*, Methuen, London, 1961.

Higgins, R., *Minoan and Mycenaean Art*, Thames and Hudson, London, 1967.

Higgins, R., *Jewellery from Classical Lands*, The British Museum, 1965.

Hoover, Herbert Clark and Ian Henry (translators), *De Re Metallica* by Georgius Agricola, Dover Publications Inc., New York, USA, 1950.

Hughes, Graham, *The Jewellery Art of*, Studio Vista, London, 1972.

Hughes, Graham, *Modern Jewellery*, Studio Books, London, 1973.

Jackson, Will A., *Jewellery Repairing*, Heywood and Co. Ltd, London, 1948.

Jessup, R., *Anglo-Saxon Jewellery*, Faber and Faber, London, 1950.

Koningh, H. de, *Preparations of Precious Metals and Other Metal Work for Enamelling*, The Technical Press Ltd, London, 1947, and Norman W. Henley Publishing Co., New York, USA, 1930.

Kunz, G. F., *Gems and Precious Stones of North America*, Dover Publications Inc., New York, USA, 1968.

Kunz, G. F., *Rings for the Finger*, Constable, London, 1974.

Lewes, Klares, *Jewellerymaking for the Amateur*, B.T. Batsford, London, 1965.

Liddicoat, R. T., Jr, *Handbook of Gem Identification*, G.I.A., London, 1962. Cf. *Gems and Gemology*.

Littledale, H. A. P., *Improvements in Hard Soldering Mixtures and Hard Soldering Processes*, The Worshipful Company of Goldsmiths, London, 1933 (British Patent 415181).

Lyon, P., *Design in Jewellery*, Peter Owen Ltd, London, 1946/56.

Mahoney, Tom, and Marcus Baerwald, *The Story of Jewellery*, Abelhard Schuman, USA, 1960.

Maryon, Herbert, F.G.A., *Metalwork and Enamelling*, Chapman and Hall, London, 1912/23/54/59, and Dover Publications Inc., New York, USA, 1955/73.

Maryon, Herbert, F.G.A., *Metalworking in the Ancient World*, American Journal of Archaeology, Vol LIII No 2, USA (Cambridge, Mass.), 1949.

Meyerowitz, Patricia, *Jewellery and Sculpture Through Unit Construction*, Studio Vista, London, 1967.

Morton, Philip, *Contemporary Jewellery*, Holt Rinehart, & Winston Inc., New York, London, Chicago and Sydney, 1970.

Neumann, Robert von, *The Design and Creation of Jewellery*, Sir Isaac Pitman and Sons, Ltd, London, 1962.

Oman, C., *Catalogue of Rings*, Victoria and Albert Museum, London, 1930.

Oman, C., *British Rings 800–1914*. B.T. Batsford, London, 1974.

Oved, Sah, *The Book of Necklaces*, Arthur Barker, London, 1953.

Pack, G., *Jewellery and Enamelling*, D. Van Nostrand and Co. Inc., New York, USA, 1957.

Rogers and Beard, *5000 Years of Gems and Jewellery*, Lippincot, New York, USA, 1947.

Rose, T. K., *The Precious Metals*, Constable and Co., London, 1910.

Rothenberg, P., *New Enamelling*, Allen and Unwin Ltd, London, 1970.

Scarfe, H., *Collecting and Polishing Stones*, B.T. Batsford, London, 1972.

Scarfe, H., *Cutting and Setting Stones*, B.T. Batsford, London, 1973.

Schwann, C., *Workshop Methods for Gold and Silversmiths*, Stechert-Hafner, Inc., New York, USA, 1950, and Heywood and Co. Ltd, 1960.

Seeler, Margaret, *The Art of Enamelling*, D. Van Nostrand and Co. Ltd, New York, USA, 1970.

Shoenfelt, J. F., *Designing and Making Handwrought Jewellery*, McGraw-Hill Books Inc., New York, USA, 1960.

Sinkankas, Capt. J., *Gem Cutting*, D. Van Nostrand and Co., New York, USA, 1962/3.

Smith, D., *Metalwork*, B.T. Batsford, London, 1948.

Smith, H. Clifford, M.A., *Jewellery*, Methuen, London, 1908.

Smith, Keith, *Silversmithing and Jewellery*, Studio Vista, 1975.

Snowman, Kenneth A., *The Art of Carl Fabergé*, Faber and Faber, London, 1953.

Spon, Ernest, *Workshop Receipts*, E. and F. N. Spon, London, 1917 (4 Vols.).

Steingraber, Erich, *Royal Treasures*, Weidenfeld and Nicolson, London, 1968.

Steingraber, Erich, *Antique Jewellery, 800–1900*, Thames and Hudson, London, 1957.

Sutherland, C. H. V., *Gold*, Thomas and Hudson, London, 1959/60/69.

Taylor, G., *Silver*, Penguin Books Ltd, London, 1956/63/68/69.

Theophilus (also known as Rugerus, Roger of

Helmarshausen or Theophilus Presbyter), *Essays on the Various Arts* (*De Diversis Artibus*), translated from Latin by C. R. Dodwell, published by Thomas Nelson and Sons, Ltd, London, 1961. Also translated by J. G. Hawthorne and C. S. Smith, University of Chicago Press, 1963, and by R. Hendrie, USA, 1847.

Turner, Ralph, *Contemporary Jewellery*, Studio Vista, 1976.

Twining, Lord, *Crown Jewels of Europe*, B.T. Batsford, London, 1960.

Ullrich, H., and Klante, *Creative Metalcraft,* B.T. Batsford Ltd, London, 1968.

Untracht, Oppi, *Metal Techniques for Craftsmen*, Robert Hale and Co., London, 1969.

Vasari, G., *Vasari on Technique*, translated by L. S. Maclehose, 1907, Dover Publications Inc., New York, USA, 1960.

Vilimkova, Milada, and Dominique Darbois, *Egyptian Jewellery*, by Paul Hamlyn, London, 1970.

Webster, R., F.G.A., *Practical Gemology*, N.A.G. Press, London, 1970.

Webster, R., F.G.A., *Gemmologists' Compendium*, N.A.G. Press, London, 1970.

Wigley, Thomas E., *The Art of the Goldsmith and Jeweller*, Chas. Griffin, London, 1898, 1911.

Wilson, H., *Silverwork and Jewellery*, Pitmans, London, 1948.

Zarchy, H., *Jewellery-Making and Enamelling*, Alfred Knopff Inc., New York, USA, 1959.

Zechlin, K., *Creative Enamelling and Jewellery Making*, Sterling Publishing Co., New York, USA, and the Oak Tree Press, Sydney, Australia, and London, 1968.

Zim, H. S., Ph.D., and Prof. P. R. Shaffer, Ph.D., *Rocks and Minerals*, Golden Press Inc., New York, 22, USA, 1957/63.

MAGAZINES, JOURNALS, BOOKLETS, RESEARCH PAPERS, LECTURES

Magazines and Journals

American Journal of Archaeology, New York, USA.

Australian Lapidary Magazine, Jay Kay Publishers, NSW, Australia.

Britannia, London.

British Jeweller and Watchbuyer, London and Birmingham.

Commonwealth Jeweller and Watchmaker, Sydney, Australia.

Craft Horizons Inc., New York, USA.

Deutsche Goldschmiede, Stuttgart, Germany.

Gems and Gemmology, published by Gemmological Institute of America, California, USA.

Gems and Materials, London.

Gold and Silver, Stechert-Hafner Inc., New York, USA.

Gold and Silver, Uhren and Schmuck, Stuttgart, Germany.

Industrial Diamond Information Bureau, London.

Jeweller, Allens (Clerkenwell) Ltd, Wheathampstead, Herts.

Journal of Gemmology, published by Gemmological Association of Great Britain, London.

Lapidary Journal, California, USA.

Retail Jeweller, N.A.G. Press Ltd, London.

Booklets

Finishing Handbook and Directory, J. S. Bean, Sawell Publications Ltd, London, 1969.

Goldsmiths Hall as Patrons of their Craft, The Worshipful Company of Goldsmiths, London, 1965.

Lost Wax, Kerr Manufacturing Co., Detroit and Michigan, USA.

Skill, Crafts Centre, London, 1968.

The Sterling Craft, Goldsmiths Hall, London, 1966.

Research Papers

Heat Treatment of Metals by P. E. Gainsbury, F.I.M., Technical Development Officer of the Worshipful Company of Goldsmiths, printed by 'British Jeweller', April 1967.

Hardening Metals by Heat Treatment by P. E. Gainsbury, F.I.M., reprinted by 'British Jeweller', May 1967.

T.A.C. News, P. E. Gainsbury, F.I.M., The Worshipful Company of Goldsmiths, London.

Lectures printed in book form, published by the Goldsmiths Hall

The Scientific and Technical Factors of Production of Gold and Silver Work – series of six lectures given at the Goldsmiths Hall, London, 1935–36:

1 McDonald, D., B.Sc.   *General Metallurgy*
2 Hutton, R. S., M.A., D.Sc.   *Working in Metals*
3 Newman, W. A. C., B.Sc., A.R.S.M., A.R.C.S., F.I.C., D.I.C.   *The Royal Mint – Heat Treatment and Annealing*
4 Hutton, R. S., M.A., D.Sc.   *Polishing*
5 Littledale, H. A. P.   *Jointing and Soldering*
6 Field, S., A.R.C.S.   *Plating and Colouring.*

Suppliers

List of USA Suppliers:

Allcraft Tool and Supply Company
22 West 48th Street
New York, N. Y. 10036
(findings, metals, gem stones,
tools)

American Handicraft Company
2920 Geary Blvd.
San Francisco, California 94118
(metals)

John Barry Company
Department C.
P. O. Box 15
Detroit, Michigan 48231
(gem stones)

T. B. Hagstoz and Son
09 Sansom Street
Philadelphia, Pennsylvania 19106
(findings, metals, tools)

C. R. Hill Company
2734 West 11 Mile Road
Berkley, Michigan 48072
(findings, metals, tools)

Francis Hoover
12445 Chandler Blvd.
North Hollywood, California 91607
(gem stones)

International Gem Corporation
15 Maiden Lane
New York, N. Y. 10038
(gem stones)

C. W. Somers & Company
387 Washington Street
Boston, Massachusetts 02108
(findings, metals, tools)

Marshall-Swartchild Company
2040 Milwaukee Avenue
Chicago, Illinois 60657
(findings, metals, tools)

List of United Kingdom Suppliers:

Tools and Materials

*Buck, G. 21 Goodge Street,
London W.1.

*Buck & Hickman Ltd, 2
Whitechapel Road, London E.1.

*Buck & Ryan Ltd, 101
Tottenham Court Road,
London W.1 and 55 Harrow
Road, London W.2.

Charles Cooper
(Hatton Garden) Ltd, Wall
House, 12 Hatton Wall,
London E.C.1.

Frost, C. R. and Son, New
House, 67/8 Hatton Garden,
London E.C.1.

*Gould & Bray Ltd, 68 Berwick
Street, London W.1.

*Picador Engineering Co. Ltd,
83 Euston Road, London
N.W.1.

Picard, Henri & Frere,
357/9 Kennington Lane,
London S.E.11.

Pike, F., 58 Hatton Garden,
London E.C.1.

*Romany, F., 52 Camden High
Street, London N.W.1.

Salvo, C.V., 39 Greville Street,
London E.C.1.

Thomas, A. G. (Bradford) Ltd,
Dept J.M. Tompion House,
Heaton Road, Bradford 8,
Yorks.

Thomas, A. G. (Bradford) Ltd,
and E. Gray & Son, Ltd,
12/16 Clerkenwell Road,
London E.C.1.

Thor Hammer Co. Ltd,
Highlands Road, Shirley,
Birmingham.

*These companies have a
limited range of jewellers' tools
and materials.

Platinum, Gold, Silver, Findings

Abelson (Hatton Garden) Ltd,
Abelson House, 16 Greville
Street, London E.C.1.

Betts, J. and Sons, Ltd,
84 Hatton Garden, London
E.C.1. and
64 Charlotte Street,
Birmingham 3.

Blundell, J. and Sons, Ltd,
199 Wardour Street, London
W.1.

Commercial Smelting and
Refinery Co. Ltd, 15 Farringdon
Road, London E.C.1.

Day, Edward and Baker Ltd,
28 Warstone Lane, Birmingham
18.

Englehard Sales Ltd, Primate
House, 57 Hatton Garden,
London E.C.1 and 49/63
Spencer Street, Birmingham 18.

Gray, E. and Son, Ltd, and Thomas, A. G. (Bradford) Ltd, 12/16 Clerkenwell Road, London E.C.1.

Georges and Co, 88/90 Hatton Garden, London E.C.1.

Johnson and Matthey, 73/83 Hatton Garden, London E.C.1.

Johnson & Sons Smelting Works Ltd, 104 Spencer Street, Birmingham 18.

Knight, J. S. and Sons, Ltd, 6/9 Benjamin Street, London E.C.1.

Mocatta and Goldsmid Ltd, 16 Finsbury Circus, London E.C.2.

Pennellier, D. and Co. Ltd, 28 Hatton Garden, London E.C.1.

Sheffield Smelting Co. Ltd and Englehard Sales Ltd, 34/36 St John Street, London E.C.1 and Royds Mill Street, Sheffield 4.

Sinclair, M., 118 Holborn, London E.C.1.

Wolff, Rudolf and Co., 26 Finsbury Square, London E.C.2.

Brass, Copper, Aluminium, Steel

Bonds (of Euston Road) Ltd, 186 Tottenham Court Road, London W.1.

Buck and Ryan, Ltd, 101 Tottenham Court Road, London W.1 and 55 Harrow Road, London W.2.

Macready's Metal Co. Ltd, Usaspead Corner, 131 Pentonville Road, London N.1.

Rollet, H., and Co. Ltd, 20/22 Howie Street, London S.W.11.

Smiths, J. and Sons, 50 St Johns Square, London E.C.1.

Gemstones

Beach, M. L., 41 Church Street, Twickenham, Middx.

Bottley, Gregory and Co., 30 Old Church Street, London S.W.3.

Buckman, D., 7 Hanover Street, London W.1.

Calipe, C., 44 Poland Street, London W.1.

Clark, D. and P., 18 St Cross Street, London E.C.1.

Couch, R. E., 30b Great Sutton Street, London E.C.1.

Dennis, F. and Co. Ltd, 15 Heddon Street, London W.1.

Drewell and Bradshaw Ltd, 25 Hatton Garden, London E.C.1.

Eaton's Shell Shop, 16 Manette Street, London W.1.

Fahy, O.D., F.G.A., 64 Warstone Lane, Birmingham 18.

Fleming, J. A., F.G.A., 18 St Cross Street, London E.C.1.

Gemmological Association of Great Britain, St Dunstan's House, 2 Carey Lane, London E.C.2.

Gemmological Institute of America. 11940 San Vincente Boulevard, Los Angeles 49, California, USA.

Gemrocks, 7 Brunswick Centre, London W.C.1.

Gemstones, 23 Hatton Garden, London E.C.1.

Gem Testing Laboratory, Greville Street, London E.C.1.

Holt, R. and Co. Ltd, 111 Hatton Garden, London E.C.1.

Hirsh Jacobson, 91 Marylebone High Street, London W.1.

Kernowcraft, Highertown, Truro, Cornwall.

King Lapidary, 1 Albemarle Way, London E.C.1.

Knowles, Norris and Co., 41 Southgate Street, Winchester, Hants.

Lindley, G., 26 Hatton Garden, London E.C.1.

Lowe, B. C., 73/5 Spencer Street, Birmingham 18.

Matthews, C. and Sons, Ltd, 14/15 Hatton Garden, London E.C.1.

Rockmin Gem Co. Ltd, 84 Hatton Garden, London E.C.1.

Shipton and Co. Ltd, 27/33 Spencer Street, Birmingham 18.

Stern, T., 22 Great Pulteney Street, London W.1.

Stern, W., 1 Hatton Garden, London E.C.1.

Thompson, E. A., Chapel House, Hatton Place, London E.C.1.

Ward, A. E., and Son, Ltd, 10 Albemarle Way, London E.C.1.

Wessex Gems and Crafts Ltd, C/o Knowles Norris & Co, 51 Southgate Street, Winchester, Hampshire.

Woods, T. G. and Sons, Ltd, 19 New Road, Amersham, Buckinghamshire HP6 6LD.

Lapidaries and Lapidary Equipment

Beach, M. L., 41 Church Street, Twickenham, Middx.

Bottley, Gregory and Co., 30 Old Church Street, London S.W.3.

Dennis, F., and Co. Ltd, 15 Heddon Street, London W.1.

Gemrocks, 7 Brunswick Centre, London W.C.1.

Hirsh Jacobson (Agents for Robilt Lapidary Equipment), 91 Marylebone High Street, London W.1.

Kernowcraft, Highertown, Truro, Cornwall.

Ward, A. E. and Son, Ltd, 10 Albemarle Way, London E.C.1.

Acids and Polishing Materials

Canning, W. and Co. Ltd,
Greenhill Crescent, Holywell
Industrial Estate, Watford.
Great Hampton Street,
Birmingham 18.
South Parade, Sheffield, Yorks.
Squire Street, Whiteinch,
Glasgow.
21 North Approach,
Kingswood.

Harrington Bros. Ltd,
12a Weir Road, London S.W.12.

Hutchinson, T. A., 16 St Johns
Lane, London E.C.1.

Spencer, Berk Acids Ltd,
Abbey Mills Chemical Works,
Canning Road, London E.15.

Casting Equipment and Materials

Cottrell and Co., 15 Charlotte
Street, London W.1.

Ferraris Development and
Engineering Co. Ltd, 26 Lea
Valley Trading Estate, Angel
Road, Edmonton, London N.18.

*Hoben Davis Ltd, Spencroft
Road, Newcastle, Staffs.

*Hoben Davis are the Agents
for Kerr Manufacturing Co.
Products, USA.

Hooker, W. J., Ltd, Waterside,
Brightlingsea, Essex.

Nesor Products Ltd, Claremont
Hall, Pentonville Road,
London N.1.

Tiranti, A., Ltd (Agents for
Dow Corning, USA), Goodge
Place, London W.1.

Precision Casters

Johnson & Matthey,
73/83 Hatton Garden,
London E.C.1.
Just Castings,
101–2 Turnmill St,
London E.C.1.
Goulaing & Bird Ltd,
58G Hatton Garden,
London E.C.1.

Rinberg, M. & S. Co. Ltd.,
56 Hatton Garden,
London E.C.1.
Sondé Jewellery,
91 Goswell Road,
London E.C.1.

Enamels and Equipment

Arts and Crafts Unlimited,
Macklin Street, London W.C.2.

Catterson-Smith Ltd, Adams
Bridge Works, South Way,
Exhibition Grounds, Wembley.

Dryads Ltd, P.O. Box 290,
Technico House, Leicester.

Enamelaire, 61B High Street,
Watford.

Gallenkampf and Co. Ltd,
6 Christopher Street, London
E.C.2.

Hatton, W. J., 285 Icknield
Street, Hockley, Birmingham.

Thomson and Joseph Ltd,
46 Watling Street, Radlett,
Herts.

Wengers, Ltd, Etruria, Stoke-
on-Trent.

Platers and Polishers

Pairpoint, W., 110 Shacklewell
Road, London N.16 7TT.

Richards, F. P., 7 Poland Street,
London W.1.

Woodhouse, Britten Street,
London E.C.1.

Plating Equipment and Materials

Canning, W. and Co. Ltd,
As before.

Cooper and Co. (Birmingham)
Ltd, Brynmawr, Breconshire,
South Wales.

Johnson and Matthey. 73/83
Hatton Garden, London E.C.1.

Electroforming

B.J.S. Electro Plating Co. Ltd,
Rhodoplate House, 346–8
Kilburn High Road, London
N.W.6.

Englehard Industries Ltd,
Primate House, 57 Hatton
Garden London E.C.1.

Electric and Pneumatic Tools

Desoutter Bros. Ltd, The Hyde,
Hendon, London N.W.9.

Expo Tools, 62 Neal Street,
London W.C.2.

Finishing Aids and Tools, Ltd,
2a Cambridge Grove Road,
Kingston-on-Thames, Surrey.

Flexible Drive Tool Co. Ltd,
Edenbridge, Kent.

Kenilworth Manufacturing Co.
Ltd, West Drayton, Middx.

Les Applications Rationnelles,
119a High Street, Teddington,
Middx.

Engraver on Metal or Seals

Betser, G. M., 15a Grafton
Street, London W.1.

Glass (for watch bezels and lockets, etc)

Bray, L. C., 68 Clerkenwell
Road, London E.C.1.

Gold Leaf, Gold and Silver Foil

Whiley, G. M., Ltd, Victoria
Road, South Ruislip, Middx.

Winter, E., and Co. Ltd,
12 Charterhouse Buildings,
London E.C.1.

Watch and Clockmaker

Lee, A., 122 St John Street,
London E.C.1.

First Aid Box

FASCO (First Aid Ltd),
88 Newington Butts, London
S.E.11.

First Aid Book, Published by
St John Ambulance
Association, 98/108 North
Street, Charing Cross, London
W.C.2.

Instant Eye-wash bottles,
Fisons, Bishop Meadow Road,
Loughborough, Leics.

Fire Extinguishers

Nu-Swift, 122 Regent Street,
London W.1.

Pyrene & Co. Ltd, Hanworth
Air Park, Feltham, Middx.

Soldering Equipment

Adaptogas, Meadow Mills,
Water Street, Stockport,
Cheshire SK1 2BY.

Dependox, British Industrial
Gases Ltd, Lea Road, Waltham
Abbey, Essex.

Microflame, Abbots Hall,
Rickinghall, Diss, Norfolk.

Microflame Inc., 3724 Oregon
Avenue, Minneapolis,
Minnesota 55426

Microweld, 110 Churchill Road,
Launton Industrial Estate,
Bicester, Oxon.

Ronson Ltd, 352 Strand,
London W.C.2, and 66 Jermyn
Street, London W.C.1.

Sievert, Wm. A. Meyer Ltd,
P.O. Box 562, 9/11 Gleneldon
Road, London S.W.16 2A.

Supa-Nova II, Henri Picard &
Freres Ltd, 34/35 Furnival
Street, London E.C.4.

Wilkes, William Allday & Co.
Ltd, Alcosa Works, Stourport
on Severn, Worcs.

Index

Frames 223
Fused metals 216
Fusing, enamel 187

G clamp 12, 222
Gainsbury, P.E. 80
Gapping file 18, 120, 132–3
Garnet 157, 215
Gas cock 16
Gas, compressed air torch 60, 183;
    oxygen torch 59, 60, 183
Gate, in casting 177
Gemstones 154, 156–9, 171
'Gilbow' shears 11
Gilding, antique 215
Gilson, Pierre 163
Girdle, of gemstone 140, 169
Glacial acetic acid 53
Gold, alloys 90–4; foil 191, 193–4;
    forming 204, improve or reduce quality
    94; leaf 194; melting point 85;
    plating solution 201; potassium cyanide
    201
Goldsmiths Hall 86
Graduated stones 150
Grain setting 152
Graining tool 21, 38, 149
Granulation 209–12
Graphite rod 196
Gravers 21, 38, 218
Gravity casting 183
Grisaille 193
Gum tragacanth 190
Gypsum 155
Gypsy setting 148

Hack saw frame 36
Hair 137
Half round file 64, 148
Half round pliers 63, 129, 141, 213
Half round wire 138
Hallmarking 63, 66, 86–9, 118
Hammers 19, 25, 38
Hand engraving 215
Hand drill 104
Hand vise 19, 25, 39, 44, 104
Hank, of polishing threads 20
Hard rolled metal 47
Hardness, of diamond 168; of gemstones
    155
Hardened silver 129
Hardwood 136
Heat, of gases 56; for hardness 121;
    for springs 129
Heavy liquid method of stone testing 173
Heel of pin 123–4
Hematite 215
Hexagonal collet 142
Hide mallet 25
Hinge 123, 131

Horn 137, mallet 19
Hot iron 197
Hydrochloric acid 53, 96–7
Hydrogen peroxide 53

Icing syringe 185
Improvized tools 217
Inclusions, in gemstones 173
Ingot mould 81–2, 197
Instrument vise 21
Intaglio 166, 193, 196, 215
Investing 179
Investment plaster 14, 174, 178
Iron betrothal rings, Roman 137
Ivory 137, 162

Jacobi 202
Jade 137, 157
Jet 161
Jeweller's Loupe 13, 171
Joint, pin and catch 69, 113
Jointing tool or chenier spacer 24, 217
Jordan 202
Jump ring 113, 116–7, 119, 148
'Jugodent' polishing motor 44, 74

Kiln 42, 44, 146, 181, 188

Laminated wood 136
Lapidary 16, 39, 45, 148, 155, 165
Lapping, in stone cutting 165
Lathe 16, 40, 45, 215; in wire coiling
    98–9
Lead 14, 185, 195–7, 219; cake 220;
    solder 53; for doming blocks 68, 136,
    219
Leather buff 197
Lemel 81, 197
Lettering 214
Limoges 187, 193
Link, of chain 100; of hollow chain 202
Light, in gemstones 172; shield 13
Littledale, H.A.P. 210
Locating pegs 223
Locket 115, 147, 217, 223
Locking tweezers 17, 42, 67, 117, 119,
    139
Lost wax casting 174, 177

Mace 223
Machine textures 215
Magnet 197
Magnifying, glasses 24; headband 21;
    lens 20
Malleability 79
Mallets 19, 38
Mandrel, for pendant drill 75; for ring
    making 20, 25, 35, 64
Marquise cut 167
Maryon, Herbert 196

Mating punches for doming dies 220
Matrix 164
Measuring devices 37
Melting 81, 183; apparatus 20, 37
Mercury 215
Mesh 197
Metal turntable 13
Metallic oxides 187
Metals 79–85
Methane gas 56
Methylated spirits 193; rouge mixture
    132
Mica 193
Micro Weld Micro Flame Gas Generator
    45, 61
Microfilm 178, 185
Microflame Weldmaster soldering torch
    60
Micrometer 19, 23, 25, 31
Microscope 171
Mill grain tool 21, 38, 150
Modelling wax 25
Mohs scale 155
Mole wrench 21, 34
Mortar and pestle 189
Mouldings 222
Mouth blow pipe 24; torch 11, 13, 18,
    24, 59

Nacre 160–1
Natural gas 13, 56–7; soldering torches
    59
Navette 101
Needle file 18, 25, 30, 129
Nickel 189
Niello 136, 188, 195
Nippers 224
Nitric acid 96–7

Octahedron 169–70
Oil stone, Arkansas 36, 222
Onyx 137
Opal 158
Organ pipe setting 143
Organic, gems 160–2; substances 137,
    159
Orthoclase feldspar 155
Oval collet 142
Overheating 13
Oxide 198
Oxidization 14, 80
Oxy-acetylene cylinder and torch 41, 45
Oxygen 56, 58, 59, 183

Paillons 50–1, 194
Pavé setting 151
Pearl 147–8, 160–1, 222; cement 147;
    drill 152
Peg and cut away setting 150
Pegs 16–17

238